STODDARD MARTIN is a critic and lecturer. He was born in Philadelphia, grew up in California and has lived in Europe, principally London, since the early 1970s. As Chip Martin, he is author of a sequence of linked novellas published by Starhaven.

The cover, frontispiece and endpiece of this book incorporate images from drawings by Fritz Schwimmbeck, Lovis Corinth and Alfred Kubin, courtesy of their owner.

I0098802

Monstrous Century

Essays in 'the Age of the Feuilleton'

Stoddard (Chip) Martin

Starhaven

in association with Quarterly Review

©Stoddard Martin 2016
ISBN 0-936315-40-7

STARHAVEN, 42 Frognal, London NW3 6AG
books@starhaven.org.uk
www.starhaven.org.uk

Typeset in Dante by John Mallinson

Contents

Books under review are listed at the end of each chapter.

Preface

Editing a small-circulation journal can be a tedious undertaking, maybe especially when that journal – *Quarterly Review* – is simultaneously illustrious and non-remunerative. The editor of such a magazine is therefore more than ordinarily thankful when he lights upon a writer who not only produces top-notch pieces, but turns them out as reliably as a factory. This is not to suggest there is anything in Chip Martin's work that is not utterly artisanal, simply that his output is as impressive by volume as it is in worth. From the moment my colleague Leslie Jones (now *QR* editor) forwarded to me a review-essay by an interesting new acquaintance, it was apparent we had struck rich.

The formerly footloose Philadelphian WASP, struggling with Hesse as he wandered enraptured across Seventies Europe, has ensconced himself on the London literary scene, and made signal contributions to contemporary culture. A multiplicity of books and articles combine deep reading with rare readability, their author vaulting agilely over the boundaries lesser writers erect for themselves. Insights from the old and new literatures of several countries jostle for space in his work – not to mention aesthetics, musicology, mythology, philosophy, poetry, politics and psychology. His subjects, even when unsympathetic in themselves, are viewed in the round, and judged with humanity. Yet he also has a strong moral impulse, as evidenced by the title of this collection. So although he can roam as far back temporally as Perkin Warbeck, and into magical regions with Orpheus, we see in his work a frequent return to more recent periods, and a nagging anxiety to explain why and how Europe went so badly wrong between 1900 and 2000 – particularly the dread duodecennium 1939-1945.

A hopeful nineteenth century turned into a monstrous one indeed, as classical restraint turned into self-realization and mildly restrictive regimes into populist tyrannies where the sourest suspicions were suddenly given free rein by politicians, often to sonorous accompaniment (the chanting of cantos, the riding of valkyries, neoclassical colonnades in concrete). The freeing of ids paralleled the flattering of national egos, new expectations the revival of old resentments, the rise of the bourgeois and working classes, the ability to manipulate them through sociology and technology. These essays are thorough-going 'inductive investigations' of how modern fruits came from old roots – examinations of the ever-tense nexus between past and present, order and 'imaginative extremity', Apollo and Dionysus, one episode or opus at a time. Like Elisa Segrave, the author patiently 'adds telling strokes to the larger picture'.

Through subtle microscopy, we see Wagner, Nietzsche, Pound, D'Annunzio, Céline and others in unexpected lights. We have all heard the charge that these inadvertently (or, as with Céline, advertently) helped unleash catastrophe upon a continent – but few arraigners truly understand the contexts from which such men could arise, nor how difficult it can be for humans to bear titanic talents. Chip not only comprehends the greater circumstances which once in a while throw up geniuses, but can also outline the personal foibles, paradoxes and problems which warp their worldviews, and so our world. This matters, because even the least winsome and oldest-fashioned of them are inseparable from ourselves. 'The past isn't dead – it isn't even past', as Faulkner wrote, and so we dissolve constantly in and out of its Cocteau-like mirror, descend at times into an oxidized underside. Resonant musics can be heard in our darkest depths (the orchestra at Auschwitz), and are the soundtrack to up-to-date dilemmas. We still struggle with the same constructs and concepts, probably always will. Wagner is in some ways still Germany – hundred year old academic memories of Nietzsche still help fuel American exceptionalism – Eliot's *Waste Land* is also ours. As the author writes with deceptive casualness vis-à-vis two Orpheans – in so doing somehow summing up the recent histories of two whole countries – 'Italians appear to be haunted by Verdi because they can't live up to him while Germans are fixated with Wagner because they can't live him down.' Few writers could fashion such steely barbs from art history ingredients.

Some cultural arbiters reject 'the West' on nihilistic principle, but Chip is invariably constructive. He is no aloof Castalian, but a man engaged in the world, trying always to see it differently, make it slightly better than it was five minutes ago. He is a liberal, but unlike many who so self-describe, he is not in thrall to any of the sects of the P. C. cult. He may be a citizen of the world, but he knows which parts can be called home. To him, even a stained civilization can be beautiful, and worthy of continuance, despite all contradictions and crimes.

As postwar, post-Christian, increasingly post-European Europe stares at itself through a glass darkly, and all literature seems at times to lessen, it is pleasing to think some stalwarts still search for meaning – and sometimes find it – among our foundations. Whether they, and therefore we, can also find redemption is a question still to be answered. But for now, we must be thankful that an age of complexes has found a complex explicator.

Derek Turner (editor, *Quarterly Review* 2007-15)

Introduction: in 'the Age of the Feuilleton'

In the counterculture of the late 1960s, the author to read – in translation, in Anglo-Saxony – was Hermann Hesse. Youths of my kind would begin with the Jung-inspired *Demian*, move on to the Brahman-ic *Siddhartha* and finally devour proto-psychedelic *Steppenwolf*. More sophisticated attention was needed for *Narcissus and Goldmund*, with its yin-yang of the man of meditation vs. man of the road. A theme of community won and lost in *The Journey to the East* seemed to chime with a mood of the early 1970s; but it was only a Happy Few who found Hesse's largest and last novel, *The Glass Bead Game*, readily accessible. I perused it more out of duty than pleasure and laid Hesse aside for four decades.

I turned to him again a few years ago in German and found the going tough for an attainment that might run to the libretto of *Tristan* with effort or achieve, say, 75% comprehension of a story by Stefan Zweig. So when it came to re-attempting *Der Glasperlenspiel*, it was to a paperback translation I'd acquired when setting out on the road for Europe in the summer of '71. If I'd struggled with the book then, I could enjoy it now with an attention I might no longer devote to the straighter, simpler narratives of earlier Hesse such as I'd been entranced by in my hot youth. I was ready for the density of analysis of a Zeitgeist I felt I'd lived through – the day-before-yesterday of the 20th century, which Hesse renders as if from a pinnacle looking back over two or three centuries' distance. *Sub specie aeternitatis* the days of our lives may seem different. The play of history – that deadly, yet death-defying game – may be turned, tried, misapprehended and turned again until we get a grip on our place in ever-widening circles of time and geography, whether terrestrial or cosmic.

So went my dreaming thoughts on returning to Hesse. But reading his last novel more closely, I came upon an issue I had not registered in hippy-era perusal of his work: profound irritation at what he calls the 'age of the feuilleton'. This had chimed little with my concerns of those days. What I recalled vividly was the death of the protagonist on leaving Castalia, the remote citadel of the rarefied 'game', to become tutor to a troubled young man. Hoping to impress the lad by joining him in a pre-dawn swim across an icy mountain lake, he plunges in instantly to sink, his heart stopped by the temperature shock. Physical life may appear refreshing after a dense career of the mind but if pursued with Dionysian lack of caution can obliterate at a stroke an edifice of Apollonian attainment. Spellbound by this ending, I felt it transmuted a message Hesse's friend Thomas Mann had conveyed decades before in the climax to his *Death in Venice*. The Nietzschean crisis[1] appealed to a strain in me harking back to boyhood immersion in Wagner and was reinforced by Visconti's contemporary film of the novel, a deep romanticism underscored with the *adagietto* of Mahler, which my companion on the road[2] in Europe-on-$5-a-day and I absorbed at a cinema in Milano across from the Fascist-era train station as we whiled away our long summer afternoon of freedom before bunking on *couchettes* up to Paris.

Hesse's 'age of the feuilleton' was the last great era of newspapers and before internet. In his view it was characterized by a shallow intellectualism catering to middle-brow minds and/or those whose attention could be caught only by trivia of dress, diet and so on – what we know well from our recent age of 'celebrity'. His practitioners of the 'glass bead game' live in a more austere space, where intellectual pursuits are purified – puritanical perhaps, or 'spiritual' if you prefer a term used by devout souls in my hippy youth. A disciple of Jung and contemporary of Rudolf Steiner, to say nothing of Krishnamurti, Hesse posited in his Castalia something like a finer form of independent scholarship, with a version of morality at home in the sublime more than in the 'human, all-too-human'. Intercourse with the latter was of course necessary, but painful

---

1 Hesse's protagonist has as his shadow a version of Nietzsche, by whom Hesse was strongly though not blindly influenced.

2 Later my wife.

and potentially debasing, thus restricted. In a locale of chaste ether, one might descry with more clarity the pattern behind all: the motives driving art, music, mathematics, language – all the games of the mind which, once amalgamated, comprise a totality of imagination... or so it seemed. Visionary heights! But we too are obliged to live in an 'age of the feuilleton', or its decadence. And as Hesse's irony never lets us quite miss, its aspirations at best may not be so foreign to what his fictive ideal ostensibly opposes. We are all Castalians in the outer reaches of mind – reaches at times so remote that we can hardly recognize their existence. So when we consider attempts to explicate our era, we may also feel a disruptive shiver of a never-quite-repressible scepticism.

Castalia, as Hesse has it, had to collapse following 'the age of wars'. It may be re-constructed, but only after time has brought into focus the horrors history has produced alongside its marvels of creation, or in relation to or even consequence of them. This is an element of the quest through, and inquests into, 20th century political and intellectual history of, say, the finer writers contributing to the premier journal in our 'age of the feuilleton', *The New York Review of Books*. For someone like the late Tony Judt books under review were a pretext in the best sense. not to be neglected, rather to be taken as starting-points for exploration of a topic and always related back to the textures of one's time and its place in larger time and place. Judt may have deprecated a Castalian 'spirit'; he could be alarmed by some of its guises. At the same time, he charged his own era with blinkered morality, self-serving forgetfulness, chilling indifference, misuse of language and glissandos re higher values in favour of 'universal abstractions' such as '"truth", "justice" and "rights"'. I read Judt and his kind with admiration, though recognizing that they too may be locked into their own time, circumstances and sensibility – their Will, Mask, Creative Mind and Body of Fate, to use Yeats's more fascinating categories[3] – as was Hesse, as am I. So it was with pleasure that, when invited

---

3 Explained and explored in *A Vision* (Macmillan: 1925/rev. 1937).

some years ago to contribute to a revived version of the grand old British feuilleton journal, *Quarterly Review*, I did. An *NYRB* approach was perhaps more in my mind than in the editors'. But they were generous and soon let me go my own way, throwing 'pretexts' at me which they judged might serve what they saw as my partly German, partly Judt-like concerns – 20th century Europe and its offshoots in history, literature and culture.

Such personal reasons as I had for these concerns belong to another discussion. Intellectually speaking, a degree in history with 20th century European emphasis no doubt resurfaced in what I wrote, and perhaps my perspectives overall, though I was less conscious of academic matters in the period when I took that degree than of, say, the music of The Grateful Dead. "'69 I was twenty-one and I called the world my own,' Jackson Browne sang. Adulthood, however, initiates one into wider perspectives, and it did not take me long to see that what had happened in Europe of the mid-20th century had to do with my life too, and that of my culture, even though I was not German or Jewish or European except by descent, but a mere American WASP for whom issues like burning Black ghettoes or the Vietnam War were the urgency of the day. Time marches on, and one's own Body of Fate. I read literature out of a desire to write. I wrote out of desire to make music of words. The sounds of the Dead did not so overcome boyhood thraldom to Wagner as to prevent my first book from being about the latter's relation to literature in subsequent generations. The problems of the 20th century loomed larger as I pursued this. I wrote about anti-Semitism and by the mid-1990s was invited to pen feuilleton-length pieces for *The Jewish Quarterly*. Not long after, I was asked to write reviews proper, the blest 600 words, for *The Jewish Chronicle*. One of these led me to the attention of *QR*'s then deputy editor, Leslie Jones. He asked me if I were willing to expand my review. Having done so, more requests came, plus a few suggestions of my own, only one of which (on republicanism) was wholly rejected. Thus the main essays in this book.

After some thought, I decided to include the *JQ* essays,

which have a thematic connection, and to exclude a couple of British-oriented ones, which mainly did not. The essays seemed to cohere in a kaleidoscopic way, illuminating a Zeitgeist one has lived in or through, and I reproduce them almost as they appeared, a difference being that they are arranged in loose historical and geographic order, not sequence as published. There may at a glance seem repetitions: I'd like to see these as leitmotival, to use the Wagnerian term, more than consequential and hope they contribute to unity of the whole. Some of the essays seemed to demand notes, others not. Of further pieces – thirty-five or so for the *JC*, in particular – I have included one expanded, two fused and three others as published, as they seemed to fill out the picture painted. That picture is of what I call a 'monstrous' century, for reasons apparent. Approaching it piece by piece may help to root deductions in something like an inductive investigation. I'd like to think so. The 19th century German scientist Justus von Liebig said that the problem with Romantic philosophers like Schelling is that they created a culture rich in word and idea but poor in real knowledge. It is a recurrent pitfall, not least in an 'age of the feuilleton'. I beg forgiveness for the extent to which I too have descended into it.

A note on italics

Subjects of these essays often invite intrusion of foreign words and phrases. Such has traditionally called for italics; I have eliminated these if usage seems familiar in English. When in doubt I have reverted to the authority of my youth, the Britannica World Language edition of Funk & Wagnall's Standard Dictionary. Proper names and titles of institutions are not italicized; sobriquets usually are.

Wagner and Verdi, compared and contrasted

Quarterly Review, Autumn 2012

After seeing *Parsifal* at Bayreuth, the symbolist critic Arthur Symons remarked that 'Wagner realized the supreme importance of monotony'[1]. Wagner himself told his wife, who obsessively recorded his words, 'The eloquent pause – that is the province of music.' Nuggets of this kind are dug out of the rich veins of ore which Peter Conrad mines in his impressive *Verdi and/or Wagner*. In almost every sentence we trip across some glittering detail, an *embarras de richesse* of knowledge seldom on display at our stage in cultural history. Conrad has lived with his subject(s) with an intensity recalling, say, Ruskin with *The Stones of Venice*. And it is in that decadent city of high Romanticism that he begins and ends his co-habitation with genius, contemplating the larger-than life statues of Wagner and Verdi which stand near to one another, though not facing, in the Giardini Pubblici.

The lagoon surrounding the 'città morta' has a fabled monotony to it, a lassitude of motion which Thomas Mann captures in his post-Wagnerian *Tod in Venedig* and Luchino Visconti set shimmering in his film of that novel to an adagio from Mahler, co-opted as *Liebestod*. Such textures may be what readers will feel on stepping into Conrad's prose, which unfurls in long, evenly-weighted paragraphs, with sentences balanced and a regularity of lilt like that of the diminutive waves of the pale Adriatic as they lap against shallow sands in front of the Grand Hotel des Bains at the Lido. Despite its appearance of depth, the book has a curious, salt-water weightlessness to it, so that at times you experience what Nietzsche feared for 'youthlets' who fell under Wagner's spell[2]: on entering his seas of 'unending melody', they would lose their footing and drown – the very fate Hollywood would depict in the lovelorn Joan Crawford of

---

1 Conrad, 196. Other references incorporated in text.

2 In *The Case of Wagner*, quoted in my *Wagner to 'the Waste Land'* (Macmillan, 1982), 7, 93.

Humoresque, who after hearing an adaptation of Isolde's blissful love-death on radio, played by her lover – a violinist who loves his music more than he loves her – walks out of her beach house and into a surf from which she will never return.

Conrad gathers and weaves motifs of this kind into his vast tapestry of two centuries of 'life' of his twinned giants, both of whom were born in the year of the Battle of Nations, and delivers us to a present in which Italians appear to be haunted by Verdi because they can't live up to him while Germans are fixated with Wagner because they can't live him down[3]. Conrad describes the absurd antics of producers in our era, including the great-granddaughter presiding over Wagner's shrine at Bayreuth. He notes how war and peace have shaped culture's responses, recalling that Hollywood has linked Wagner to evil ('The Ride of the Valkyries' in *Apocalypse Now*) and Verdi to humaneness (*La Traviata* as *Pretty Woman*). He recollects ingenious parodies – the Marx Brothers' trashing of *Trovatore* in *A Night at the Opera* – and catalogues their precursors in Modernist revolt: Marinetti hacking *Parsifal* into forty tiny bits, Dali twisting *Tannhäuser* in *Bacchanale*, Lang wresting the Nibelungs back to *Ur*-savagery, Cocteau's contemporizing the original Tristan in *L'Éternel retour*. Presenting this record of an afterlife to genius, Conrad is gentle with comment so that we are able to weigh for ourselves the merits of envy, exasperation and contumely. Where it will end, he does not predict. Perhaps it would not do to suggest that the postmodern era he has flourished in has led into the murk.

There are scraps to suggest it. For example, Conrad is no admirer of Auden's attempt to blame World War II on Wagner. 'Today the anti-Wagner orthodoxy belabours his politics,' he remarks, choosing a verb to impute tedium to a hackneyed approach. Wagner's anti-Semitism he hardly touches on, noting near the start of his book that the composer was probably son of Jewish actor Ludwig Geyer (in fact, Geyer was only partly Jewish, if at all, and his paternity of Wagner has never been proven) and including among his illustrations an 1875 cartoon lampooning

---

3   Conrad is particularly interesting on this topic, 342 etc.

the composer by morphing his profile into that of an orthodox rabbi from Leipzig. Conrad's argument vs Wagner, which otherwise is relentless, pivots on aesthetic and/or personal taste. Near the end of his book he claims that 'the ideals of Bayreuth' were 'always spurious', which by this stage a gently narcotized reader may be prone to accept without more comment; in any case, there is none. The silk-dressing gowns and perfumes from Paris have long stood as symbols of the turpitude of *Der Meister*, just as muddy boots have of a contrasting authenticity in the farmer of Sant' Agata. For those who find such forensic data other than spurious in respect to ideals, Conrad's book will make persuasive reading. For those who do not, it may seem somewhat fantastic. For purer souls, it may not be read through at all.

They may balk after the first few chapters. This is because, whether out of desire or fact of being a man of his times, Conrad cannot resist devoting a hundred pages or more to gossip, vignette and post- or sub-Freudian analysis of the foibles of genius. That many have loathed Wagner with vehemence is well-known: Nietzsche started the trend and manifested a cause – shame at being 'taken in' and subject to a god who (shock, horror!) turned out of to have feet of clay. That Wagner was a man, and an errant one, may be fascinating; that he was a titan of musical theatre is surely what counts. Why then, we may ask, does an author of Conrad's stature and skill not concentrate on the latter and leave the tattle in its place, as a kind of debris, of secondary, tertiary or even no importance, rather than delving into it with a glee that recalls the genre of *Hollywood Babylon*, turning stretches of his book into a prequel as if of such scurrility – a tactic akin to the eagerness of those who, disliking Wagner, brand his work 'not real music' but mere anticipation of film scores[4]?

Exploring a rich inheritance in soundtracks by Max Steiner, Mikos Rosza and Erich Korngold, Conrad shows himself to be no snob of this ilk. In his use of Verdi vs Wagner, on the other hand, we often hear the thwack of a blunt instrument. Whether

---

4 An opinion I once heard from a former chairman of the Royal Opera.

it is Falstaff vs Hans Sachs, Boccanegra vs Wotan, Violetta vs Isolde or what have you, he pounds with the force of a Siegfried at *the* idea: Verdi is for mortals, Wagner for Übermenschen; Verdi is for consolation, Wagner for aggravation of pain; Verdi is for the world as it exists, Wagner agitates for one that does not; Verdi is a realist, Wagner out with the fairies; Verdi is for love, Wagner for sex; Verdi is for Life and Wagner for Death or, if not quite that, or that always, at least for the Beyond – and so on. This seems to me *vieux jeu*, easy game. Moreover, to sustain parlour oppositions of the kind for over 350 pages is to enter a realm of artifice and subjectivity of such proportions that a receptor might reasonably ask if the exercize has much worth beyond its display of a game-master's indisputable brilliance and/or exposition of his personal prejudgements about what constitutes Greatness.

The reader who persists is likely to be ravished by a chapter mid-book which gets down to music and methods. Trivia and prejudice fall away and we remember why we should be interested in these figures. Somewhere mid-book we also get glimpses of Conrad's admiration for aspects too often overlooked: Wagner's 'species-ism', for example, which anticipates concerns of our era. There are countless bravura descriptions – of *Falstaff*'s finale (192), of the significance of the Norns' rope (242) – and citations of rare insight – Mazzini on individualism (82), Cosima Wagner on the 'ideality' of London (132). Occasionally, however, the platter of gems turns up a paste stone: D'Annunzio staged his coup at Fiume two decades after writing *Il Fuoco*, not one (251); Stella Artois is advertised not by the 'Vergine hymn' from *La Forza del Destino* but by a wandering tune (356), and the Leonora who is fed by Padre Guardiano is the one from that opera not her namesake from *Il Trovatore* (171). To cite such slip-ups is not mere nitpicking. They accumulate into a frustration that goes to the heart of how one is liable to react to the game-master's marvellous congeries.

His book, as I've said, pivots on fact and quotation, with nuggets a dozen a page; but *it has no notes!* Cosima quotes Richard in her diary – what year, what season, what circumstance? not to be found. Verdi suffers from composer's block; Boito suggests a device out of Wagner; the old man explodes – where? when? Can we read more? Not a chance. Not unless we know as much about the sources as the author, and even then possibly only by flipping through hundreds of pages. There is an index but no bibliography, only a list of illustration credits. Is this the publisher's choice? 'We don't want to appear academic; puts off the punters.' Was the author consulted? If so, could not one of Conrad's eminence have resisted or at least offered an authorial apology? *Niente.* Such absence leads one to wonder: is Conrad himself aspiring, consciously or not, to be that godly type of creator who, in James Joyce's semi-satirical phrase, 'stands above and beyond events paring his fingernails'[5]; who, having composed *his* work of genius, says 'that's that – you take it or leave it'?

If you do the former, you must ask finally not just about Verdi and Wagner but about Peter Conrad: who is he, and why should we care? These questions have an interest but produce no firm answer, because he is liable to shape-shift. In his finest chapter, that one about music, he indicates without quite stating what Peter Gellhorn used to teach about Verdi[6]: that, despite Romantic content from Byron or Schiller or Shakespeare, the forms are essentially classical and rarely remodelled or radically re-patterned, unless and until his alleged 'wagnerization' by Boito late in career. So creativity *chez* Verdi is implied to be less than in Wagner – beyond which aperçu lies a piquant thought: does Conrad admire or perhaps, à la Nietzsche, *love* Wagner more than he dare to admit? There is a moment in the back-and-forth between the upright, straightforward Italian and the sinuous, 'effeminate' German when one could almost imagine him evoking the portrait of some ideal gay marriage. But let that and other unknowns of referred autobiography drop into

---

5   In the finale of *A Portrait of the Artist as a Young Man.*

6   The former conductor gave a lecture on this topic at Burgh House in Hampstead in 1997.

the pile of detritus where one would have preferred him to leave his animadversions on Wagner's silk underpants[7]. What is important is that 'knowing' Wagner as he does, and Verdi, and every jot of their lives and works, Conrad is, like many know-alls, still locked out from an essence. He cannot, it seems, penetrate into their souls – not sufficiently, consistently or with full understanding or sometimes even much apparent feeling.

This element of heartlessness, un-self-detected, along with delight in externals – those brilliant surfaces – reminds us why Conrad's name is familiar and what he has been. As lead reviewer for *The Observer*, he existed for years above the struggles of artist, or warrior, or impoverished bohemian man-of-theatre nursing prima donna egos or rash lover of too many women, let alone iconic modellers of new nations, partly inventing new language, culture and body of values. He has been, outside of a world of newspapers, an Oxford don, residing in book-lined studies, holding forth from wide armchairs. He is in short not of *them*, which of course is not disqualifying or to be expected. But what may be is that he should respect the fact, acknowledge the limitations it imposes and pay *them* the respect of trying to view their careers in terms approaching those by which they might have viewed themselves. Peter Conrad *is*, after all, a man of our era and writing for it. His constituency is his audience, not his subjects. Yet to produce a great book about those subjects, which this one in its majesty of scope and ambition and style ought to be, requires an author who in terms of what he has taken on sees the appropriateness of a less antic, more reverent perspective.

Verdi and/or Wagner, Peter Conrad. Thames & Hudson, 2011.

---

7 He notes that Wagner suffered from a bacterial skin condition, erysipelas (135), but it does not evoke sufficient sympathy to keep him from indulging in the usual barracking about Wagner's sartorial extravagance.

Ride of the Wagner Debunkers

Quarterly Review, Winter 2010-11

In the old, bad days, hero-worship, idealization. In the new, 'good' era, desecration, or at least jokey debunking. This seems a leitmotiv within the recent contemporary German arts establishment. The prologue to Oliver Hilmes' biography of the first mistress of the Bayreuth Festival describes with sardonic awe the Great and the Good which every year ascend the Grünen Hugel in Upper Franconia for latest productions of works by Richard Wagner. Portentously it alludes to a snatch of conversation overheard about the 2005 *Parsifal*, directed by iconoclastic Berliner Christoph Schlingensief. Cognoscenti are alerted to the Scylla and Charybdis of taste through which a 36-year-old author has had to steer his craft.

The *Meister*'s final work, a 'stage-consecration play' for his purpose-built theatre, has ever held special status for the Wagnerian devout. For two decades after his death, his widow protected it from 'exploitation' elsewhere; then 'enemies' staged it at the Met in New York – America was not yet signatory to the Berne Convention on copyright. Cosima's motive in 'saving' *Parsifal* for Bayreuth was to sustain an aura of piety around it, the festival and Wagner at large. This was an era characterized by the malaise Nietzsche summed up in his famous phrase, 'God is dead but for millennia to come people will spy his shadow in their caves'[1]. Heterodox Christian shadows cast by Wagner's last work appalled the philosopher, but others felt differently, including a Nazi Chancellor who, fifty years later, would tell Cosima's successor as 'Lady of Bayreuth' that he wanted to use *Parsifal* as the basis for a new Aryan religion.

The approach of Schlingensief and Co. suggested the subtext: 'Hitler was taken in by this stuff, so we won't be'.

---

1   In *La Gaya Scienza*, III, 108, tr. following Thomas Common's in *The Complete Works of Friedrich Nietzsche* ed. Oscar Levy (Edinburgh & London: T. N. Foulis, 1909-13), vol. x.

The Berliner[2] reduced the 'sacred text' to a farrago of childish magickings, a stuffed rabbit being handed round stage and the eponymous hero killing both Amfortas and Kundry with the Holy Spear before being stabbed in the back with it by an undead Klingsor. As songs of servitors of the Grail ascend into the dome of their chapel (Verlaine's 'voix des enfants chantant dans la coupole', quoted by Eliot in *The Waste Land*), a black-and-white scrim comes down to reveal a dying hare being eaten by maggots. Why did the then 86-year-old master of Bayreuth, Cosima's and Richard's grandson Wolfgang, invite such abuse? It is a question for analysts into attitudes of the second-rate towards their more illustrious forbears[3]. The production was boo-ed by pilgrims who'd travelled far and paid dear, but cries of '*Schweinerei*' delighted Schlingensief and friends, who longed evidently for scandal[4]. Those who argue that one production does not a Zeitgeist make might consider the gratuitously offensive offering mounted by Calixto Bieito at Stuttgart shortly after, or an earlier 21st century production at Munich in which Grail Knights paraded in bloodied Masonic aprons, suggesting that purity requires self-castration.

At first glance Oliver Hilmes' book seems to belong to this school of response to Wagner. It measures Cosima's mid-19th century upbringing by later middle-class standards, a tactic reminiscent of Paul Johnson's hatchet-jobs on Rousseau, Shelley and other liberal romantics in *Intellectuals*[5]. Cosima's parents are censured for their near total absence, her father Franz Liszt performing through Europe as a pop-idol, her mother the Countess Marie d'Agoult hosting a salon in Orléanist Paris, penning articles as 'Daniel Stern' and avenging herself on her lover in a roman à clef. Both were serial adulterers, their children

---

2 That he died of cancer last summer at age 49 perhaps informs his approach, but does not justify it.

3 Nike Wagner, *The Wagners: Dramas of a Musical Dynasty* (Weidenfeld, 2000), is acute on this topic.

4 A more traditional production in the recent repertoire has mollified some.

5 First published in 1988.

illegitimate. Cosima and siblings were brought up first by their Liszt grandmother, a simple Hungarian at sea in sophisticated milieux, then by their mother's onetime governess, a septuagenarian Frenchwoman who, like Joseph de Maistre, had had her ancien régime values bolstered by extensive sojourns in reactionary St Petersburg. Hilmes has little trouble in making Mme Patersi de Fossombroni's régime of high etiquette and rigid Catholicism seem preposterous. It is mainly by inference that we take it as grounds for Cosima's eventual devotion to, and acumen in, organizing her late husband's legacy.

Liszt went on to set up a relatively stable household at Weimar with the cigar-smoking Ukrainian Princess Carolyne von Sayn-Wittgenstein, part wicked stepmom, part role model as grande dame for a teenaged Cosima. With her brother dying at age twenty and her sister not yet thirty (leaving a grieving husband who would become premier of France on the eve of Franco-Prussian war), the 19-year-old girl attached herself to her estranged father and pleased him by marrying his star-pupil, Berlin aristocrat Hans von Bülow. Bülow was cynical, sickly and afflicted with low self-esteem, not least evidenced in his idolatry of Liszt's confrère in the 'artwork of the future', Wagner. Cosima bore Bülow two daughters, was neglected by him and allegedly beaten, and began to yearn for a saviour. It did not take long for Wagner's roving eye to spy this: Bülow was his constant acolyte at the time; and once Ludwig II had invited the composer to settle in Munich, the group embarked on a near ménage à trois. Hans was installed as court conductor – he would direct the premières of *Tristan* and *Meistersinger* – and Wagner turned to comforting the wife. The affair was covert, neither party wishing to offend Liszt, Bülow or above all the king who, though homosexual, valued appearances and was catching enough flack from his minders for patronizing Wagner in the first place. Cosima had three more children, and by the time Ludwig discovered that none were by her husband, the group had been sent packing, Bülow to Berlin to be first conductor of the famed Philharmonic, Cosima, children and second-husband-to-be to an *Asyl* on Lake Lucerne.

Wagner maintained relations with the king sufficiently to build his bespoke theatre in a northern corner of the Bavarian realm. Cosima was executive partner in the enterprise from the outset, and Bayreuth's atmosphere owed much to her. The religiosity mentioned was part of it, also a nationalism typical of the decade of triumph over the French and German unification. Cosima was as vociferous against the land of her origin as in an anti-Semitism which became unbending. Regarding origins of the latter, Hilmes breaks into the first person to say, 'The last thing I want to do is to criticize Cosima or turn her into a psychotic study'; he then proceeds to do something like that, with results that are not clear. What is is that Wagner's prejudice was less consistent than his wife's. Some of his *dicta* in this phase sound like sops to her hunger for fatherly precepts; others give off a scent of opportunism – nationalism to collect subscriptions for his theatre, reprinting 'Judenthum in der Musik' to foment controversy and capitalize on a popular trend, composing 'Kaisermarsch' to win Wilhelm I's presence at the first festival. This event, in 1876, entailed endless receptions for philistine aristos and bourgeois plutocrats, as well as the general 'beer-drinking Germanness' which drove Nietzsche to flight, beginning a career of denunciation of his onetime idol. Hilmes opines that the philosopher failed to see that Wagner was as put off by the whole song-and-dance as he was but had to go on with it to insure that his *Ring of the Nibelung* could be presented at last and on something like his own terms.

This aperçu reveals Hilmes as not quite of the school of desecrators and, as he continues, one might even begin to imagine Wagner as a victim of Wagnerism and Cosima as his unconscious victimizer. The composer would accept Ludwig's fiat that his new court conductor, Hermann Levi, direct *Parsifal*; he chose another Jew, Paul von Joukowsky, to design sets; he relied on a third, the idolatrous Josef Rubenstein, to help finish the score. Some of his Jew-baiting – serving 'Hebrew wine' to Levi when he came to lunch, for example – seems calculated less to persecute than to tease; but with humourless Cosima, it was never so. Though her husband had been exiled from Germany in 1849 for manning the barricades with Bakunin and had spent his most productive years in Switzerland and France, she kept up her hyper-nationalism, speaking ever of 'us Germans' and declaring the French and the Jews in that order to be inimical to a 'German spirit'[6]. This would be typical of the Bayreuth politburo (Hilmes' term) until beyond her death. From the turn of the century she would rely on a transplanted Englishman to set the ideological tone, Houston Stewart Chamberlain, whose bestselling *Grundlagen des Neunzehnten Jahrhunderts* would impress many top Nazis[7] and whose marriage to Wagner's younger daughter, Eva, a spinster of forty, was calculated to gain power in the clan. Until his demise from neurological disorders in the '20s, Chamberlain's star was ascendant, with tragic consequences for Wagner's elder daughter Isolde among others[8]. Power then moved to the young wife of Wagner's son, Siegfried, a composer-manqué who died within months of his mother in 1930 – Winifred Williams, English too: born in Hastings, German via adoption by another Liszt protégé.

Hilmes sees these later guardians of the grail as having progressively less in common with its progenitor. The subtext is that, though he dreamed of a princely establishment upholstered with trappings of a *faux* church, Wagner was at heart a Wandering Jew. Hilmes does not ponder if he was Jewish in part, son of Ludwig Geyer rather than his named father, a theory floated by Nietzsche and credible enough that prominent Jews in New York would include Wagner in a slim vol. of illustrious forbears

---

6 According to Nike Wagner, Cosima persuaded her husband to insert Hans Sachs' 'Deutsches Kunst' warning at the end of *Meistersinger* in order to introduce a serious ideological element into the essentially comic work. It may be the one passage in Wagner's dramas which explicitly looks forward to National Socialism.

7 Works by Party ideologue Alfred Rosenberg derive from it, as does *Mein Kampf*.

8 The 'politburo' denied her inheritance from Wagner on grounds that Cosima had been married to Bülow when she was born, making her *de jure* his child. She was banned from *Wahnfried* and, abandoned by a self-seeking husband, died of lung disease in penury in 1917. Her invalid mother was not informed for a decade.

privately printed in 1927[9]. On the other hand, Hilmes notes how towards the end of his life Wagner grew weary of the sycophants and ideologues around him and longed like Nietzsche to fly to the south. He wintered on the Amalfi coast and in Palermo (Cosima's younger Bülow daughter married a Sicilian count) and died at Venice, an event fictionalized by Gabriele D'Annunzio in his 1900 novel *Il Fuoco*[10]. This connection Hilmes might have pursued instead of spending pages on the un-provable rumour that Wagner's last heart attack was brought on by a row with Cosima over a flutter he'd had with the flower-maiden Carrie Pringle during the previous summer's *Parsifal*. A most influential literary apostle of Wagner, D'Annunzio provides a direct link to Fascism, being its exponent before Mussolini. It is piquant too that, when the Italian state had to put him out of political harm's way following his coup at Fiume in 1920, they installed him in a villa on Lago di Garda where Cosima's elder Bülow daughter had once lived and the grande dame visited after her own heart issues forced her to resign as head of the Festival in 1907.

Connectives to National Socialism are better known. Hilmes tells of how Chamberlain and Winifred became party members in the '20s, also Chamberlain's wife though not Winifred's husband – Cosima may have counselled her heir as head of the Festival to stand aloof. Chamberlain provided Hitler with paper on which to write *Mein Kampf* while in prison; Winifred grew attracted to Der Führer, possibly out of disappointment with her older, probably gay husband, Hilmes avers[11]. Elation in Bayreuth

---

9   Michael Estorick inherited a rare copy of this book, which I've perused. In its catalogue of why each figure is included, Wagner's sole listed claim is authorship of 'Judaism in Music'!

10   The Italian's most extensive work, which Joyce and Proust admired, focuses on a dramatic poet who longs to develop a version of Bayreuth in his country. A central scene shows him helping Cosima convey Wagner into a boat after the composer has had a heart seizure on the Lido. The final scene has him helping to carry the dead Wagner's coffin to the gondola which will take it to the station and train back to 'la collina bavarà'.

11   This is not a new idea. Nike Wagner subscribes to it, citing among other sources Josef Goebbels' diaries.

when the Nazis took over is where his book ends, with the phrase 'But that is another story'. Does this mark Hilmes' ambition to follow his biographies of Cosima and of Alma Mahler with one on Winifred? In the arena of grande dames of the post-Romantic era, the first 'Lady of Bayreuth', flawed though she was, hardly merits such company. The position Cosima created and upheld with rigour was disgraced by Winifred's blind Nazism and handed on to Wagner's grandsons as a polluted chalice. In this light we might view Wolfgang Wagner's bow to Schlingsief and Co. as a result of continuing shame and hope for closure. What comes in the era of his daughters Eva and Katarina (first signs, not good[12]) will be gazed on with a cold eye by Cosima from her grave in the garden of the family home *Wahnfried*, now run by the Bavarian state. The ghost of her husband seems to have flown long ago, in quest of fresher airs elsewhere.

Cosima Wagner, the Lady of Bayreuth. Oliver Hilmes, trans. Stewart Spencer. Yale University Press, 2010.

---

12 Katarina's inaugural production, of *Meistersinger*, infuriated traditionalists nearly as much as Schlingensief's *Parsifal*; nor did a subsequent production of *Lohengrin*, set in a laboratory for experiment on rats, please many. Her great-grandfather also knew the principle *épater le bourgeois* but did not apply it meretriciously.

Stefan Zweig: Yesterday's Man

Quarterly Review, 22 ii 2013

The fall of Hapsburg civilization was a catastrophe for some; for others it was cause for rejoicing. The ways of life emanating out of Vienna had for some time seemed to belong to no *Leitkultur*. A German-speaking majority felt insecure in a federal state where half the official dicta were in Magyar, much religion in Latin, musical culture in Italian and literary in French, service in a ragout of Slavic dialects and mercantilism in Yiddish or – by the turn of the 20th century – makeshift English. A sense of *mélange adultère de tout* was abroad, to use T. S. Eliot's phrase re Europe post World War I[1], in which Vienna was the great loser. A capital city grown so multi-kulti was in the end loved mainly by a precious few whose privilege diminished as its territories split off and raison d'être vanished. The many would shrug and carry on in the semi-depressive state they had always served in, half-unnoticed by narcissistic masters, surviving on trickle-down. In a vertiginous epoch of change they had at least the catharsis of schadenfreude in watching their 'betters' brought low.

Stefan Zweig's career spanned this epoch, and its progress affected his subjects. His mature books on *Joseph Fouché* (1929) and *Marie Antoinette* (1932) were in effect studies of further types of calamity about to descend on an order into which he'd been born. His historical dramas *Jeremias* (1918) and *Das Lamm des Armen* (1930) were successes in part because bourgeois audiences saw in them analogues for their deteriorating situation. Yet the received notion that Zweig and kind wished their late Hapsburg delights to continue unmolested may be soft thinking, at least at the outset. *Wöllust*, a term comprising what the French call 'volupté', allied to what Mrs Thatcher used to brand 'wet', marked the youth of many like Zweig[2]; but war altered much,

---

1 A poem of this title appears in the pre-Wasteland *Poems 1920*, some of which are (notoriously) anti-Semitic.

2 Zweig uses the term to describe the 'Art Infektionsphänomen', 'Theatremanie'

and Zweig's fevered work on masculinist icons such as Balzac, Nietzsche, Dostoyevsky and Casanova – to say nothing of Bonaparte's police chief – suggest unease with an identity as a *kuchen-und-sahne* Baudelaire. Like Emil Ludwig's contemporary *Napoleon* or Leon Feuchtwanger's *Jude Süss*, Zweig's *Baumeister der Welt* series was, despite liberal professions, read as avidly by journeyman Nazis as by carpet-slippered aesthetes[3]; and Zweig's vast productivity, not least in creating this pantheon, may (in a nod to his revered Freud[4], another target of biographical essay), suggests displacement activity mixed with wish-fulfilment.

Zweig's own biography turned out more eventful than initially promised. Second son of a wealthy Moravian Jewish mill-owning family with Italian banking connections, he cut his teeth in the Vienna of Johann Strauss waltzes and haut bourgeois networking. Teenage was spent in the milieu of Schnitzler and Schönberg, Schiele and Secessionist renegades. This was the era of anti-Semitic, pan-Germanist Mayor Karl Lüger, whose speeches inspired another young Austrian of provincial extraction pursuing not dissimilar aesthetic dreams on meaner streets; and beside unknowns like Hitler, 'self-hating Jews' such as Otto Weininger and Karl Kraus were part of the scene, along with others who sought to evade populist noise and get on, such as Gustav Mahler and Hugo von Hofmannsthal. Young Zweig hero-worshipped, stood at theatre doors to collect autographs, ran after celebrity, left family affairs to his brother and enjoyed the light Don Juan-ism of a *jeunesse dorée*. He translated francophone poets – Verlaine, Émile Verhaeren – solicited manuscripts from the famous and set about acquiring those of the great dead. Imitation begat style, inauthentic yet

---

and 'absurd Enthusiasmus' he felt as a young man. *Die Welt von Gestern* (1941), Frankfurt: S. Fischer Verlag, 1944, 27, 45, etc.

3 Zweig suggests that his *Fouché* encouraged Goebbels and Göring. Ibid., 342.

4 He put Freud beside Mesmer and Mary Baker Eddy in *Die Heilung durch den Geist* (1930). This annoyed the doctor, but in thanking Zweig for a copy he merely said, 'I could object that you overemphasise the element of petit-bourgeois rectitude in me – the fellow is a little more complicated than that!' *Three Lives*, 248.

conscientiously à la mode. The life choice *de jour* was to be an artist, literary above all, and Zweig pursued it with a Rastignac-like concentration[5] until his name became known.

Whatever his true north as sexual being – and much has been speculated[6] – Zweig wrote semi-erotic novellas and became involved by age thirty with a married woman, herself an aspirant author. Professing complaisance about his touted liaison with a shop-girl in Paris and his less specific adventures in bosky Schönbrunn, she separated from her husband and pursued Zweig with a zest. Zweig married her suddenly towards the end of the war, thus acquiring two spoiled stepdaughters as well as a 'top bunny'[7] to establish his writer's *asyl*[8] in a château on a hill overlooking Salzburg. The choice was prescient. In the calm that descended over Europe by the mid-20s, a beau monde arrived to parade itself at the newly-established music festival. Protected by his wife, Zweig became a virtual writing factory and used his proceeds to collect ever more compulsively, accumulating one of the most remarkable caches of manuscripts in Europe – eventually he bid for a speech of Hitler's and for the original of 'Deutschland über alles' as well as for Beethoven's violin and ink-pot. His rooms were ordered to perfection, every book he could want near to hand, shelved from floor to ceiling. Yet continually he fled - to Paris, to Belgium, to north Germany, to the Soviet Union and further afield.

Ostensibly this was to avoid festival crowds or to fulfil

---

5 Balzac's hero. Zweig's essay in the *Baumeister der Welt* series ascribes Balzac's genius to an immense power of will manifesting itself in tireless concentration on his subjects and work.

6 Zweig's brother thought him 'a stranger to passionate love, merely observing it in others'; Fontana called him a 'detached voyeur'. Zweig boasted to his future wife that only adventures with risk appealed to him; during their courtship he wrote in his diary, 'The cards of perversion [were] put ever more openly on the table'. Later he mused, 'I must make sure that it doesn't become all about sex... sexual passion frightens me'. After his death, she would claim that he had been 'no Don Juan'. *Three Lives*, 77, 82, 117, 121, 258.

7 Her prideful description of herself. Ibid., 147.

8 There may have been a mutual fantasy that she play Cosima to his Wagner.

invitations to launch books, read, lecture, speak at congresses, rehearse plays or research new topics. Emotionally, however, obscure restlessness drove him, a Nietzschean 'wanderer and his shadow' or, one may guess, a formerly contented bachelor bibliophile who marries an apparently docile housekeeper only to find her morphing into a monster to make his life hell – the scenario of the novel *Die Blendung* (*Auto-da-Fé*) by young Elias Canetti, which Zweig helped to get published. Zweig's domestic idyll, in short, may have been something other than idyllic; yet who really knows what goes on behind the closed doors of a marriage? What is indisputable is that once the 1930s had begun to impel Jews, liberals, pacifists and others to take stock and then flight, Zweig was quick to liquidate his paradise, selling as much of his collection as he could, and get out, first to Switzerland, then to England where he proposed to settle, leaving wife and stepdaughters behind. Eventually – to her dismay and even denial[9] – he divorced her and, as the receding skies of the continent grew darker, applied for a British passport.

The BBC, imagining its nation honoured, set up an interview with 'Dr Zweig' only to have him explain that he had moved to London because its libraries were good, there was plenty of music and you could work because no one bothered you[10] – hardly a ringing endorsement of the land and its beauties, culture or inspirations. England proved a refuge *tout court*, and how could it have been otherwise after the mountains of Salzburg and a Viennese lad's lifelong pursuit of versions of Parisian *vie bohème*? In this exile, Zweig acquired a young female secretary, also Jewish, a refugee from Silesia. Once his divorce was final, he married her and they bought a house, in Bath. It was grey. When the war came, they were restricted in movement and put on an

---

9   There were 'fierce and protracted arguments'; she 'refused to accept that their life together was over'. Zweig let her keep his name, and after his death she 'tried to cover that [he] had remarried'. Ibid., 13, 306.

10   A transcript is in *Three Lives* (303-5). On his first trip to London in 1906 Zweig, coming from Paris, compared the change to 'stepping out of the bright summer sunshine into the cool shade'. Ibid., 75.

aliens list. It was not long before the old restlessness impelled Zweig to move on, this time to New York – just as important for a writer's career and repute as London, maybe more so, though no more paradisal. Zweig could not settle down there, nor upstate by the Hudson. Evidence suggests that his health – he was now in his 60th year – broke down with the effort. So he ended by retreat, or advance, to the most exotic and colourful locale he had encountered during his years of wandering as a literary lion: Brazil.

Here *was* paradise. It had the best coffee on Earth, but... where were the cafés, the artists, the literati, the musicians, the feuilletonistes, the politicos – that 'world of yesterday' Zweig had thrived in, the grand *monde* he had known? In a green and warm suburb amid gorgeous hills above Rio, he finished his memoir, labouring as Nietzsche had said that the superman must 'at the edge of exhaustion'. 'Give me only books that are written in blood because blood turns to spirit!' Zarathustra cried[11]. Zweig's memoir was one; and he must have known it. In a real sense it was *the* work he had lived to write. So, mission accomplished and affairs put in order, he overdosed himself – his young wife too, it seems, though when a servant entered the bedroom to discover the bodies, hers was still warm.

Zweig wrote letters implying that the reason for his end was political – the horrors abroad in his vanishing world. Others have used this explanation to place him near the head of a list of writers driven to take their own lives directly or contingently by Nazis. Such a list might include Zweig's friends Ernst Toller, Josef Roth and Irwin Rieger, whose ambiguous deaths preceded his by only a brief spell. It would surely include Auschwitz survivors Jean Améry and Primo Levi[12], as well as other Jews whose careers were turned upside down by events – Romain Gary comes to mind, even at a further stretch Arthur Koestler, who shares with Zweig complicity in the simultaneous snuffing of a younger, suggestible consort. Suicide solo is ghoulish

---

11 *Also Sprach Zarathustra*, I, vii. My translation.

12 I discuss this in 'Jean Améry and multiple identities' further on in this book.

enough; *à deux* it raises worse spectres. Hitler and his younger wife took their own lives too, but which one took whose, and in what sequence and under what coercion? Such macabre questions may seem in bad taste, but in the case of a writer with a moral agenda – as Zweig decidedly had by the time of his dramatic end[13] – they require exploration.

Oliver Matuschek's biography does not take the hunt far. An archivist and documentary film-maker, the youngish author conscientiously musters sources and facts but declines to take the kind of speculative leaps that Zweig-as-biographer never shied away from. Matuschek gets something of the 'lebenskurve' which his subject sought in *his* subjects but fails to show how the 'innere Seele lodert und glüht'[14]. He tells us that Thomas Mann suspected a sexual kink in Zweig had resurfaced, of which he could not face the consequences[15]. This semi 'death in Venice' scenario invites a stray idea of a Zweig-ian inspiration for Mann's famous novella, written years before at the time of Mahler's death[16], but its non-specificity leads Matuschek only to muse on unsubstantiated rumours of Zweig being a serial exhibitionist[17]. The most credible explanation for Zweig's suicide may be a feeling of exhaustion of his powers and/or sense that

---

13 By the '20s his politics were pacifist, socialist and pan-European, these shared with friends such as Romain Rolland, whose later Stalinism he did not go along with. He became a member of German PEN in exile but at an international congress in 1936 found its 'carnival of vanities quite repulsive' (*Three Lives*, 298). He disliked Zionism, believing Jews had a key role in creating an international order. Subtitling his memoir *Errinerungen eines Europäers*, he states that for forty years he had worked for a free European Union and what did war or his own death matter if this should still come into being? (*Welt von Gestern*, 394-5).

14 Zweig sets down these principles in his *Einleitung* to *Mary Stuart* (1935).

15 Mann floats this in a letter to his patron Agnes Meyer. *Three Lives*, 288.

16 Zweig wrote 'Gustav Mahler's Wiederkehr' on return from America on the same ship that brought the ailing composer home to die. Mann absorbed the 'dramatic pathos' of the essay before writing his novella. Mahler did not die in Venice as Wagner had, but Visconti's film of Mann's work (1971) links Mann's inspiration to him.

17 *Three Lives*, 285-8.

his best words had been written and more could only mean less – something like what drove Hemingway to a similar act at the same age almost exactly two decades later.

This is to ponder. For others it will be issues and tendencies in the man's work that most matter[18]. So: what of them? The *Wöllust* and self-indulgence of Zweig's early phase, passing through the crucible of World War I (in which Zweig served as a propagandist), became harder, more spare and clear in the '20s[19], a shift not unlike that of his bestselling, near contemporary Gabriele D'Annunzio from overblown aestheticism in *Il Fuoco* to a laconic soldier's eye-view in *Notturno*[20]. Another parallel might be to the transit of Somerset Maugham from *Of Human Bondage* via war experiences as a spy[21], reflected in the Ashenden tales,

---

18 A scholarly account of them is offered by Rüdiger Görner, head of the Centre for Anglo-German Cultural Relations at Queen Mary's College, London. His *Stefan Zweig: Formen einer Sprachkunst* (Sonderzahl, 2012) reviews in succinct chapters Zweig's attributes as poet, tale-teller, travel writer, dramatist, librettist, essayist, memoirist, political and aesthetic thinker. Görner emphasizes Zweig's pan-European, internationalist and pacifist ardours – his Erasmus impulse, if you will. At the same time Görner's portrait is of an obsessive in the great sense, a late or post-Romantic type of genius – driven, idealistic, Angst-filled, finally tragic. Through his eyes, Zweig becomes what he inevitably must seem in the 'Nerven' of the type of sensitive reader with whom he wished to set up 'Dialog': a kind of emissary of the spirit; a voice urging as if from within, like Nietzsche's 'shadow' or Kierkegaard's conscience, impelling one on dangerously, eyes open, looking backward or forward through error, towards what in civilization and/or personal experience has been or may be for the Good – a condition which can hardly be defined otherwise than by its fraternal Platonic attributes: Beauty and Truth.

19 'After the war I told myself everything must be vehement, intense, hard-hitting.' *Three Lives*, 230.

20 I discuss this in 'Hemingway & D'Annunzio' further on in this book.

21 Was Zweig a spy? At the outset of his career in Berlin in 1907, he met future Weimar Republic Foreign Secretary Walther Rathenau, who suggested that he go to India and America to view the Anglo-Saxon 'colonial' system from the inside. He was given letters of introduction by Baron von Münchhausen and teamed up with a journalist to play Hobhouse to his Byron. Encouraged to send cards and photographs back to 'important friends', he was able to place every article he wrote in leading journals. In India he communed with geographer Karl Haushofer, seconded there by the military and inceptor of Lebensraum theories later beloved

to the bestselling *Moon and Sixpence* and *Cakes and Ale*. Zweig shared with Maugham an ease of access into the imaginations of the middle-brow. His fictions can be marvellously finished but on inspection fall prey to charges of manipulation and sentimentality: the war-traumatized amnesiac of 'Episode an Genfer See' or the blind collector in 'Die unsichtbare Sammlung' are examples of each. The 'moral' behind such constructs is Dickensian in emphasis on charity. Zweig also shares with Erich von Remarque, Romain Rolland and Hermann Hesse[22] a modish 1920s turn to pacifism.

In texture Zweig's style is ever self-conscious, whether ornamental or spare. The biographical works which increasingly absorbed his energy became strikingly rhetorical, as if anticipating or mimicking great flings of speechmaking by a Mussolini or Goebbels, yet always in housebroken mode, as if uttered as lectures out of the pit of a darkened cinema where a silent film is simultaneously being unreeled. Coffee was Zweig's tipple and Balzac his pace-setter. His narratives have a velocity evoking the 'young man in a hurry' which another bestselling contemporary, Jack London, depicts in his writer-hero Martin Eden – also a suicide[23]. Zweig entitled his sole novel *Ungeduld des Herzens*[24] and remained faithful, one could say, to a fin-de-siècle

---

of the Nazis. Zweig's first wife, who would supervise his practical affairs, had been daughter-in-law to a high official in the Austrian foreign service, to whom she remained close. Zweig's work for the imperial 'hero factory' in World War I morphed at the war's end into lecturing abroad for the rump state. This raised his profile, and by the '20s the powers-that-be in Central Europe clearly found him useful to promote their ideas of culture worldwide. Kosher to a variety of régimes, Zweig found the last phase of his life marred by a rumour that the Brazilian government had subsidized him to write a book about the country in order to lure him to live and work there.

22   The latter two were friends and mentors to Zweig in pacifist and pan-European politics (see 13 above).

23   London's eponymous novel, by some considered his finest, was published in 1909. In an apprentice phase, Zweig had written a novella with similar plot, which was never published. *Three Lives*, 42.

24   *Impatience of the Heart*, released in English bizarrely as *Beware of Pity*.

creed of 'burn with a hard, gem-like flame'. If describing his achievement in terms of so many parallels and potencies seems pretentious, it is unlikely that he would have objected. A Valhalla of genius is where he longed to dwell, as one might guess of a fetishist of handwriting who pored over pages of Goethe or Mozart or even the hapless Mary Stuart before sitting down to purple ink and featherweight paper at Beethoven's writing desk.

Zweig's *Drang nach Grandeur*, noticeable also in book layouts and bindings, lured his language into what many saw as rhapsodic, *exaggeré*, showily seasoned with foreign or exotic locutions; and when Alfred Rosenberg's Nazi Kulturbund für deutsche Kultur got a grip in the 1930s, it was branded 'un-German'[25]. Fifteen of Zweig's books were banned by the Deutsche Buchverein in the autumn following Hitler's access to power. Too popular for suppression (50,000 copies of *Marie Antoinette* had sold the previous Christmas), they were restored to circulation in 1934, only to be banned again throughout Germany after the première of Richard Strauss's *Die schweigsame Frau* in 1935. This opera, marking Zweig's début as successor to Hofmannsthal as librettist to the greatest living German composer, caused a crisis in the Nazi arts hierarchy. In normal circumstances, Hitler would have travelled anywhere to attend a new work by Strauss, but – with text by a *Jew*?[26] Excuses were made; 'events' held the Führer in Berlin. The performance was a triumph but after two more, it was banned and Strauss obliged to step down as President of the Reichsmusikkammer.

To Zweig this débâcle was cognate with police turning

---

25 An article in 1930 accused him of 'crimes against the German language'. This was not just anti-Jewish rant; Kraus had made a similar attack on him earlier, and Hofmannsthal had once described Zweig as 'sixth-rate'. Of his biographical work it was said that 'he was always a storyteller first, not a historian', yet an early review of his stories by his friend Hesse damned him in that genre with faint praise: 'He has a singularly amiable personality... which is worth more than all the technique in the world'. *Three Lives*, 65, 73, 261.

26 Hofmannsthal was partly Jewish, but *Der Rosenkavalier* had been turning in the repertoire for so long and was so popular that the Nazis did not dare ban it. See 'Music in a Nazi Slumberland' later on in this book.

up at his house at Salzburg in search for weapons meant to be hidden on behalf of a socialist terrorist group. None were there, of course; the true terror was at the door. Of similar kind were the swindles, half-swindles and chiselling attendant on sale of his collections and the pusillanimity by publishers in discontinuing to market his work[27]. Zweig was too prescient not to have foreseen this dénouement and was already gone before the worst came. Transposition, however, was never sufficiently more than in body. As his swansong and elegiac masterwork *Die Welt von Gestern* shows, there was – beyond memory and the covers of fine books – no *elsewhere* to hold him, not finally, not fully, certainly not in the kind of voluptuous embrace he had enjoyed during the long adagio of *crépuscule* over disintegrating Hapsburg domains.

Three Lives: A Biography of Stefan Zweig, Oliver Matuschek (2006), trans. Allan Blunden. Pushkin Press, 2011.

---

27 Pusillanimity was not always on one side. In 1933 Zweig agreed to write for Klaus Mann's exile journal *Die Sammlung*, but he pulled out once he realized it would make sale of his books in Germany more difficult.

Fame and its Pursuers

Jewish Chronicle, 5 xi 2015

One associates struggling young writers with Parisian garrets and *La Bohème*, but Vienna of the fin-de-siècle was perhaps their great heyday. Hugo von Hofmannsthal and Stephan Zweig apprenticed themselves there. Slightly older was Arthur Schnitzler, best known now as the playwright of *La Ronde*.

Schnitzler mixed with theorists such as Freud and Herzl, also the 'second Viennese school' of musicians and 'Secessionist' visual artists. Like the Schönbergs and Schieles, he and his kind fancied themselves rebels: men of manifestoes, sure of their 'genius' almost before it had been put down in ink.

Late Fame is Schnitzler's never-before-published novella about this milieu. Translated by Alexander Starritt, it appears in an elegant edition from those fine exhumers of overlooked classics, Pushkin Press. It tells of a sexagenarian civil servant who wrote a slim volume of poems in youth, only to be neglected. One day a representative of 'Young Vienna' arrives at his door to inform him that he is now a heroic exemplar.

The old man visits the 'Enthusiasm' Society, which meets in a smoky café. Members represent all writerly identities – poet, novelist, playwright, critic, lecturer. Out-of-work actors attend too. In pique at general lack of attention, they devise an evening in which all may have fifteen minutes of fame. The old poet is to be lead-turn in this enterprise. He imagines himself on the verge of an adulation he had forgotten he deserved. In truth, he is being used mainly to promote younger men's work.

Schnitzler's protagonist moves between the self-styled avantgarde and amateur versifiers in an old duffers' pub. Pretentions of both are skewered: the backbiting of bohemians, the self-protective scorn of the settled bourgeois. At risk of being ludicrously out-of-time with the one and alienated by conventionality from the other, the old man gradually realizes that whatever poetic urge he had in youth has vanished, as if it belonged to another person entirely.

This is no tragedy, except perhaps to one shy acolyte who posits faith in his judgement. Seeking advice on whether he should take the risk of becoming a poet, he is told: 'If something was very beautiful or very bad, I might be able to tell you the difference; but to say whether you have talent or not? I don't understand the first thing.' Calloused humility at last must be learned. Caprice and chance lurk behind artistic success. Recognition of true talent is ever a crap-shoot.

Lost Fame, Arthur Schnitzler, trans. Alexander Starritt. Pushkin Press, 2015.

Father to the Man

Quarterly Review, 2 iii 2014

In this year of the centenary of the start of World War I, the dinner-party topic *du jour* in Britain is: should we have fought, and who was to blame? The consensual answer, with which 'sound' types are meant to agree, is the conventional one: Britain was noble to have devoted blood and treasure to a just cause (technically, the inviolability of Belgium), and the villain was German militarism. In this self-serving gloss, almost nobody mentions that it was Russian mobilization which set the alliance-system dominoes falling, or that the cause of that sudden show of force was Austro-Hungary's ultimatum to Serbia and its belligerent reaction when its tiny neighbour didn't immediately click heels in abject assent.

Austro-Hungary was the sick man of Europe. Presided over by the octogenarian scion of a dynasty that had reigned at the heart of the continent far too long, it could hold together a fissiparous mass only by a bureaucracy best known via Kafka and a military whose pomp was in inverse proportion to its performance, from Sadowa back to Austerlitz. Even the puny Prussia of Frederick the Great had done rather well against it in the salad days of Maria Theresa. Cultural drift reflected this long goodbye in political dominance, with the brio of the age of Mozart, Haydn, Beethoven and Schubert giving way to an era 'when joy had become a subtle form of pain'[1] – Mahler, Schönberg, Berg, Webern and the decadence Richard Strauss deftly rendered in music for the *Salomé* of Oscar Wilde (1906).

This pullulating period produced Secessionist artists specializing in borderline porn: the self-frigging females of Klimt, masturbatory self-images in Schiele. The prurient imaginings of Stefan Zweig reflected desires concealed beneath the perfume of the bourgeoisie, so too an endless discovery

---

1 The phrase is Arthur Symons' in an essay contrasting the era of Beethoven to that of Wagner and after.

of sexual motivation behind conduct recorded by Dr Freud. Vienna gave in to temptation and elected an anti-Semite as mayor, mirroring its majority's loathing for so many non-native-German speakers in its midst. Odium lurked beyond its favourite Strauss (Johann) waltzes until even the avantgarde Strauss (Richard) was persuaded to change tune and glorify nostalgia in *Der Rosenkavalier*. This overlong swan-song for an epoch was produced in a year when Adolf Hitler was eking out his living selling painted postcards of quaint olden buildings. Vienna was rotten and Austro-Hungary already breaking up, though few yet quite admitted to it. Soon all would turn worse, the 'nation' dismembered, its half-a-millennium-long monarchy deposed, the perverse delights of a Zweig giving way to the monstrosities of, say, Elias Canetti – *Die Blendung* (1935).

The greatest literary figure of this parlous place and time is seen by many to be Robert Musil. His long, unfinished masterpiece *Der Mann ohne Eigenschaften* (*The Man without Qualities*) is often ranked with Proust's *À la recherche du temps perdu*, Joyce's *Ulysses* and Mann's *The Magic Mountain* as a 'book to go beyond all books'[2] of an era. Musil painted his world in intimate detail, recording its vices undauntedly, analyzing with profound curvature, using language like a master and tapping into the new-ish frontier of inner life with a candour which arguably surpassed that of his rivals. Like Joyce and the others, his great work was preceded by a Bildungsroman exploring the young artist in embryo or a persona very like him – Proust's Jean Santeuil, Joyce's Stephen Dedalus, Mann's Tonio Kröger. *Der Verwirrungen des Zöglings Törless* – *The Confusions of Young Master Törless* as Musil's 1906 work is entitled in its latest English translation – describes a crucial year in the development of a bureaucrat's son at one of the empire's élite academies. The milieu may seem familiar to English readers knowledgeable about public schools, from the playing fields of Eton on down.

---

2 The phrase is Nietzsche's (*Gaya Scienza*, III, 248) and would likely have been familiar to all of these authors, with the possible exception of Proust, who might have known better a similar dictum of Mallarmé's.

Yet the power struggles and sadism which Musil's protagonist encounters will shock the sensitivities of graduates sentimentally still wedded to a roseate notion that schooldays are mainly an epoch of memorable fellowship and pastoral growth.

Törless's institution is far off in the countryside, an isolation meant to protect its students from urban vice. In fact, it is a perfect setting for worse. There is a village nearby, but the peasants who frequent its sole tavern are brutes; and when not performing as work-beasts, they spend their hours drinking themselves silly and abusing the local prostitute. The schoolboys evade these frightening males but visit the whore too, unsure of what to do with her but boasting otherwise. The most epicene of them, impecunious Basini, accumulates debts from his visits and services them by pilfering cash from his classmates' lockers. A clique discovers his 'crime' and initiates a cycle of intimidation and blackmail as his punishment, leading to repeated homosexual rape, beatings and torture. Törless is at first no more than an observer of these violations: he is a straight-arrow who is simply outraged by Basini's theft. However, when all the other boys are away on a long weekend, leaving him and Basini virtually alone at the school, a curious erotic attraction leads him into his own heartless liaison with his abused fellow. A mixture of existential indifference and free-floating anxiety follows.

The plot is marked by graphic, occasionally lubricious descriptions which take it well beyond what the north German Mann had intimated in his homoerotic *Tonio Kröger* four years before or would in his more mature *Tod in Venedig* five years on. The latter shares in identifying temptation and downfall with the beauty of a teenage boy, an Italian penumbra behind him – Basini's name, Mann's novella's location – yet revealed sex and its consummation are not even imagined. Nor are they importantly depicted in the début novel Joyce would begin in the Austro-Hungarian port of Trieste in the year of *Törless*'s publication. What *A Portrait of the Artist as a Young Man* (or *Stephen Hero* as it began life) shares with Musil's novella – Mann's too in its ways – is a blending of philosophy and metaphysics into the account of moral awakening. In Joyce's book these grow out of arguments with religion and nation to assume centre-stage and proceed to a weighing-up of aesthetics as the way forward. In *Törless* similar arguments and weighings-up are opaque. Religion does not figure and nation is unmentioned, possibly because the 'nation' in which the action takes place is no longer much more than a theoretical amalgam.

Its mélange is reflected in the identities of the book's principal characters: Reitling, Germanic, given to command, oratory and manipulation; Beineberg, possibly Jewish, given to science of mind, hypnosis and the occult; a Viennese prince; a Polish count; the indeterminate Törless; Galician peasants and of course the hapless Basini. It seems portentous that abuse is doled out to this non-Austrian, an incomer from one of the empire's peripheral provinces, a foreshadowing perhaps of the roles that subject nations of Hapsburgia would play within a decade and their disintegrative effect on the whole. Törless, through whose eyes we see, does not interpret matters so prophetically; but Musil's intentions are subtle. He arranges his dramatis personae in such a way that we are invited to sense it as representing larger forces. At the very least, the supporting characters embody fundamental tendencies of mind around which the relatively passive protagonist must find his own way. Yet, try to do this as he vaguely does, the young man can achieve no firm direction. Törless remains a dreamer who is happiest when lying on his back in the grass observing infinity in passing clouds or is fascinated by imaginary mathematics and the writings of Kant without managing much true understanding of either.

This unsettling book, revolting at turns, is sinister in its power of seduction. In a useful afterword, its new translator says that 'much of [its] impact derives from Musil's poetic and incisive prose'. He describes enthusiastically a style 'littered with idioms from French and the many different national languages of the Empire – and *Kanzleisprache*, the intricately formal parlance of the omnipresent Austro-Hungarian bureaucracy'.

Said bureaucracy is strangely absent as the terrible plot unfolds: again and again one wishes that some prefect or master would step in to prevent evil; yet none appears until the end, when Törless musters the gumption to tell Basini to alert them. Meanwhile, the richness of language which the translator extols is not conveyed easily in English. He may be correct that 'the narrative often resembles a combination of an epic poem and a ministerial briefing document, leading us through a maze of subordinate clauses where foreign words and phrases suddenly explode like fireworks'; yet foreign phrases are few in his version, and fireworks, epic poetry and bureaucratese hard to discern. The style of subordinate clauses as presented here either leaves us groping for meaning or is broken into shorter, more comprehensible sentences. Read the book in the original German, if you can, or at least with it alongside. Otherwise, you may suffer an antipathetic experience without consolation of its redeeming aesthetic brilliance.

The Confusions of Young Master Törless, Robert Musil, trans. Christopher Moncrieff. Alma Classics, 2013.

Mussolini and the murderous madame

Quarterly Review, Summer 2010

Assassination was a traditional political tool revived in the neo-Borgian epoch of Fascist Italy. Precursor of its dramas, in which Mussolini played *Heldentenor*, was decadent writer and famed lover of Eleanora Duse, Gabriele D'Annunzio. His apotheosis as political hero came during World War I when, with financial assistance from the French[1], he helped persuade Italy to dump the Triple Alliance and support the other preeminent Latin power. Creating Greater Italy vs. 'twin threats of pan-Germanism and pan-Slavism' was his cry; dropping leaflets from planes over Trento and Trieste made him 'the best propaganda instrument Italy had'; being shot down and blinded in one eye increased his celebrity. When Italy was 'betrayed' at Versailles by not receiving her 'left lung' – i.e., Adriatic territories once held by Venice but assigned by Woodrow Wilson to a new 'Jugo-slavia' – he led irredentist *arditi* in a coup at Fiume and propagandized for government based on a 'contract' of universal suffrage, schools free of state and religious propaganda, free press, free trade unions and 'a kingdom of the human spirit' encouraged via music and poetry.

Socialist as well as nationalist, D'Annunzio remained popular in Italy well after Rome was obliged to relocate him to a villa at Lago di Garda once occupied by a stepdaughter of his early idol Richard Wagner[2]. 'De-Germanizing' the place, D'Annunzio recast it as the Vittoriale, a Bayreuth-like shrine to his own ideals of art and heroism. Despite nights marked by 'attacks of lycanthropy', the ex-soldier-of-fortune settled into relatively mild days of editing his oeuvre and entertaining

---

1 See John Woodhouse, *Gabriele D'Annunzio: Defiant Archangel* (Clarendon, 1998), 273-89. D'Annunzio left Italy in 1912 to evade debts and settled near Paris. In 1915 the French government 'restrained his creditors' and encouraged him to return to Italy, along with a battalion led by the grandson of Garibaldi.

2 D'Annunzio's longest and most important novel, *Il Fuoco* (1899), pivots around Wagner's death in Venice. See note 10 in 'Ride of the Wagner Debunkers' above.

mistresses. His continuing clout worried Mussolini, who had kept a low profile during the Fiume affair; and while praising him in public, the *Duce* was privately unperturbed when, shortly before his March on Rome, D'Annunzio fell from a window during a party at which a Fascist agent was present, nor when rumours were spread that the writer had been groping the sister of his mistress while out of control on cocaine[3]. Once in power, Mussolini sent D'Annunzio gifts at the same time as Fascist *squadristi* were beating up his supporters. In a year when four attempts on *his* life helped him to establish full dictatorship, the *Duce* made a pilgrimage to the Vittoriale and declared it a national monument, assisting the chronically indebted writer and buying his complicity. In his inner circle Mussolini was known to remark that D'Annunzio was 'a broken tooth which had either to be eradicated or covered in gold'. He did the latter, but the gilding may have proved inadequate. Ever Francophile and hostile to Germans, who in his view 'treated Italy like a museum, a hotel, a place for vacationing, a horizon painted Prussian blue', D'Annunzio mocked Hitler. Though aging and ill, he travelled to Verona to meet Mussolini's train on its way up to Brennero to warn against the 'Pact of Steel'. Did this hasten his end? A young Tyrolean woman serving at the Vittoriale vanished into his bedroom for days a time, doors locked. When one of these supposed sex-and-drug sessions went on for too long, the room was entered and D'Annunzio found dead but she nowhere. Mussolini and Co. arrived from Rome within hours; the body was buried with small ceremony and no inquest made. Weeks later the braided Tyrolean was spotted in Berlin, working in the offices of von Ribbentrop.

---

3   Saunders mentions the event in *The Woman Who Shot Mussolini*, 103-4, but unlike commentators then and since sees nothing sinister in it. In general she is not interested in D'Annunzio, whom she dismisses with a quote from a secondary source as an 'unreadable' writer, producing 'trashily plotted novels about supermen figures who are transparently the author himself'. In his day international literati felt somewhat differently, as essays by Henry James, Arthur Symons, James Joyce and Ezra Pound *inter alia* would attest. See the following chapter.

It was an era of Mata Haris. A different incarnation was Violet Gibson, subject of *The Woman Who Shot Mussolini*. After *Who Paid the Piper?*, which scrutinized CIA operatives in the cultural Cold War, and *Hawkwood*, which assayed the prototype of rogue mercenaries such as we know via Blackwater etc., it is apt that Frances Stonor Saunders should have turned her attention to this third type in a timeless theatre of political skulduggery: the apparently lone fanatic willing to martyr him-or-herself in a 'higher' cause. Gibson was a younger daughter of Lord Ashbourne, onetime Lord Chancellor of Ireland and a familiar of George V's before the latter became king. Though privileged, Violet's youth was a weary trudge through turn-of-the-century Anglo-Irish frustrations, political and otherwise. One beloved brother became a casualty of the trenches; another grew active in the Gaelic League. Conventional marriage unavailing, Violet took up Theosophy and feminism before converting to an edgy Catholicism, illuminated by the lives of the saints. Spinsters of her era often occupied themselves in religious or human rights charities then springing up; Violet instead chose to travel to Europe, adopt the faddish extremities of a Zeitgeist and like Nijinsky or Virginia Woolf descend into mental vagary. She spent time in confinement but was not ill enough to remain. Ideas of killing the Pope morphed into shooting Mussolini as he emerged from a meeting in Rome, April 1926. Was Violet induced into this act, and if so by whom? Marxists? 'pre-mature anti-fascists'? dissident moderates such as the Duke of Cesarò, whom she claimed to have been in love with and to have received signals from? The complex of pathologies and motives offers no assured truth, but that may be just the point. In weird anticipation of what happened to Silvio Berlusconi on the eve of Saunders' book appearing, the Italian leader escaped with a grazed nose, spurting a dramatic quantity of blood and thereby evoking a convenient outpouring of national sympathy.

New opportunities had arisen in the era of Freud. Culture was becoming willing to see personality as erratic, potentially damaged or blocked into patterns incapacitating right thought.

Individual culpability could now be questioned, even in its own terms and to itself. Acts once ascribed to evil or possession – 'the devil made me do it' – yet nonetheless punishable might float into realms magically as if beyond judgment or blame. With inception and motive buried under shards of a putatively fractured psyche, Gibson's act could be called 'mad'. But was it truly? Might she have not simply simulated rage and delusion to evade punishment for what had been coolly planned? Did it suit others for her to fake lunacy? Was her 'diseased will' strong enough to keep up an act through unpredictable years of incarceration? If so, for whom? those who might profit from Mussolini's end? Or was her attempt only ever meant to wound; in which case, cui bono? Britain's establishment feared Bolshevism. In this year of the General Strike, it favoured all anti-communist movements. As early as 1916 Samuel Hoare had urged the Treasury to funnel money into Mussolini via his socialist newspaper *Il Popolo*. In the following decade Foreign Secretary Austen Chamberlain would come to treat *Il Duce* with something resembling homoerotic awe. It was, in any case, essential to Britain that this high-born lady's act not be allowed to stir the Italian regime's hostility. Conversely Mussolini felt obliged to stay in Britain's good graces during a period in which he was liquidating opponents and all action against him was being co-opted to secure the Fascist dictatorship. Both sides, in short, had reason to spin Violet Gibson as mad, bad, sad, deserving to be sent home and confined.

Forms had to be observed even if conspiracy theories abounded. Investigation by Superintendant Epifanio Pennetta[4] moved rapidly to unearth what underlay Violet's deed. His eagerness was shared by both the Crown Prosecutor and the *Intransigenti* – enthusiasts of a harsher, swifter *fascistizzare,* led by Roberto Farinacci. Dictators need outriders to be restrained to create an appearance of magnanimity and pragmatism: Hitler had the Strassers, too socialist; Röhm, a threat to traditional

---

4 Surname resembling that of the present [2010] CIA Director, as readers of *Who Paid the Piper?* might find piquant.

military; even Julius Streicher, too anti-Semitic. As in many touches, Mussolini anticipated his Austro-Germanic imitator: to show clemency to Miss Gibson was to rise above petty rancour; but it had to be done deftly and to milk maximum benefit. Pennetta pondered Violet's history of odd excursions prior to her attack, of suspect encounters, of unusual sums of money flowing through her account; but when interrogation produced her claim of contact with the Duke of Cesarò, who had served in Mussolini's first, not fully Fascist cabinet, it was dismissed as fantasy, and gradually investigation was sidelined in favour of psychologizing. Enrico Ferri was brought in to argue that a person might be sane and insane at the same time. A sudden flare-up in prison – Violet took a hammer to a fellow-inmate's pate – assisted a 'defence' that she was unfit for trial. A hearing was called before a set tribunal; motions were gone through; the result was a foregone conclusion. Following an assurance from Gibson's family that she would be locked up in England, Mussolini's agents secured her deportation. They took care not to reveal the day or the train lest overzealous *squadristi* be tempted to practice their usual vigilante justice.

The story of Violet Gibson fuses two seemingly incompatible types: the would-be martyr/assassin and Englishwomen of privilege who normally withdraw to Jane Austenian lives of small pleasures, even in 'quiet desperation'. Deviance in the latter may for generic reasons interest Saunders more than matters of a larger, contemporary world; it may also constitute a good publishing wheeze, attracting female readers to what might seem yet one more history of a repugnantly masculinist era of Machiavellianism and mass murder. Should we take it as more? a portent, say, of how English womanhood might behave in times of decadence and activism? Saunders does not state this. What she does argue is that her composite type, like both of its halves, found in Mussolini the perfect *monstre sacre*; further, that in its capacities for fanaticism and 'living dangerously' at least, his type represented a perfect obverse. This veers close to the position of Ferri, which Saunders mocks: that there are 'borderlands of the mind' on one side of which a Darwinian supertype may appear, capable of 'superior expression of political thought and action', while on the other a possessor of 'sick will power' may fall prey to 'slow invasion of the homicidal idea' – i.e., the exceptionality which led to heroic leadership in *Il Duce* could in a lesser personality produce a Violet Gibson. In accepting Ferri's line of thinking, the tribunal prorogued further inquiry, dismissing the assailant as too unreliable to justify following up clues she gave as to her motive, her preparation or her sources of 'slow invasion'. It was, as Saunders says, in any case self-evident to judges under Fascist supervision that 'nobody in their right mind could want to stop Mussolini in his historic tracks'.

Such arguments might pass in Italy of 1927. That they should have impressed official Britain to the extent that it made sure the Gibsons institutionalized Violet on repatriation may be understood best on the hoary grounds of 'national interest'. Why then no change after 1936, when Italy's invasion of Ethiopia lifted the scales from Brit eyes? Wouldn't her act from that point seem prescient? And after Italy's entry into the Axis and its opportunistic invasions of Nice, Albania, Greece and Tunis, mightn't Violet have been embraced as a heroine? In 1943, when the Fascist council deposed its leader, or in 1945, when Mussolini's Salò Republic collapsed and he and his mistress were strung up by their heels, couldn't a septuagenarian heart-patient have been released? Was Violet simply the victim of a grand family's urge to keep an embarrassment hidden away, akin to the five maternal cousins of the present Queen who, Saunders notes, were shut into asylum and effaced from *Burke's*? That would be, relatively speaking, an easy answer. Larger questions may have to do with how régimes deal with unstable persons who may once have seemed useful for covert policy or national hedging-of-bets. We know how literary apparatchiks persuaded Ezra Pound to plead insanity in order to evade trial for his support of Fascism; he too was locked away and freed to return to his beloved Italy only once he had become a snag-toothed oldie descending into cryptic silence. Saunders wondered in *Who Paid the Piper?* to what extent James Jesus Angleton, 'legendary' counter-intelligence chief of the CIA, had a hand in Pound's incarceration and release[5]. Was Angleton interested merely because he read poetry, or had the author of *Jefferson and/or Mussolini* long been a person the powers-that-be had kept in their sights lest fortunes should change and realpolitik demand new directions? Could Violet Gibson have been in an analogous position, if in her relation to Fascism reversed? If so, why did her minders not let the harmless bird fly? mere carelessness, or did some inconvenient old truth make it seem just too risky? This is a type of question for which a proper answer may remain permanently obscured.

The Woman Who Shot Mussolini, Frances Stonor Saunders. Faber & Faber, 2010.

---

5 Granta, 1999, 248-51. Saunders moves into her speculations via Allen Ginsberg's 1978 fantasia 'T. S. Eliot Entered My Dreams'. Angleton when a student stayed for an extended period in Rapallo near Pound and participated in his 'Ezuversity'. A decade later, almost to the day when Pound was sent from the U.S. Army Detention Center in Pisa to Washington D.C. to have his treason judged, Angleton returned to Italy to direct postwar counter-intelligence for the OSS.

Gabriele D'Annunzio – flame of the former future

Quarterly Review, 25 iii 2013

When living in lascivious pleasure in post-Napoleonic Italy, Byron wrote to his publisher, 'Scribbling is a disease I wish myself cured of'. Within a few years he was famously dead in the cause of Greek independence, and for a century after writers regularly chafed at the bonds of their profession, wishing to transform themselves into men of action. A leap out of art and into history usually involved adopting a messianic cause, which if frustrated could produce antinomian outbursts, even crime. W. B. Yeats, who dreamed of glory and dabbled in Irish revolution and later fascism, spotted the danger – 'Did that play of mine send out/ Certain men the English shot?'[1] Nonetheless he was among the host of literati of the early 20th century who found inspiration in their Italian contemporary Gabriele D'Annunzio. Henry James, George Moore, James Joyce, D. H. Lawrence, Marcel Proust, Ernest Hemingway[2] all admired his prose. Ezra Pound perhaps came closest to him in morphing literary prominence into political activism. In Pound's case, failure of the cause led to disaster. In D'Annunzio's, at least in his lifetime, it produced even greater celebrity.

Named for an archangel and seen by some as a devil, he appears to have been born under a lucky star. His father, a licentious man and skilful networker, was mayor of Pescara in the backward province of Abruzzi; his mother, like Lawrence's, was of more refined stock. The child was doted on, educated above his station and subsidized through his first literary efforts, which rendered him into a Wunderkind as poet by age twenty. Adept at networking too and striking-looking, if small, he set about climbing the social and literary ladders of Rome via shrewd love-affairs and journalistic alliances. Newly unified Italy needed geniuses, and patriotic Gabriele perfectly combined the

---

1 'The Man and the Echo'.

2 See 'Hemingway & D'Annunzio' later in this book.

persona of coming young man with respect for an older order of rank. Parisian decadence, Dostoyevsky, Nietzsche, Wagner and other artistic fads of the fin-de-siècle were mixed easily by him into a specifically Italian penchant for beauty and tradition. Turning to novel-writing, he became by age thirty one of the leading literary names of the age. A very public affair with the actress Eleanora Duse vaulted him by the turn of the century into world celebrity.

He wrote gargantuan plays for his mistress, though on one occasion infuriated her by offering the lead to her rival Sarah Bernhardt, whom he may also have bedded. His reputation was such that he felt at ease in spurning collaboration with Puccini, whom he saw as not high-brow enough to do his work justice. Published simultaneously in French and Italian, he became a figure to envy in the then citadel of the arts and relocated there in 1910 to escape debts he had racked up in a notoriously extravagant lifestyle. In the salons of Paris he was lionized by the Count of Montesquiou, once inspiration for Huysmans' Des Esseintes and shortly for Proust's Baron Charlus. Debussy was allowed to set music to his *Martyrdom of St Sebastian* and Ida Rubenstein to play the lead. Cross-dressers and lesbians appealed to his increasingly jaded sexual taste, and along with Rubenstein the American painter Romaine Brooks joined the list of his lovers. In the demimonde they moved in, the chief slander from which a woman could suffer was to be said *not* to have had a liaison with D'Annunzio.

All this Lucy Hughes-Hallett catalogues with eyes on stilts. She is fascinated to uncover what this bald little man in goatee did with and to women to attract them in droves. Delving into the wealth of letters he left, which his lovers failed to destroy, she details the foods and the fabrics, the flowers and scents, the acts and afterglows which attended his clandestine post-midnights and *cinq-à-septs*. Cunning in seduction, D'Annunzio was also blithe in discarding what he had done with; thus a trail of children and ex-paramours was left in his wake as he set out on the greater adventure of his career – to persuade Italy to fight on the side of its Latin sibling in World War I and to demand a larger share of the spoils than the Allies were willing to give at Versailles. Having promised his country all that it had asked for in order to abandon the Triple Alliance, France and Britain reneged under cover of Wilson's Fourteen Points. D'Annunzio, who had been instrumental in engineering Italy's volte-face and became its lead propagandist during a fight in which 600,000 of his countrymen died, was, not surprisingly, outraged.

He had preached war as the crucible out of which glory was forged and blood as a libation needed to fertilize the soil of an expanding new nation. He himself had lost an eye in one of many exploits in modern chariots of battle: the airplane and the motorized attack-boat. Gutsy as a diminutive Napoleon, he had become a hero for millions, his rhetoric fanning their war-cries, his commitment to fight on for territories 'unredeemed' rallying their postwar bellicosity. When he staged a coup in the sub-Istrian port of Fiume, proposing to make it a bulwark against what he saw as a trumped-up southern Slav kingdom, demobbed soldiers and unemployed thugs flocked to his banner. Over them and others enraged at the 'unfair' peace and the pusillanimity of official leaders, he ruled as a quite benign dictator. Promulgating his own post-democratic political charter, he presided for a year over a festival of art, sex, drugs, expressionistic glamour and larceny until the 'eunuchs' of Rome, under pressure from the West, forced him to step down.

On this episode Hughes-Hallett focuses her most excited attention, and for a spell D'Annunzio's experiment in Fiume indeed dazzled the world. His mesmeric speeches evoked mass adulation, and the trooping of *Arditi* and other young irregulars through the piazza of his mini-state impressed women and men alike. Here was chutzpah incarnate, Nietzschean exuberance rather than the threat of proletarian excess, which Lenin and Trotsky were fomenting in Russia or Bela Kuhn and Kurt Eisner closer to home. D'Annunzio was no enemy to Western civilization *tout court*, rather its prospective defender, an antidote to its torpor – or so many imagined. Others noted a jack-booted edge to the performance. Mussolini, who slyly did not get involved, wrote in tepid support from his editor's desk at *Il Popolo*. D'Annunzio had become far and away the most charismatic political figure in Italy: he could be neither opposed nor fully adhered to by a younger man with rival ambitions.

D'Annunzio might have spread his revolt from Fiume back into and down the national peninsula. In the post-Versailles atmosphere, discontent was so rife that action against the men of Rome might have been propitious. But the man dithered. Hughes-Hallett tells how at crucial moments he would slip away to luxuriate in his bath, thence to a long *crépuscule* of aesthetic delights – he had his own string quartet to serenade him – entertaining the de rigueur mistress or two amid an overlord's gaudy display of mufti and trinkets. Perhaps he was just too old by the time for action – 60 to Mussolini's 40. In any case, despite professions that he would die for Fiume, he let himself to be pensioned off to Lago di Garda, where he spent the final seventeen years of his life creating a private Xanadu out of a lakeside villa once owned by the art-historian Heinrich Thode, husband of Cosima Wagner's daughter Daniela, complete with a piano whose ivories had been tinkled upon by her womanizing celebrity grandfather Liszt[3].

D'Annunzio remained a figure of notoriety through these later years. Mussolini feared his political intervention and did all possible to keep him shut up in his shrine, eventually dubbed the 'Vittoriale', a word intimating the role its inhabitant had played in victory over Austro-Hungary and as 'phraser of the dialectic of fascism'[4]. Major differences might have set him against the *Duce*, not least the Latin racism which inclined him forever against the 'Teuton' and Slav; Hughes-Hallett, however, rejects the story that he could have been murdered by a German agent out of fear of his opposition to the Berlin-Rome Axis.[5] She attributes

---

3   Liszt, Cosima and Wagner all figure at crucial moments in D'Annunzio's largest novel *Il Fuoco*. See also note 10 to 'Ride of the Wagner Debunkers'.

4   Hemingway's tag, in *Across the River and into the Trees*. See note 2 above.

5   See the first paragraphs of 'Mussolini and the murderous madame'.

his fatal heart attack to chronic abuse of cocaine and a penchant for orgy even at age 74. Shades of Silvio Berlusconi spring to mind, 'bunga bunga' being a demotic version of what went on in the Vittoriale's warren of dark-draperied rooms. Berlusconi, however, has only outrageous eccentricity in common with his arguable precursor, for D'Annunzio was until the end a serious or at least self-conscious artist.

Hemingway revered *Notturno* and owed inspiration to it. Proust subsumed the inwardness, self-analysis and narrative abundance of *L'Innocente* and *Il Fuoco*, a title which Hughes-Hallett renders as *Fire* though Hemingway and others of the epoch would have read as *The Flame*. The latter indicates the dominion of Duse over the novel, but Hughes-Hallett may prefer a 1960s tinge to her version. This hovers behind her account of long-haired bad boys roaming the streets of Fiume, hot nights of fornication in alleys or on wharf side – young masculinist fun that both prostitutes and slumming patrician ladies abetted. Hughes-Hallett views this with indulgence, as did its true begetter. Her dictator of Fiume might be a sibling to the 'wickedest man in the world', the equally bald Aleister Crowley, practising 'sex magick' in a commune in another port town at the far end of Italy. Licentiousness was abroad and D'Annunzio a fount of it. His example no doubt encouraged other Anglo expatriate writers to preach it during their own sojourns in Italy of the time – Lawrence in 'Sun', Pound in his 'Circe' cantos.

Hughes-Hallett's enthusiasm for this aspect of her subject prompts her on occasion to make explicit parallels between the carnival that was Fiume and the 'new age' of the '60s. On BBC3's Private Passions, aired to coincide with her book's launch, she identified herself as of a generation which grew up when Eros was defined by the Rolling Stones and chose as her one non-classical inclusion Mick Jagger's seductive if provocatively misogynist 'Under My Thumb'. No sentimentality here, rather challenge, effrontery. Hughes-Hallett's treatment of the D'Annunzio phenomenon in this way has a likeness to her friend Ann Wroe's 'biography' of the applicable archetype in her recent *Orpheus*, which interrupts serious discussion to notice a rock busker in the London Underground and paints the inceptor of music as a spirit of dark shades, a lover of all yet above all of himself with a sinister streak that makes it seem almost apt for him to have been ripped apart by inflamed maenads in the end[6].

A sado-masochistic element in D'Annunzio's work coloured his exploits as much as his décor and arguably assisted his courage. The awful side of it affected the imagination of great Italian artists to come – in film, Pasolini in *Salò*, a town within sight of the Vittoriale, and Visconti in *The Damned* as elsewhere. But post-Fascist Italy and postwar cultural judgement sought to downgrade this once titanic figure, a re-rating Hughes-Hallett partly seeks to correct, though she fails to provide enough space to his serious work. A page or two each for *L'Innocente* and *Il Fuoco* seems derisory in a book whose main text runs to 650 pages. These are major novels, as Henry James knew when he broke off writing his own most D'Annunzian effort[7], set partly in a *Fuoco*-like Venice, to dictate an extended essay about the Italian for *Quarterly Review* [8]. The paucity of Hughes-Hallett's treatment makes one wonder if she did much more than speed-read what now are considered unfashionable texts.

In the genre of trade biography, big name authors often favour sensation and eschew any whiff of the academic. Editors concerned with sales encourage this, and writers whose day job may be mainly journalism fear if not loathe experts who might take them to task over this fact or that. Some mix of such motives may be what brings Hughes-Hallett, her editor or both to confine references to summaries of the sources read for each chapter. These 'notes' are prefaced by an invitation to those wishing exact citations to contact the author via the publisher's website. I wonder how many have done so and, if so, have been

---

6 My essay on Wroe's book appears at the end of this book.

7 *The Wings of the Dove*, 1902, two years after *Il Fuoco*. D'Annunzio may also hover behind *The Golden Bowl*, 1904, not least the character of Prince Amerigo.

8 This appeared in QR April 1904. It is omitted from Penguin Classics of James's literary criticism on the grounds that 'D'Annunzio is so little read nowadays'.

responded to to their satisfaction, and how quickly. The tactic seems designed to chill scholars hot on the trail of the origins of the many myths which inevitably grow up around figures of D'Annunzio's charisma. The approach might encourage loose tale-tellers to legerdemain, if not outright dishonesty, and in this respect, as in its tightness of narrative, John Woodhouse's 1998 biography *Gabriele D'Annunzio: Defiant Archangel* shows a steadier hand. In any case, it has a better title.

'Pike' refers to a quip made by D'Annunzio's onetime friend the writer Romain Rolland, whose politics became pacifist at the same time the Italian's became militarist. The fish in question is a predator which lurks in wait for its prey; D'Annunzio, said Rolland, ever lurked in wait for ideas – in style, in content – fresh models to swallow and vomit back as his own. Well, great writers steal, they don't borrow, T. S. Eliot famously said; moreover, D'Annunzio was as sinned against as sinning in the practice – Lawrence, Joyce, Proust, Hemingway on the one hand vs. Nietzsche, Dostoyevsky, Huysmans and Wilde on the other. Had D'Annunzio's politics not disgusted Rolland, the epithet might never have been applied, and the fact that Hughes-Hallett uses it only once or twice in her introductory pages suggests that it was an afterthought, encouraged perhaps by editorial concern that her book not appear too much in thrall to what post-Fascism has deemed a rebarbative subject. One is reminded of the blithe coda tacked onto the end of *Don Giovanni*, which fails utterly to efface a dominant impression of what went before: the awesome spectacle of a libertine to whom daring is all and the consequences of being pulled down into flame is faced with a roar, not a whimper.

The Pike, in short, is not about D'Annunzio being a 'pike', it is about him being a dangerous exemplar of genius. His courage, allied to sensuality in extremis, is what attracts the author and gives her text a narrative drive and flavour far beyond what the less affected Woodhouse conveys. An Italian commentator said of D'Annunzio's most youthful novel that you could sense an excess of semen about it; Hughes-Hallett daubs in the 'orgasmo' with which women responded to this 'seminal' figure of a modern *Italianità*. The book is prurient and would be less if it were not so, for the erotic within the aesthetic is essential to what Italians have called *dannunzianismo*. The sanguinary is here too, and towards it Hughes-Hallett's moral compass is spot on. D'Annunzio's war-mongering – '*Morire non è basta*'[9] – was appalling and the results terrifying. He too of course suffered – impaired vision, headaches, hallucinations – and his emphasis on remembrance of the dead in the elegiac *Notturno*, as in the Vittoriale itself, is impressive. But no part of Hughes-Hallett's book is more moving than her account of the ghastly, unnecessary carnage that went on on the Isonzo and the Piave from 1916 to 1918.

Her descriptions of war have a Goya-esque grandeur. Add them to Hemingway's in *A Farewell to Arms* and you begin to understand modern Italy with a profundity that elbows aside the blithe jokes about Berlusconi or Beppe Grillo that are common currency nowadays. For this alone Hughes-Hallett's book is worth reading. Alongside Amanda Foreman's treatment of the carnage of the American civil war in her recent *A World on Fire*, it makes one wonder if a new age is at hand for history written by women – an age in which the matter of blood and destruction wreaked by men is weighed up and grieved over, yet with a fine objectivity, by the sex that largely did not participate in it. Here may be a writerly equivalent to the advent of Hillary Clinton, Susan Rice and 'Oestrogen Power' into the arena of war-making policy[10]. Let us hope women do better. Certainly it is hard to imagine D'Annunzio's Nietzschean cries for Dionysian glory in death issuing from the lips of the greater or sometimes lesser beauties he spent so much of the rest of his career longing with purple vehemence to kiss.

The Pike: Gabriele D'Annunzio, Poet, Seducer & Preacher of War. Lucy Hughes-Hallett, Fourth Estate, 2013.

---

9   As Hemingway quotes, again in *Across the River and into the Trees*. Note 2 above.
10 On this see Ilana Mercer's 'Libya: a war of the womb' in *QR* (Spring 2011).

Cultural Disease Diagnostician

Jewish Chronicle, 18 ix 2015

Late in his short life Joseph Roth deliberately spoiled a pair of trousers which his better-off Viennese fellow-writer Stefan Zweig had bought for him. Loath to accept charity, he died an alcoholic early in 1939. Best known for his novel *The Radetzky March*, he had supported himself mainly by penning feuilleton pieces for German-language newspapers. Adept at spotting cultural disease, his decline was hastened by a cancer he diagnosed from the start. Its mark was the swastika.

Roth inspected graffiti on bullet-pocked walls and scabs on bodies politic hurtling between catastrophes. His pieces are pictorial: literary equivalents to sketches by Grosz or Chagall. Their range is broad: from the mud of peasant Galicia to the smoke-binding undifferentiated cities of the Ruhr. He locates social parables in a blond black French soldier or a secretary fallen into morphine-induced street-walking. The bourgeois angst of Zweig's carpet-slippered milieu interests him little. Troublous expressionisms of the dispossessed are his patch.

He style is quick, dashed with colour and rendered vivid in English by Michael Hofmann. In an explicit labor of love, the distinguished translator draws his favorite bits of Rothiana into a multi-hued fresco of a raucous time and place. The disparate morphs into a coherent whole, and a new classic is born for all of us struggling still to comprehend the Europe of an epoch that beggars belief.

Pathos, irony, prose poetry and bottled rage decorate Roth's depictions. Of villeins sleeping 4th class on a Volga steamer, he muses: 'All the faces look like open gates through which one can see into clear white souls.' Of an aristo whom revolution has chased into exile, he states: 'Even though I knew him to be a leading anti-Semite and a figure in the exploitation of the peasantry, there was still something moving about him.' The head never abandons its link to the heart. Yet it is scathing about political systems 'missing the regulating consciousness'.

Spies are ubiquitous. In Mussolini's Italy Roth's host fears his own janitor. In a hotel the porter insists on posting Roth's letters, which thus reach their destination late. (How much easier surveillance in an era of email!) Any presence of strangers causes alert; each new wave of refugees renders the natives less welcoming. Sound familiar? Roth's period pieces show a crooked timber of humanity that remains evergreen.

Of Albania in 1927, he observes: 'It is impossible to judge the circumstances of an Oriental state, whose history is oppression, whose ethics are corruption, and whose culture is a mixture of the native bucolic and archaic-romantic naïveté and the recent importation of intrigue, by the criteria of a Western democracy.' – This might be scripture for policy-makers brainstorming away our successor century's destiny.

The Hotel Years, Joseph Roth, trans. Michael Hoffmann. Granta, 2015.

Music in a Nazi Slumberland

Jewish Quarterly, Autumn 1995

Culturally speaking, Nazism was a reaction against modernism and 'decadence'. Its extremity, racism and ideological dogmatism set it apart from similar reactions which occurred at the same time in other countries, including Britain. We had our censorious Eliots, our xenophobic Waughs, our Sitwellian imitators of the collaborative opportunist Cocteau. Our internationalism was shallow then, as it is now. We still have Paul Johnson to rant from the pages of *The Spectator* against experimentalism in the arts; and the 'Fairest Isle' series on Radio 3, as well as ubiquitous Britten and Elgar revivals, show that we are not immune to glorifying our own perhaps more than is deserved. How many talking heads have in recent years been heard to make slighting remarks about Wagner, or even Beethoven? In the wake of the challenge from Classic FM, our state-owned serious music station sometimes seems to make this the norm. What celebrations of kind, what provincial pettifogging disguised as scholarship, what nativist propagandizing has obtained in a Majorite era of a nation at unease with itself?

Let us make no mistake: the Holocaust was no absolute inoculation against the type of absurdities which afflicted a great European culture in the 1930s. It is a matter of degree and of temperament that led Germans to respond to their depression and sense of national breakdown with extreme spasms; that and a collapse of political will in the face of appallingly mediocre leaders. According to Erik Levi in his *Music in the Third Reich*, Alfred Rosenberg was chief villain in the attempt to drive culture back into a nativist ghetto; beside him, his rival Dr Goebbels seems partly pragmatic and a man of taste. To Rosenberg anything redolent of Judaism, modernism, Catholicism or Mediterranean influences was *verboten*, or should be. His wing of the party sought to suppress French classics with as much zeal as American ('nigger') jazz. On the 'positive' side, its efforts produced such bizarries as the promotion of Belgian-born César Franck above francophone rivals because of a discovery that his forbears were German. Bizet, despite the irrepressible popularity of *Carmen*, had to endure a whisper-campaign about his ancestry.

Turf battles between Rosenberg and other Nazi leaders are among the most intriguing aspects Levi brings out: worthy of our present-day Tory party. A characteristic procedure of National Socialism was to foment chaos in order to impose order, and this was not least true within the Nazi hierarchy. Hitler looked on in shrewd complacency as his party ideologue battled with his minister of propaganda for control of opera houses, recording studios and concert halls. Minister of Education Bernhard Rust played a part in this struggle too, as did official union boss Robert Ley; walk-on roles were taken by other officials and gauleiters small and large, including the great and gross president of the Prussian state, Hermann Göring. He managed to make the Berlin Staatsoper his private fiefdom, despite Goebbels' dual claims to it as minister for the arts and gauleiter of Berlin. As a personal showcase, the good doctor had to settle for the other premier musical institution of the Reich, the Berlin Philharmonic.

Conscious of world opinion and vain about the figures they cut, both Goebbels and Göring could on occasion rule with a light hand. Furtwängler at the Phil was allowed to part with Jewish soloists at his own speed, despite demands for a quick and full purge by the Kampfbund für deutsche Kultur (Rosenberg's fanatical 'Fighting League'). Hindemith was allowed on the programme for his *Mathis der Maler* despite having a Jewish wife and 'ill-advised' anarchistic antics in works of his Neue Sachlichkeit youth. Operas by Richard Strauss continued to be performed despite the fact that his librettist, Hugo von Hofmannsthal, had been partly Jewish. *Elektra* was vilified; but *Rosenkavalier* was too popular to be suppressed, and nothing could prevent *Arabella* from being the most sought-after new work of the period. Still, even a composer as pre-eminent and unambiguously German as Strauss had difficulties: his opera *Die schweigsame Frau* was attacked because its librettist was the banned Jewish writer Stefan Zweig; and Strauss was forced to resign as president of the Reichsmusikkammer after the Gestapo intercepted a letter from him to Zweig in which he claimed that he was 'only aping' being head of this quango.

Strauss continued to be the most performed composer throughout 'Greater Germany'; the other titan of early modernism, Gustav Mahler, fell from second place in 1932 to total oblivion. Wagner's unfortunate outbursts re 'Judenthum in der Musik' were taught in schools, and his early rival Meyerbeer was dropped from programme lists. History was rewritten so that Schumann gained anti-Semitic credentials despite his sympathies with Mendelssohn. Excuses were offered for why Handel had written his oratorios on Old Testament subjects; efforts were made to 'aryanize' the three great Mozart operas which had libretti by that 'grimacing' Venetian Jew, Lorenzo da Ponte. Mozart in German may have caught on a bit; but, in spite of numerous attempts, no substitute could be found for Mendelssohn's incidental music to *A Midsummer Night's Dream*. 'Even if one has legitimate doubts about Mendelssohn's work,' one Nazi-sanctioned critic confessed, 'it cannot be denied that his representation of the magic in the forest remains unique.' (Magic, don't you know. Well, perhaps it was OK to let a Jew seem adept at *that*.)

The 'legitimate doubts' often began with Wagner's warning that 'a thousand years' of European culture had lost out to 'the plastic demons for the decline of mankind' and ended with the paranoid belief that Schönberg's twelve-tone system was a deliberate plot to destroy the last vestige of the traditional Nordic musical soul. Musicologists wrote tracts to prove that the German peoples naturally used a diatonic system and that the advent of the chromatic had introduced an alien 'Orientalism'. Again Wagner was cited: the drowning of the Pilgrims' Chorus by the Venusberg bacchanale in *Tannhäuser* was a metaphor for the threat under which German culture laboured. This argument might at a stretch find supporting passages in *Lohengrin* or *Meistersinger*, though contradicting ones are available too. But what about *Tristan und Isolde*, the most revolutionary of Wagner's works, in which chromaticism is generally seen to have done away with the old diatonism forever – indeed, to have ushered in modernism in music? Nazi musicologists had to skirt around this. Yet it is only one of the many impasses at which their dogmatic and bogus 'racial' aesthetic arguments break down.

The case of Wagner may in fact provide the most satisfying illustration of the fatuity of the Nazi musical cultural enterprise. Despite his ingratiating diatribes against the influence of Jewish impresarios or in favour of the Second Reich as it grew, it will be obvious to anyone familiar with his music dramas that their success depends on a *balance* between so-called German and so-called Oriental elements (he was, after all, a 'Parisian decadent', according to Nietzsche); between diatonism and chromaticism, with the latter, as said, gaining the upper hand; between stolid 'bourgeois' characters and 'plastic demons'. There would be no *Tannhäuser* without Venus, *Lohengrin* without Ortrud, *Ring* without Alberich and Mime and Wotan, *Parsifal* without Klingsor and Kundry. Such personae, variously regarded as sinful, disintegrative, anti-German or Semitic, are as essential to 'old Cagliostro's'[1] magical mix as Iago, Shylock or Richard III to Shakespeare's. Perhaps more to the point, they were as essential to Wagner's own multi-faceted personality as less ruthless, more 'feminine', Germanic or Celtic types such as Elisabeth, Elsa, Tristan and Parsifal.

In his status as revolutionary in music, Wagner did, arguably, more to destroy the supposed old German forms than his successors and partial disciples of the Second Viennese School, the modernists Mahler, Strauss or Schönberg. His obsession in prose writings with a typological Jew, whether wandering or established, victimized or exploitative, was, like Shakespeare's

---

1   The characterization is Nietzsche's from *The Case of Wagner* – ever the *Ur*-text for Wagner critique.

fascination with Machiavellian types, a projection of a powerful dramatic counter-self or selves. So too, analogously, is Hitler's in *Mein Kampf*: an obsession and fascination subsequently thrust on a nation whose nature, it was told, had been fatally passive, feminine, abstract, idealistic and thus manipulable. The nation was enjoined, like the individual self, to whip itself up into its opposite – active, 'masculine', materialistic, realistic, manipulative – by extirpating those very elements in its midst, or their stand-ins, which were depicted as the alien 'other'. It was all high dramatics, loaded with irony. Tragedy marched off the stage and on to the streets – and the correct response to it aesthetically, if not ideologically, may have been the Neue Sachlichkeit 'operas' of Brecht and Weill. But of course they had to be banned as well.

Satire, parody and 'Entartete Kunst' had to make way for humourless, narcissistic bourgeois self-inflation. Bolshevist, 'Jewish', decadent, modern, *Die Dreigroschenoper* and *Mahagonny* went the way of twelve-tone, jazz and other experimental modes of the Weimar period. In came operetta, though not even the best of that sub-genre, such as Offenbach's or the Johann Strausses' (antecedents Jew). Philistinism, self-pitying or anodyne, reigned so supreme that by the end of the 1930s even the hallowed Wagner had slipped down the ranks. In 1938-39, not one of his works was performed with more frequency than two of Lortzing's! A saccharine, fairy-tale world was what a gently narcotized public wanted to escape into; and Dr Goebbels, even attuned to what could make the régime popular, obliged by encouraging this lowest-common-denominator fare, even if he might have preferred a modernized Romanticism with a hard, stylized edge. His other constituency, let us not forget, was A. Hitler himself, a man whom his propaganda sought to depict as petting dogs or giving flowers to secretaries; who was called 'Uncle Wolf' by Winifred Wagner's sons at Bayreuth; who wanted to relocate the capital of European music from 'decadent' Vienna to Linz; and whose idea of the zenith of musical culture was the work of Anton Bruckner.

Who says that National Socialism was fascinating? How could it have been when its ultimate arbiter was a figure whose artistic taste was about as high-brow as that of Richard Nixon? When the 37th President appointed a second-rater to the Supreme Court of the United States, a Republican senator defended the act by saying that most of the American people were mediocre and needed to be represented too. Nations, alas, sometimes get what they deserve. The Germans of the '30s were, by and large, all too willing to accept their Führer's banal impressions of *Kultur*. What was more important to them: the loss of a few great Jewish conductors like Otto Klemperer and Bruno Walter, or the flattering assurance that their 'native' music was once again supreme (as if it had not been in the Weimar period and, even if it had not, so what)? Opera houses, music journals, academies and concert halls were able to re-establish assured employment for thousands of 'Aryans' who had been thrown out of work because of the Depression (engineered by Jews in New York) or the advent of sound in films (once again an alien enterprise). Little jobs for the boys were handed out with as much attention to connections as opposed to merit as some jobs in the British establishment are for an Oxbridge cabal.

It all became quite cosy, and suffocating: a hot-house atmosphere in which only designated cultivations could grow. A lively panorama of it is given by Levi, drawing on recent German scholarship and adding a good deal of his own. Nor has the phenomenon vanished in all aspects, as I say. Believers in cultural multiplicity have not won every battle since 1945. Modernism remains under attack, even decades after its death[2]; provincialism, like nationalism, continues to offer a comforting retreat for little spirits who find the world rife with confusion and change. Second-raters and power-hugging placemen of the control industry may be by nature ever liable to wish us to inhabit

---

2 I think here, for example, of John Carey's *The Intellectuals and the Masses* (1992), which poses as scholarly but in fact resembles Paul Johnson's style of journalistic attack and perhaps derives its title in part from Johnson's notorious debunking of greater modern figures from Shelley to Hemingway, *Intellectuals* (1988).

slumberlands of illusory order and calm. Sometimes they are unconscious of their own muffling philistinism. Sometimes they even imagine themselves as 'liberals' and would be outraged by comparison of their techniques with those of the National Socialists. But what happened in the Third Reich is only a grotesquification of what could happen elsewhere anytime. It behoves us to be alert and aware.

Music in the Third Reich, Erik Levi. Macmillan, 1994.

Upwardly Mobile Couple

Quarterly Review, 5 i 2015

A petty bourgeois element runs through the history of National Socialism, with counterpoint from its traditional obverse – the bohemian. Himmler came from suburban Munich and had the provincial's suspicion of the uncleanness and un-Germanness of the metropolis – Berlin. His eventual wife and later a secretary by whom he had two illegitimate children both lived there, and his early letters to the former are seasoned with disparagements of it. She, Marga Boden, responded with pleas that he be not too hard on her home town, and in course of their courtship he softened his tone about a place soon to supplant Weimar as capital in a new Reich, whose erection he tirelessly worked for. Ironically, the Bavarian bourgeois grew adjusted to radical Berlin just as his spouse was acculturating to the new life on the outskirts of Munich which he offered, eventually transmuted into a comfortable villa by a lake in the foothills of the Alps. Marga turned out to be better-suited to this transit than had at first appeared. Having described the most prominent of Berlin Nazis, Josef Goebbels, as 'a Jewish type' – this mainly because of how he combed his hair – and her (Jewish) boss at a clinic she worked in as not paying properly (money frets were a constant theme), she seemed in general to find other people antipathetic; thus what she got could be seen as a kind of liberation – a household far from the madding crowd, with fruit trees and vegetable patches to cultivate, a dog and a few sheep and goats to husband, as well as a variety of fowl.

The bucolic retreat was an ideal pen for the bohemian bourgeois to herd his 'little woman' into, especially once she had bred him a child. It was an anchor too for him as he pursued peripatetic activities on behalf of the new party, a homestead to long for and return to when away on what constituted – in political terms – increasingly eccentric, sometimes dangerous missions. In fact, after a supposedly dominant Jewish bourgeoisie, the group Himmler expressed himself most as despising was the petty bourgeois – more than ironic when you consider how dutifully he marked his parents' birthdays and fests such as Christmas plus all that went with them, purchase and giving of gifts not least. At these observances the conventional chap never failed, even while keeping a frenetic pace of building up his ruthless movement and later the apparatus of one of the most monstrous modes of governance ever seen. *Sitzfleisch* in the common man clearly annoyed him. Promulgation of revolution was preferable to living peaceably in one place doing small offices as a professional or perhaps civil servant. Constant travel from one end of the land to another, or more – Austria for the Bavarian was of as much interest as the Prusso-Baltic northeast – intoxicated him, and the petty bourgeois virtues of sobriety, exactitude, adherence to hierarchy and love of rule could readily be set to serve the Party's 'bohemian' ends. Above all loomed a Führer who, with quasi-religious doctrine set down in *Mein Kampf* and iterated from numberless speaking pulpits, enabled the little man to exult in perhaps the most urgent of all his petty bourgeois virtues: a worshipful loyalty.

Yet one always had to take care to make the 'right' choices. Himmler began in the Party under the wing of fellow Bavarian Gregor Strasser. Strasser and his brother Otto were close to its helm through the '20s, near equals to Hitler, for whom Gregor sometimes deputized, and major contributors to its advance. With Goebbels, who was neither a South German nor an Ur-Party member, the Strassers developed left-of-centre policies to compete with dominant Social Democrats and Communists in the German electorate. When these policies were slung out at the start of the 1930s, it triggered signal events. Under new and opportunistic influences, Hitler summoned Otto Strasser to a tirade famously lasting four and a half hours, after which the younger Strasser stormed out of the Party, declaring its 'socialist' aspect dead. His brother stayed loyal, declining in 1932 an invitation by President Hindenburg's military associate Kurt von Schleicher to split the Party by entering a coalition in order to solve the crisis brought on by the Depression. By then the Party had grown attractive to folk with names prefaced with 'von', both landowning and industrialist. Goebbels as ever saw how the wind was blowing; Himmler, now trusted by Hitler for his organizational skills, evidently saw too. Flattered by invitations from aristo new Party members, not least to a hunt, the petty bourgeois also saw that his wife enjoyed taking tea with Gräfins, from whom she did not have to fear being sullied by low human nature. In any case, Himmler recognized that loyalty could not be divided. So on the 'Night of Long Knives' he demonstrated his merit by liquidating not only the old style military man who had had the temerity to discuss splitting the Party with the elder Strasser but also that hapless Strasser himself, who had committed the treason of allowing such discussion to take place.

This history we are reminded of not by correspondence between Himmler and his wife, but by the commentary stitching it together, forming this volume into a kind of biography. Himmler does not burden Marga with details of his political activity, nor does she appear to want to know them. She is concerned for his digestion, he that she gets sufficient sleep. She tells him about her garden and complains about the hired help; he sends her compotes and chocolates and informs her where and when his train or car is going to deliver him and what sort of rally or meeting he must attend. (Mention is made often of tea with 'the boss'). Himmler had studied agronomy, thus is keen to share with his Frau the latest research he has discovered or commissioned on the value of this herb or that kind of animal husbandry. These are among the few matters of substance of interest to both husband and wife, but Himmler does not go on to share the implications of various breakthroughs in cod-science that will eventually be applied to what he sees as the betterment of the human species. For Marga and their daughter he is ever and mainly provider/protector, and for them this is proper and enough. Marga will feel neglected in time, not least after it becomes clear that she can have no more babies. But she will make no fuss with 'Heini', not fractiously, not even when he comes to have offspring by another. Frau Himmler remains Frau Himmler and wifehood her job, requiring its own front and loyalty. When asked at Nuremburg if she knew of Himmler's second family, Marga's response was that she assumed he had fathered more children, but not by whom or how many. 'Lebensborne', a policy Himmler helped to create, enjoined healthy SS men to 'haveth childers everywhere'[1]: a greater German world needed good Aryan stock, especially once its new territories had been cleared of their lesser inhabitants. This Marga presumably had come to regard as normal. Her deliberate ignoring of her husband's bastards is shared by his great-niece and her co-author, who do not mention their fate in an epilogue to this book, which details the afterlives of Marga, her daughter and the Himmlers' 'step-son' (they 'adopted' the child of a murdered SS man in the '30s) down to the present day.

Happy families!

It is difficult to have much sympathy for Marga Himmler. Like others privileged under Nazi rule – Winifred Wagner comes to mind – she failed through years of de-Nazification and after to show much remorse for or even recognition of the hideousness that went on, notably under her husband's aegis. England had caused the War in her view, and Himmler's efforts on behalf of the German people were uniformly heroic. This cost her. Her home by the lake with its chattels and heirlooms was not restored to her and she spent much of her postwar existence under supervision in an unfamiliar part of north Germany. A negative personality, Marga may also have been a borderline depressive, whose original attraction for Himmler had been superficial: blond hair, blue eyes – the theoretically perfect 'master race' breeding type. Such had a kind of fatal attraction for the often stumpy, dark-haired, Celtic south Germans: a fantastic, illusory ideal. The energy of Hitler's criminal regime was of course driven by types unlike this – Goebbels, for

---

1 The phrase comes from *Finnegans Wake*, Joyce's contemporary (1939) bohemian bourgeois work of excess. It is one of various sobriquets for the 'hero' Earwicker, whose initials are HCE.

instance, whom Marga imagined as 'Jewish' – thus the whole race clap-trap may be turned topsy-turvy. Yet the often slyly intelligent Himmler seems not only to have believed in it but to have pursued it with more system and efficiency than any other of the 'bonzos'[2], gaining credit and advancement and in the end allegedly more trust from a beleaguered and exhausted nation than other remaining early Party leaders and pin-ups such as the buffoonish Hermann Göring.

It makes one wonder. Significant parts of this story remain untold, at least in the confines of endless billets-doux and sweet nothings in a grit-and-intelligence-free correspondence between husband and wife. What transpired in those equally endless meetings and conferences and teas with 'the boss' that Himmler neglected family life to get on with? In policy-making sessions of the petty bourgeois bohemians, what was the dynamic? How much of what was decided was made on the hoof, hepped up by blood-sugar rushes or abuse of caffeine? How much was late-night competitive brainstorming the font and origin of disastrous miscalculations leading to the death of tens of millions and whole nations crushed, including *Die Heimat* itself? What petty rivalries, behind-the-hand snickers, rolling of eyes, histrionics, rising voices and temper and trumping male swagger were likely to carry the day? In a régime born out of bohemian audacity who or what but the most outlandishly audacious ever wins? Thus the plague of ideas-men. Give us the boring, the gradual and careful, even those scared of their shadow. Postwar Germany right up to the ultra-circumspect Frau Merkel fills the bill. The children and children's children have, at least until now, 'learned the lesson'. Whatever is next?

Heinrich Himmler d'après sa correspondance avec sa femme, 1927-1945, ed. Michael Wildt and Katrin Himmler, traduit de allemande par Olivier Mannoni. Plon, 2014.

---

2 Slang for 'bosses'. Their presence in Tegernsee and environs earned it the nickname 'Lago di Bonzos'.

Josef Goebbels: Chronicler of a Catastrophe

Quarterly Review, 4 ix 2015

There are possible revelations to be inferred from Peter Longerich's exhaustive biography of Josef Goebbels, but when I started out on his long, rich account I had to ask myself why I was going over this terrible history once again. When, I wondered, is the world going to tire of fascination with Nazis? In answer came the rhetorical questions: when will little boys give up asking daddy to play scary baboon? When will teenage girls cease to titter about the antics of rogue males? When will policy wonks on 'national security' sofas stop being swayed by the most audacious voice among them?

The most audacious voice among Nazi jostlers for power was often and finally that of club-footed, simian, non-Aryan looking Goebbels. Unlikely you may think next to blue-eyed Rudolf Hess or 'matinée idol' World War I hero Hermann Göring. But the Chaplinesque little Rhinelander had drive – call it need to prove himself, if you wish, or 'narcissistic personality', if you need to resort to the day-before-yesterday's psychobabble. Longerich protects himself with this lingo on occasion.[1] Yet while armchair analysts may enjoy speculating about motivation, historians must deal in known acts. For them the question may be not so much *why* as *how* did he do it?

Energy is an answer. Hess decamped early; Göring grew drug-ridden, indolent; Hitler withdrew into indecision, even invisibility, as National Socialism's triumphs morphed into disaster. Goebbels, a radical and fighter by nature, angled and maneuvered against rivals early and late – the Strassers as left leaders, Rosenberg as ideologue – to dominate an agenda, becoming Reich Plenipotentiary in the last year of 'total war'. His main backing, Longerich makes clear, came always from

---

1 Longerich takes this up in his 'Prologue', xv etc., and alludes to recent German studies of the matter in his bibliography and notes, but it is not really central to his text. One wonders if nods in this direction aren't the result of editorial suggestion after the digging, sifting and writing up of historical research had been completed.

Hitler. Quid pro quo was Goebbels's expression of faith in a *Führer prinzip*. The Reich's minister for propaganda never deviated from this in public. In private the profession often may have been tortuous.

We know this courtesy of the diaries Goebbels kept throughout his Nazi years. They are an ultimate product of his early ambition to be a writer. Avid reader in youth – favorites included Hamsun and Hesse, as well as Dostoyevsky – young Josef gained a doctorate in literature and laboured through his twenties to make himself a lead voice of the Weimar decade. A lower middle class provincial who deprecated the era's establishment, he was not well-placed to achieve it; his Bildungsroman *Michael Voormann* was disregarded, and two plays of his were performed only perfunctorily in Party-backed theatres. Eventually, like Hitler diverting his ambition as artist to other ends, the writer-manqué found his niche in a new brand of rhetoric. He became warm-up act for the Führer as Party speech-maker and, when Hitler descended to near silence towards the end, virtual voice of the Reich. At the same time he came to make Clintonian sums from book-writing and journalism[2].

Longerich leans heavily on Goebbels' diaries to tell his tale, buttressing well-known passages with new material unearthed in the past decade as well as deconstruction of subtext. Posterity may ever have to rely on these diaries for its most substantial insider view of a terrible régime, but the propagandist was always a spinner of fact and as time went on increasingly sensitive to how truth had to be massaged or even kept from his audience, sometimes possibly even from himself or at least from the secretaries to whom he dictated. Reader, beware. One must also bear in mind that, despite occasional quotation from Nietzsche, the little doctor was no superman. Subject to skin disease, kidney disorders, bouts of melancholy or depression, he was in such weaknesses not so different from Hitler, Göring

---

2 These were arranged for him with Hitler's backing by Party publisher Max Amann. Whether for skill or by patronage, the writer-manqué thus became one of the highest-paid German-language authors of his day.

and others of the régime's surprisingly fragile bosses. He does, however, seem to have exceeded them in capacity for rallying against downturns, profiting possibly from his own diatribes to the *Volk* about need for maintaining morale – if not in 'mood', then at least in 'bearing'[3].

To a considerable degree Goebbels was able to believe his own bullshit. Yet the strongest streak in his nature appears to have been a kind of sado-masochistic pragmatism. In periods when Nazi dogma failed to cohere, such as the 'socialist' vs conservative arguments of 'the years of struggle', he glommed onto anti-Semitism as a handy glue – this despite having a half-Jewish girlfriend for years, being himself considered a 'Jewish' type by some[4] and rarely harboring racist views during his school or university days. The sadistic dogma would return with a vengeance as war began to shatter national fortunes and again operated as a kind of ideological glue, this time to bind otherwise apparently opposed enemy identities of Western plutocracy and Bolshevism. Both were part of the 'international Jewish conspiracy', don't you know? – Goebbels had read *The Protocols of the Elders of Zion* and, though sophisticated enough to accept that they were probably faked, maintained that they must have been put together by authors who had gleaned an essential truth.

The mass cruelty which derived from this attitude is well-known, also Goebbels' role as cheerleader of it. The obverse – a masochistic aspect of his pragmatism – becomes clearer from Longerich's book than it perhaps ever has been before. It centers on Goebbels' marriage to Magda Quandt, grandmother to the present-day BMW clan via a son from her first marriage. An ambitious and apparently exacting seductress whose own Jewish connections (stepfather) remained in the shade, Magda married

---

3 *Haltung* in German, as Longerich points out in his impressive discussion of how skillfully Goebbels adapted language to the shifting requirements of persuading a people to continue a war which a majority of them – including the Propaganda Minister himself – had never supported with much optimism.

4 Himmler's wife, for example. See previous chapter, first paragraph.

Goebbels in 1931 and over the next decade produced five further children, to all of whom she gave names beginning with 'H'. These children, eldest and youngest daughters notably[5], were doted on by a godfather / protector to the family at large, another 'H' – Adolf Hitler. About the presence of this 'third party' in the Goebbels' marriage, Longerich provides copious detail. He does not indulge in what the detail invites: obvious speculation.

Hitler was infatuated with Magda from first meeting. She could hardly have been but flattered by the attention of this yet greater star, whom her principal suitor idolized and was dependent upon. Whatever may have transpired in early days, the three soon enough 'came to an agreement', and Hitler stood witness at the Goebbels' wedding. The newlyweds' domestic life became stormy: rows, goings and comings, makings-up, new pregnancies / babies, bigger houses, faster cars, more extensive holidays and expensive gifts. The 'Boss' doubtless in mind, Magda would chide Josef to make more progress in Party hierarchy and prestige. All the while, her households were visited by said Boss, announced or not, with full entourage or solo. The Goebbelses would be summoned on sudden whim to the Führer's eyrie on the Obersalzburg; Magda might be invited to stay on if Josef was called back to Berlin on Gau business. She was also known to spend the night at the Führer's Chancellery in Berlin, companioning him until the wee hours after some reception or concert which she had attended with him, Josef being out of town on ministry affairs.

Goebbels' goings and comings were determined ultimately by Hitler. Whenever large marital issues arose, Magda would turn to him for advice, whereupon he would summon his

5 At the birth of the first, when Goebbels expressed disappointment that it was only a girl, Hitler said he was 'thrilled' and called Magda 'the loveliest, dearest, and cleverest of women'. When the child was six, Hitler remarked that 'if Helga was 20 years older and he was 20 years younger she would be the wife for him'. At the birth of the last child, Hitler 'shared in the family joy' and on Magda's birthday shortly afterwards 'surprisingly arrived in the afternoon to offer his congratulations'. Longerich, 189, 361, 473. Such details my seem unremarkable in themselves but as they accumulate begin to imply more than is said.

reliable underling to broker a solution, Goebbels' status implied in the balance. On one occasion when Magda was giving birth, Hitler turned up at her hospital bedside before the apparent father.[6] After a subsequent birth, the apparent father expressed jubilation on seeing a 'true Goebbels face'[7]. Such details[8] almost invite us to ask, if we haven't already, what are we to make of this? Longerich does not go so far as to line up probable dates of conception with Magda's visits to or from Hitler, but one is tempted to ask whyever not? Might he fear giving offense to present-day Quandts? Is the world not ready for the possibility that Hitler as sexual being was not quite the eunuch of lore? Would it humanize him, glamorize him to discover that for years he was participant in a kind of ménage à trois, cadging covert *cinq à septs* with a mistress and subjecting her husband to a half-willing, half-outraged cuckoldry? Did he perhaps even father one or two of her kids?

Such things are not unknown. Among Fascist contemporaries with an artistic bent, consider Mussolini, or Ezra Pound. Bourgeois cover may have been expected for the *Volk*, but bohemian arrangements had long been a norm for 'genius'. Hitler's idol Wagner took as mistress the wife of his conductor Hans von Bülow, fathering two daughters by her before Bülow, who idolized his *Meister* and needed his patronage, gave up being complacent and decamped. Goebbels clearly suffered from Magda's lack of connubial devotion, of mind, body or both; thus the rows, thus his retreat to solitary guest houses or private lairs on one or another of their estates, thus his eventual affair with the actress Lila Baarova and decision during the darkening days of 1938 to end his marriage. But he couldn't. The Boss wouldn't have it. Magda as ever scurried to Hitler for protection, and Hitler, preoccupied with the Sudeten crisis and perhaps with his own needs, as well as the requirement that top

---

6 At the birth of the second daughter. Ibid., 253.

7 At the birth of the third child, a son. Ibid., 306.

8 There are more – such as that news of the birth of the next child, a daughter, reached Goebbels only via Hitler, to whom Magda sent a telegram. Ibid., 380.

Party bonzos[9] not be seen as licentious or corrupt, summoned the little doctor and decreed that the status quo must remain. Goebbels was obliged to break off his affair with Baarova; she in this process lost patronage of a lover who by then was calling most of the shots in cinema as well as other arts in the Reich.

Goebbels was disconsolate. He turned to others for advice, even Göring whom he had hitherto disparaged and despised[10]. Sympathy was offered, but reprieve was in nobody's gift but the Führer's, and he would not budge. Goebbels swallowed hard, then worked rapidly to re-cement his relations with his Boss, including by heightening the anti-Semitic rhetoric that led to *Kristallnacht*. Magda later confessed to her husband that she had had an affair with his state secretary, Karl Hanke, another confidant and sometime liaison between the Propaganda Ministry and Chancellery. Goebbels expressed fury, but by now what he was telling his diaries may have become code or part fiction. Magda, it is known, had a history – adultery had been a reason for break-up with her first husband – and whether Hanke was truly her lover during her second marriage, a sole lover or mere cover for somebody else cannot be more than surmised from what Longerich relates.

About her great protector/admirer, this is known. From the later 1920s, Hitler had shared his Munich flat with his niece Geli Raubel, with whom it is assumed that he had or was having an affair.[11] Geli hero-worshipped a relation whose trajectory was becoming stratospheric; at the same time, some of Hitler's mentors and backers took a dim view of a connection close enough to suggest incest or in any case that of a mature man with a suggestible girl hardly out of her teens. In due course

---

9 Slang for 'bosses". See note 2, previous chapter.

10 During the war, and especially as its fortunes deteriorated, Goebbels turned to other top-Nazis to brainstorm policy and 'help' an overworked Führer, who was increasingly at the front and sequestered by military chiefs. Göring was nominal overseer of these discussions but Goebbels' only really effective interlocutors, especially after the 20 July 1944 plot, were Himmler, Bormann and Speer.

11 *Hitler and Geli* by Ronald Hayman (Bloomsbury, 1997) investigates this topic.

Geli was found dead – suicide, it appeared: shot with Hitler's pistol when he was out of town. Yet who knows? What had been whispered by whom into whose ear? that if Hitler cared for his career, such an amorous adventure had to be off the menu? that if Geli truly cared for her 'great man', she had to clear out? Did Geli need telling? Did Hitler? Did either of them listen? What did the aspirant leader, ever an intriguer for power, tell himself? – Whatever, he was left in evident grief: feelings of guilt perhaps (was the man capable of it?), but grief nonetheless. Goebbels witnessed it close-hand, Magda too – she was by then on the scene. Hitler's place in their life began on this note and would be forever after predicated on a notion of the poor soul's isolation – his deprivation of family, his inability or time to find suitable partner. Nor was it long before he was expressing the idea that one in his position could not afford to be 'married' to anyone but the German people.

Is this to be taken at face value? Scabrous tales such as that Hitler had only one testicle are about as credible as that Napoleon was only 5 feet tall. (He was 5'6", as Andrew Roberts has corrected for a happily-deceived Anglo audience.[12]) There is no real reason to believe that in the sexual department the Führer was less of a man than another. He did, after all, ultimately marry Eva Braun, a younger woman again and by most accounts attractive. Are we to suppose that for the decade or more which separated Geli from Eva, he never felt an urge, nor, being the most powerful man in the land, found means to satisfy it? If he were 'married' to the *Volk* and dared not risk its jealousy or ire by appearing with a rival, what better option that to indulge in a covert affair with a married woman whom he fancied and whose husband was bound to indulge it? If this were the truth about him and Magda – and nothing Longerich tells us discourages such a hypothesis – it would explain why Goebbels was obliged to accept Hitler's continual intrusions as 'part of the family', why Hitler would invite the family as one or in part to the Obersalzburg – a privilege not accorded

12   In his recent biography *Napoleon the Great* (Allen Lane, 2014).

to others, or certainly not with such frequency – and why he was ever involved in the Goebbels' finances and disputes which might threaten to 'upset the apple cart'[13].

What did others know? There were apparently rumours, for which Magda's confessed affair with Hanke could have been cover. We don't know exactly what Goebbels told Göring etc. when Hitler forbade him to leave Magda in 1938, but all of Goebbels' confidants were either high Party members or sufficiently dependent on the Führer's favour to keep shtum. The further and more shocking questions suggested – whether Goebbels' unusually large number of children were all his, whether one or more of them may have been Hitler's, whether this may explain the unusually fatherly attitude the latter took and the former's occasional Joseph-like backgrounding – seem crucial to understanding the core natures of two of the most demonic movers of 20th century history, and one is amazed that they have not been mooted before and are not now taken up by Longerich, despite that all he has laid out. Would it not have been in character for Hitler to have played manipulative God-the-father, equally for the ultimately opportunistic, Führer-bound Goebbels to have abased himself into the requisite masking role? Sharper light on these matters may also illumine any rationale we can concoct for what on a personal level may be the darkest of all dark crimes of the Nazis[14]: murder of all five of the Goebbels children, eldest age 14, in the bunker in Berlin just after Hitler took Braun's life and his own and before their mother and Goebbels himself dutifully followed suit.

What kind of mother performs such an act? What kind of father? When Goebbels told Hitler that Magda had decided that the whole family would stay with him in Berlin 'til the end, the Führer replied that the sentiment was 'admirable' but he could not encourage the act. In a version of the tale of Solomon with

---

13 Among plays Goebbels rated was G. B. Shaw's of this name, *The Apple Cart*, which he saw in January 1938. Goebbels and Hitler both thought Shaw the greatest living playwright: 'he lifts the veil from English hypocrisy'. Longerich, 354, 838.

14 On a historical level such an egregious act is trivial compared to the Holocaust.

two mothers, does this reveal who the true father was? the one who might at all cost want to save his innocents? In the analogous cases noted – Wagner, Mussolini, Pound – the biological father kept watch for his illegitimate offspring, creating protection for them throughout his lifetime and beyond[15]. Yet by the stage we have arrived at in this history, Hitler had, according to Goebbels, become 'frail'[16] and in many respects a broken man, indecisive, less than willful. Might this explain why he let himself be overruled by a 'father' only too eager to prevent the children from surviving into a world bereft of an ideology and régime in which he still professed fervid faith? Goebbels left a testament to the effect that the children, had they been old enough to choose, would have opted for death. So Magda and he chose for them, flattering themselves that they were joining an auto-da-fé that would inspire future generations, symbolic of the undying commitment of the best of their kind. In truth it testifies to a wanton cruelty that not even a cornered a simian might resort to.

Why do we continue to pay attention to Nazis? Humans can be the most perverted of beasts. Yet evil, alas, is ever fascinating – often especially for the cosseted and immature who have never been seriously threatened by it.

Goebbels: A Biography, Peter Longerich, trans. Alan Bance, Jeremy Noakes and Lesley Sharpe. The Bodley Head, 2015.

---

15 Wagner's children inherited his folly at Bayreuth, which remains one of Europe's great cultural attractions. Pound's daughter, age 90, still presides over courses devoted to his work at Schloss Brunnenburg in the Südtirol. Mussolini's descendants have been active in Italian politics; Longerich (609) notes how Goebbels was 'surprised' when Hitler told him 'for the first time' in 1943 that *Il Duce*'s daughter Ella, married to his foreign minister, was brought up by his wife as if hers yet was in fact the love-child of his previous liaison with a Russian Jewess.

16 Shortly after the 1944 assassination attempt, Goebbels mused,'"The Führer has gotten very old" and is making "a really frail impression".' (643).By autumn Hitler had fallen ill with jaundice or worse. He more or less gave up speech-making, even on radio, despite the damage this threatened for national mood. It was in this period that Goebbels became Reich Plenipotentiary. Hitler left a will at his suicide naming Goebbels his successor as Chancellor, but it was not to be.

Hitler's Architect

Quarterly Review, 11 iii 2016

In the rogue's gallery of National Socialism, good boy Albert Speer usually gets short shrift. As a rogue, he seems on the surface deficient – none of the public prancing of a Göring or Goebbels. He possessed neither the flair of slumming aristos nor the gangsta chic of working-class thugs who vaulted the Party to power. He was younger than most and of a privileged, though social-climbing middle class background. His rise was almost entirely as Hitler's pet. His fall was padded by an excuse that he had fundamentally not been much more than an 'artist' – Hitler's architect – and certainly no ideologue or principal policy-maker.

Martin Kitchen sets out to change an impression created by postwar Speer and by two influential commentators who knew and wrote about him: Gitta Sereny and Joachim Fest. The time has come, Kitchen believes, to demonstrate that the later Speer's touted 'battle with the truth' is 'unconvincing' and that Sereny and Fest were more or less willingly 'misled'. Kitchen's case *is* probably convincing. He lays out evidence with lawyerly skill and in bulk, even at the risk of occasional repetition and less literary than lawyerly style. One is reminded that we are well into a second generation of writers about the War and related topics. Anthony Julius in his celebrated indictment of the gentlemanly anti-Semitism of T. S. Eliot was one of the first to inaugurate this lawyer-scholar equivalent of a 'tough Jew' approach[1]. Oddly, just at the point in history when one might expect revisionists to flourish, *less* tolerance for the monstrosities of the mid-20th century seems to have obtained. Kitchen is to Sereny and Fest what Julius was to first generation postwar Jewish literary scribes such as the urbane John Gross. Understanding the odious becomes akin to pusillanimity in an era brought up on the politically correct.

---

1 See 'Pre-eminent (and anti-Semitic) modernists' later in this book.

That said, one does not cavil at this rerating of Speer. Almost a man without qualities, one has to pause to recall why he was a colleague so attractive to A. Hitler. The latter was of course petty bourgeois and provincial – not even German! – which made the higher bourgeois manners of the young Rhinelander seem admirable. And since young Speer dutifully admired in return (though how sincerely may be questioned), it was easy enough for the older fellow to feel flattered. Add to that or not as you will the scent of homoeroticism that swirls around so much Nazi posturing, especially as it relates to the arts. The number of nude statues, predominantly male, which Speer used to decorate the cavernous chancellery he designed for his Führer typifies this tendency in a Zeitgeist. But the architecture of that palace and of the 'Germania' project is key. Hitler was 'an artist'. He longed for another, part acolyte, part executor, as pal. Speer rose from near nothing to, within short years, being 'master builder' of the Reich. What young man would not revel in such a rise, and truckle to the god who had engineered it? Only one who 'doth ambition shun'. In student days Speer is said to have been 'an amiable loafer'. But in a Depression-haunted Nazi New Age not even the most ardent former *Wandervogel* could afford to continue in that vein. Idlers, malingerers *raus*! – except when the Führer required companions for his lengthy, ruminative luncheons or country weekends in the Obersalzburg.

On Speer's qualities as architect Kitchen makes a case that he was largely derivative, purloining or plagiarizing from Heinrich Tessenow and Paul Ludwig Troost. Kitchen's thesis is that Speer mainly added theatrical touches to these masters' ideas, flattering Nazi delusions of grandeur – the famous pillars of light for Nuremberg rallies – or elements of kitsch preferred by a Führer whose aesthetics were stuck in Vienna of the 1890s. Regarding the first Kitchen cites a Goebbels tale: when Hitler asked Troost's widow what she thought of Speer's work, she answered that if the Führer asked for a building 100 metres wide her husband would think about it overnight and return the next day to say that, for structure and style, it should be 96 metres, whereas Speer would retort immediately, 'Mein Führer, 200 metres!' and get the job. Hitler apparently laughed. He would not have been so amused at Speer's private comment on his artistry. As a gift for work on the chancellery, he presented Speer with a watercolour of a church in Vienna that he had painted in 1909. Ever a closet modernist, Speer would brand the painting 'pedantic', 'lifeless', 'nondescript' and 'painstaking'. Nonetheless as young court favourite, he invariably incorporated the Führer's amateur architectural designs into plans for the new 'world capital' both fantasized for Berlin.

To advance this project Hitler appointed Speer General Inspector of Buildings, a role which led to Speer's first instance of complicity in Nazi anti-Semitic crime. To build 'Germania' thousands of buildings had to be demolished in Berlin's centre, yet the city had a chronic housing shortage which the Party, especially its 'socialist' left, had long promised to address. Solution: a large Jewish population, which remained in the centre as late as 1938 and still had tenancy protected by un-repealed Weimar laws. Threat and pogrom were needed to speed clearance until more dispossessing legislation could be risked. *Kristallnacht* was part of this, and really only a beginning. Well into the '40s, Gauleiter Goebbels was complaining that some 70 or 80,000 Jews still lived in Berlin. Himmler's assistance in relocating them to the ghetto in Litzmannstadt (Łódź) could only proceed at a logistically realizable pace – troop and armament transport was higher priority. Speer chafed at the speed-limit to his mandated project while at the same time profiting from the enforced labour he was offered by Himmler and temporary office space he was able to grant to Goebbels and other Party satraps eager to be close to the beating-heart of the wartime Reich.

Kitchen rightly regards the contention that Speer knew little of the ultimate fate of those he helped to dispatch on trains to the east as disingenuous at best. Moreover, even if this 'gentleman' among Nazis was not at home with a 'vulgar' element that promulgated the Final Solution, it is incontrovertible that he was complicit in dispossession of tens of thousands – indeed, a prime mover of it. That this was only in service of the Führer's megalomaniacal building scheme is a threadbare defense given Speer's role both in incepting that scheme and as supremo for its execution. When does a supposed instrument of policy become a policy-maker? This question, first apparent in Speer's role in Berlin's projected remaking, becomes core once his 'soundness' as Hitler's lackey and perceived efficiency as 'can do' man earned him a role of minister plenipotentiary for armaments in 1942, the year Nazi victories ended and a nation settled down to what was billed as a long military struggle for survival.

The death of Troost had advanced Speer's career as Hitler's architect; a plane crash killing Fritz Todt vaulted him into position as 'economic dictator of the Reich'. The story of this phase of his career involves the now well-known counter-intuitive truth of the so-called totalitarian state: envies, rivalries, passive-aggressive stances – the endless fissiparous forces which could only increase as defeat became the elephant in the room. Holding all together was a Führer who always made a specialty out of playing subordinates against one another, giving total powers to one and then blocking powers to someone else, failing to take decisions or taking and then rescinding them, given to tirade and personal prejudice – he suspected the military, disliked bureaucrats and often edged Party colleagues into the background in favour of mannerly parvenus. Speer succeeded in this fatally whimsical milieu, until he didn't. He played as ruthlessly as another, sure in his knowledge of Hitler's favour, until that unreliable backup was withdrawn. But during his ascendancy he was able to shift power crucially out of the hands of Party bosses and military planners and into those of the third force that made the Reich tick: the industrialists.

Speer was their paladin. Porsche, BMW, Thyssen, Krupp, Daimler, Siemens and other names which would continue as 'household' in West Germany of the postwar *Wirtschaftwunder* were given tax breaks, subsidy, supplies of cheap or forced labour, *diktat* over schedules – a kind of free rein in order to mount the total war that in their eyes was necessary to assure triumph of a 'capitalist' system over its arch-rival: Bolshevism. They did not believe that Stalin could match them in productivity or quality of product. They feared an apocalypse in social and economic structures if he did. That they would lose against him was unthinkable, though it happened, despite Albert Speer's best efforts. Yet he was 'one of them': it could not have been his fault. So a case for Speer's relative innocence began to be seeded just as his most egregious acts of culpability were taking place. Kitchen notes his encouraging presence at major speeches by Goebbels and Himmler promising a final solution to 'the Jewish problem'. He records meetings Speer was looped into re construction at Auschwitz and other concentration camps. He catalogues Speer's complicity in policies of slave labour and of working prisoners, foreigners and undesirables to death, along with the minimalism in nourishment, habitation and sanitation that assured it. Of course privation was advancing through all the beleaguered Reich as bombing shattered Hamburg, the Ruhr, Berlin and more; and of course Speer did what was practical to keep essentials available not only for German burghers, on whose faith the regime depended, but also on workers who – if too reduced in health – would be of no use. A manpower crisis became central to his struggle. He worked with Goebbels to hold morale up. He prevaricated about 'secret weapons'. He lied. He intrigued.

There were plots against him – the 'three kings' Bormann, Lammers and Keitel resented his accumulation of power and access to Hitler. Göring, Goebbels and Himmler were inconstant allies – Speer would later suggest that the SS Führer's doctor tried to murder him. Through 1944, as re-positioning took place, he oscillated from fantasizing himself Hitler's successor to preparing a persona as demon's dupe. Illness at the start of that year gave his enemies an opening. Documents suggesting that the Stauffenberg conspirators wanted to keep him as minister increased suspicion about him once their plot failed. Hitler's own precipitous decline in health hardly worked in Speer's favour. He became more and more the advocate for 'industrial self-determination', code for coterie capitalism after the regime collapsed, which by the end of '44 all self-interested operatives expected. Jockeying for postwar position had commenced, yet still Speer would lie to maintain combatant morale. Came the brutal winter of 1944-5. How much damage was done to Germany in those months alone? how much need for eventual rebuilding assured, with all the architectural plans and construction contracts for Hochtief etc. to go with it? Did Speer foresee someone's bonanza? There is no suggestion of it, but what intelligence trained in forward planning could have missed such an outcome? It is legend that Speer and industrialist friends helped block a mad policy of 'scorched earth' as Party fanatics tried to ignite *Götterdämmerung* at the war's end. It would seem a mitigation of crime in some quarters – a precious commodity in later 1945.

An ambiguous character it was which sat next to devils in the dock at Nuremburg. Speer was supposed to be the face of efficient production in the Reich, yet he had often sacrificed quality for quantity to impress or bamboozle a mad Führer. He was supposed to be the civilized one among many, yet he not only presided over a policy of dragooning workers from concentration camps but also of punishing shirkers by sending them there. He was meant to be a genius at developing new weapons, but the V1 was ineffective, the V2 never really operational and the so-called English Cannon unable to fire a successful shot. That Nazi Gauleiters and ideologues didn't like him may appear in his favour, but they liked him least for opposing aspects of their programme which were local, socialist and partisan for the small businesses later called the 'Mittelstand', characteristics of a mixed economy of which postwar West Germany grew justly proud. Oddly enough, this un-flamboyant middle class fellow was at heart perhaps the most 'totalitarian' of the lot, which may be why great plutocrats and near monopolists remained his most reliable friends. Did they save him from the gallows? Did they have the power to do so?

There is no evidence of it that Kitchen brings to light. On the other hand, the eighteen months between Speer's arrest and his sentencing to twenty years' imprisonment was a crucial period of postwar repositioning. The Iron Curtain was dropping, and the Speer/industrialist fears that Western Europe was in danger were coming to be shared by the Allies. From the first Speer was seen by American interrogators as distant from 'the primitives' and a man from whom it might be possible to extract technical known-how, names of key personnel – in Mrs Thatcher's phrase in a later context 'a man with whom we can do business'. Kitchen demonstrates how the American prosecutor Robert Jackson tread lightly on some points, such as Speer's knowledge of and implication in the fate of Jews, and emphasized others, such as his efforts to counter the Nero Order (Hitler's edict re 'scorched earth'). The president of the court, Lord Lawrence, hardly damaged Speer's cause by giving short shrift to the Russian prosecutor, most hostile of the four. British and French prosecutors, no doubt with the Stalinist spectre in mind, resisted putting Speer's feet to the fire; and when the vote on sentencing came, their judges were able to persuade U. S. Attorney General Francis Biddle not to join the Russian in calling for Speer's execution. What manoeuvres lay behind this Kitchen does not speculate upon. A dimmer view of Speer was advanced among Brits by lawyer Hartley Shawcross, journalist Sebastian Haffner and the major who was instructed to read his indictment, Mrs Thatcher's later mentor Airey Neave. He thought Speer an embodiment of 'smooth hypocrisy' and 'more beguiling and dangerous than Hitler'. In the end a kind of pragmatism prevailed.

Was this meant in part as a signal to other implicated yet educated, intelligent and socially well-placed Germans? No doubt most industrialists shed no tears at the death sentence handed down to eleven of the seventeen defendants – who at that point could defend the likes of Julius Streicher? But the Allies were perhaps wise to show discrimination and possibilities for clemency, given the *Weltpolitik* they were now facing. Speer went with Neurath, von Schirach, Funk, Raeder and Hess to Spandau, a former Gestapo prison. This handful of Nazi 'bonzos' were guarded by 400 soldiers and fifty gaolers. Visits from family were allowed but provided little comfort for Speer – the cold workaholic hardly knew his six children and had no capacity to be soul-mate to his neglected wife. He gave himself to gardening and to composing a diary; backbiting with fellow detainees faded as they departed prison or into their own dreamworlds. Speer's assets, initially sequestered, were released by the West German government in 1953, rendering him a rich man, but he insisted that family expenses not be paid out of them, rather from a 'tuition account' set up by friendly industrialists. The diaries were smuggled out to a former associate, whose Jewish mistress – her family had once been evicted from their Berlin home on the General Building Inspector's order – set about to transcribe them.

The aim of Speer as writer, Kitchen argues, was to suggest that twenty years in prison absolved the criminal of all crime. If Todt had not died, Speer opined, he might have become a great architect; but now his country was being rebuilt by 'subaltern confectioners', and there was no room for 'the last classicist'. Speer mused about his identity as perpetual 'stranger' and cultivated an appearance of interest in theology – post-prison interlocutors included a pastor, a monk and a rabbi. Ego decreed that, as memoirist, the former 'artist' be seen as a new Benvenuto Cellini. There were interviews on television, with *Der Spiegel* and even *Playboy*. Speer alternated between a persona of wearing a hair-shirt and revelling in fees, royalties and celebrity as Germany's runaway bestseller. It is tempting to see his lionization as part of the 'springtime for Hitler' of the early 1970s. Warhol admired his Germania, Bowie wore jackboots in Berlin and there was *Cabaret*. Homoerotic chic in black leathers and swastikas… that era, I suppose, was the real revisionist heyday. David Irving had not yet been unmasked. Fest and Sereny sat at Speer's feet.

The point of Kitchen's book is to remind us of the mendacity in spin and perversion of perception that allowed Albert Speer to become a kind of penitent pinup for decades. We don't like to imagine that smooth, mannerly, educated middle-class technocrats can be the most dangerous and slippery individuals of the lot: it doesn't sell newspapers or make good daytime TV. And where would the West be if we had to admit that the Soviet Union came far closer to nailing this banal Mephistopheles than we were willing to do?

SPEER: Hitler's Architect, Martin Kitchen. Yale University Press, 2015.

At the end of a world

Jewish Chronicle, 4 xii 2015

Here is a tale familiar in the sense both of already known and of family. The place is a run-down manor near a main thoroughfare in East Prussia. The time is frigid January 1945. The protagonists are normal, quite civilized yet blinkered gentry. The fearful thing is approach of a vengeful Red Army.

We live the quotidian in a manless household, its relative ease. Visitors arrive: a painter of war scenes returning west, a Jewish bookbinder fleeing east. Each new arrival brings disaster closer for the German family, if (perhaps) liberation for its Ukrainian servants. Suspense builds: the end seems nigh, but comes not yet. Will it ever? Can't the Wehrmacht hold it back? Königsberg has been flattened, but may not remoteness spare this rural enclave with its rich mementoes of happier days – fine porcelain, hallmarked silverware, antler chandeliers, ancestral portraits and a library so untouched by recent events as to contain titles by Heinrich Heine?

A Nazi apparatchik from a nearby housing estate casts a resentful eye over aristocratic privilege, threatens, requisitions space for some favoured Baltic refugees. Delicacies are hidden, rumours pondered. Did those things really happen in the East? Will the Jews take revenge? The family, extended, has a last supper – Beethoven on the piano, recitation of Goethe, cigarettes, chocolate, a precious bottle of Barolo. Meanwhile guns are rumbling in the east, skies glowing red, carts crowding the road west, bitter cold... Should we flee? Hesitation. Dilemmas.

The châtelaine is arrested for having harboured the bookbinder, now captive. The Baltic refugees are swept off in an official car, while the Ukrainian servants pack a cart and coach for the others. Most set out; a few foreign workers stay; opportunists lurk to loot. On the road chests go missing. The cart disappears. The coach is overturned by a bomb, its driver – an auntie just short of sixty – instantly dies. One arm is blown far from the body; from its fingers rings quickly vanish. Corpses lie frozen by the road. Horses fall through ice when trying to cross to a strand and safe passage. Main roads are blocked – flight in the other direction. SS troops patrol, some keeping order, others intent on stringing up deserters and thieves, especially those easties – the ever untrustworthy Ukrainians, Czechs, Romanians, Poles.

A sole member of the family survives, a boy of twelve, too young for the Hitler Youth, thus death with gun in hand. By luck more than cunning – or perhaps authorial trick – he is taken onto a last dingy out to a last ship ferrying surviving trekkers to Denmark or elsewhere west. It is an epic of exodus, timely for our days, reminding Germans of what in their past has prepared them to be welcoming – the horrendous cost of a misguided war. East Prussia had a population of nearly three million in 1940. By 1950 less than 200,000 native Germans were left. No wonder this book has sold 100,000 copies in Germany. A bestselling novel there back in the most terrible days was *Gone with the Wind*.

All for Nothing, Walter Kempowski, trans. Anthea Bell. Granta, 2015.

Fuzzy Math

Quarterly Review, 10 x 2013

Literature to do with the Holocaust implicates all of us. Any responsible person who has ever felt a twinge of anti-Semitism or other unwelcome prejudice reads with a growing unease: isn't he too hiding a guilty secret? Disquiet of course travels further: what would he do were his society being directed by authorities who demanded a certain line of orthodoxy from him *or else*? When old Nazis were asked 'Why did you participate in such horrors?' and responded 'We were just following orders', how many of us can truthfully say we would have stood out and not done the same? How many of us are willing to imperil our careers or the welfare of our families, to say nothing of our lives, in such heresy? The stakes are indeed high when one deals in literature of this genre, for the writer, for the commentator, even for the reader. A slight deviation in tone and one may produce the wrong inference. Terrible discomfort may afflict partial doubters. Descent into denial threatens moral collapse and/or relegation into a category of sociopath. An apt response may seem that of Martin Bormann Jr.: to relieve himself on his father's picture.

Laws in Germany and Austria outlaw denial. In less implicated countries legislation seems extreme and, beyond cultural suasion, we are left to the mercy of our own intellectual/emotional responses to the evidence set before us. This is why veracity of memory is crucial and David Cesarani and other historians of the topic have worried about survivor accounts that bake facts, elide, exaggerate or otherwise distort, however innocently or – if not quite that – understandably. There are still fearful glissandos in this terrible saga – how many millions? Five, six or, or... Many will say that to argue over figures is ghoulish and in any case beside the point: a massive state-sponsored crime. Yet perhaps it does matter to posterity that a chief executor of the horror first claimed that only 10,000 had perished, then later signed an affidavit saying two and a half million and was finally charged with and hanged for the death of 4,000,000. How justice got to producing this staggering last figure is material to anyone used to weighing the reliability of evidence.

The executor in question was Rudolf Höss, a lower middle class Swabian, wounded in World War I, associated with Martin Bormann in dissident postwar activities and sufficiently trusted by Himmler during the Third Reich to become commandant of Auschwitz. On a dark night in March 1946, Höss was captured in a barn on the Danish border by Hanns Alexander, an officer in the British army of privileged Berlin Jewish origin. By order and desire Alexander was impelled to hunt down war criminals. *Hanns and Rudolf* is a double biography of him and his prey by a great-nephew who knew nothing of Alexander's war work until after his death in 2006. Thomas Harding (his branch of the family changed name) is a scrupulous young man who has used all available means to unearth the truth in these matters, including testimony from Höss's children and other relations, two of whom joined him in a visit to the death-camp. The account he gives is thus full of contradictions slight and grand. At one point he asks a Belsen survivor whom his father helped how 'people who experienced the same event from the same point of view could have very different recollections' and she replies, 'You can ask ten people who were in the same place at the same time and you will get ten answers.'[1] If this is a norm, how can truth be made stable? 'Through the research process,' Harding says in a postscript to his book, 'I came to learn that history – like the story of the blind men describing the elephant – is never as clear as you would expect.'

When Hanns tracked down Rudolf on that cold night in 1946, he was leading a posse armed with axe-handles and motivated by 'hatred for the bastards'. Höss was stripped naked and beaten, until a doctor told Alexander to 'call them off unless you want to take back a corpse'[2]. As a prisoner, Höss was treated

---

1 Lucille Eichengreen. See note 314-15.

2 243. Höss's wife divulged his whereabouts on being told that a train was about

with not much more kindness nor interrogated with more gentleness than you would expect. One consequence of this, as the late Harold Pinter[3] and other campaigners against torture might predict, is recorded by Harding in an endnote:

> Those ten minutes of abuse, along with allegations of further attacks by British hands, would be enough for scores of Holocaust revisionists to argue over the years that Rudolf Höss' testimony was tainted. Their argument goes like this: Höss' testimony was beaten out of him and therefore his evidence at Nuremburg, and later his autobiography, could not be relied upon. This led them, supposedly logically, to argue that because the 'story' of the Final Solution relied so heavily on Rudolf Höss' testimony the Holocaust never really happened.[4]

Harding is right to imply illogic to the deniers' conclusion. On the other hand, he follows many in seeing the testimony of Höss as crucial to the Nuremburg process – a much-needed 'smoking gun'. He also sees the figures Höss eventually signed up to – the two and a half million, to say nothing of four million mooted in Warsaw (a Russian inflation) – as beyond credibility. 'According to many historians,' he says in a further note, 'including those at the Auschwitz Museum, the most likely figure is that 1.3 million people died at Auschwitz, of whom ninety percent were Jewish.'[5] This estimate ought to satisfy reasonable readers. It is compromised, however, by a previous note in which Harding says, 'According to the Auschwitz Museum... 1.3 million or more people [were] deported to Auschwitz'. Did all of them die? The literature is now rich with tales of survivors. So between 'died' and 'deported to' which is the more accurate verb? What is the spectrum of probabilities?

---

to take her 14 year old son to Siberia and that she would never see him again.

3   The Nobel Prize winner's views about torture were vociferously expressed in person, speeches, plays and his work for English and International PEN.

4   See note 318-19.

5   See note 310. The apparently contradictory note which follows is on 299.

Höss himself in both trial and memoir[6] dismissed some of the larger figures as technically beyond the capacity of the killing apparatus he apparently so efficiently set up. His children, somewhat surprisingly given the atmosphere of admission and atonement in the culture they grew old in, maintained that – despite living within meters of crematoria – they never knew what was going on. They put this down to having been kids at the time, but how easy is it to keep from a child's eye all trace of crimes on the scale of even the lowest estimates now generally accepted? It is of course understandable that children should wish to retain doubt about evils ascribed to a father whom they prefer to recall as kindness itself. It is also understandable that, when pressed, they like others should retire behind a defence that he was only a cog in a machine, a soldier carrying out orders, and would have been punished had he behaved otherwise, perhaps even executed. And yet...

We are in danger of being led into a moral quagmire, a confusion hardly helped ex post facto by knowledge that successors to the victorious overlords of 1945 have seen fit to 'sex up' Gulf of Tonkin resolutions, weapons-of-mass-destruction dossiers and the like in order to pursue military adventures of dubious justification. Thomas Harding is a young man alive in a post-Watergate, post-Tony Blair era of unstable certainties. He is a Jew of a generation which has been enjoined to assert 'never again' and to believe that the 'tough Jew' is a necessity that too many of his great-grandparents' era in Europe failed to credit, to their terrible cost. But what that cost was exactly his book is too even-handed to clarify. Prejudice, discrimination, threat, expropriation, extortion and exile are all established beyond doubt: these things happened to his forbears or were witnessed by them with their own eyes. The rest, with all its subdivisions – how many to disease, euthanasia or starvation; how many to causes also being meted out to half a continent during the winter of '44-'45 – relies on report, documentation, evidence

---

6   This was written largely in Warsaw when Höss was awaiting trial and was encouraged by the authorities there.

and testimony; matters that require to be tested in court and in judgements whose probity must be validated not by the hot breath of immediate press report[7] but by the cold eye of long-term history.

David Cesarani and others have been right to voice concern. No book on this topic can afford to be loose, let alone tendentious or sententious, understandable as the temptation may be. As we move on in time and new generations look back, more and more clarity, it is hoped, will emerge. Thomas Harding is an honest man who has done his best against the odds to find a human dimension in an arch-enemy of his forbears and to take a cool measure of a family hero driven in part by outrage, vengeance and hatred and with a penchant for pranksterish deception[8]. None of this is easy. What it produces for us to ponder is, if not unpalatable, in any case a bitter pill. Little is resolved fully. Possibly it never can be. We are like blindfold horses turning the wheel of a mill, circling round and round imagining our progress to be towards clover-filled pastures, which we may never reach[9]. It is easy to see how a writer may come to feel, as Anthony Julius confessed in the last paragraph of his six hundred page tome on anti-Semitism – *Trials of the Diaspora* – that he had staggered through 'muck' for long enough and hoped he would never have to deal with the topic again[10]. Mystical and idealistic aspects of Jewish tradition are the pastures which those who truly care for this people may readily prefer to attend to.

Hanns and Rudolf: The German Jew and the Hunt for the Kommandant of Auschwitz, Thomas Harding. Heinemann, 2013.

---

7   Harding describes how Höss's testimony at Nuremburg was reported instantly around the world, 259-60.

8   Hanns enjoyed pulling pranks from an early age, not least ones based on identity with his twin brother Paul. This could provide comic outcomes, often in fooling girls whom one or the other wished to seduce.

9   See Shusha Guppy's 'memoir of a Persian childhood', *The Blindfold Horse* (1988).

10   *Trials of the Diaspora: A History of Anti-Semitism in England* (Oxford University Press, 2010), 587: 'Anti-Semitism is a sewer. This is my second book on the subject and I intend it to be my last.'

A doomed deal – the Jew who tried to
negotiate with the Nazis

Quarterly Review, Winter 2009/10
expanded from *Jewish Chronicle*, 10 iv 2009

Ladislaus Löb's *Rezső Kasztner,* which was shortlisted for the
Wingate Award earlier this year, is a hybrid historical work
mixing personal memoir of escape from Nazi-occupied Europe
at age eleven with a defence of the individual who engineered
his salvation, along with that of 1,670 other hand-picked
Hungarian Jews, many of them members of the community's
elite. Löb's eponymous hero is the controversial 'Jew-saver'
of Budapest, who became principal leader of the 'Zionist
mavericks' of the Vaada – a refugee and relief organization
operating independently of the official Jewish Council – after
the British had arrested his cohort Joel Brand on suspicion of
being an enemy spy during a trip to Istanbul in late spring of
1944 to consult with officials of the Jewish Agency there on
matters proposed by Adolf Eichmann and possibly Himmler.

German occupation of Hungary in March of that year had
led to the swiftest round-ups and deportations of Jews from
any Axis or associated country. At the same time, it seemed to
open ways for negotiations to save Jewish lives. In April and May
Eichmann had made propositions to Brand to the effect that for
every armoured truck the Vaada could supply from the West
for 'exclusive' use on the Eastern front, the SS would eliminate
one hundred Jews from the lists of those to be transported to
Auschwitz or elsewhere. 10,000 such vehicles were requested.
Brand, and later Kasztner, were to transmit this offer not only
to Zionists in the Middle East but also to Jewish organizations in
Switzerland and the U.S. and via them to the Allied command.

Huge questions are raised by this story. Were the offers
genuine? Did Eichmann have authority to make them, let alone
to enforce agreement if entered into? Was he acting alone?
Could Himmler, if behind it, have pushed such a policy past

Hitler? Given the state of Nazi prospects by that stage, wasn't opportunism a main motive – i.e., for certain Nazis to position themselves as covertly 'friendly' to Jews in order to emerge on the top after a débâcle they could now clearly foresee? Such questions remain ripe for speculation. What we know is that a game of cat-and-mouse ensued, in which the train transporting Löb and other Jews to 'freedom' was used as a carrot and the non-cancellation of round-ups of other Jews in the Hungarian provinces as a stick to get money and material via the Vaada out of such contacts as it could persuade.

The Allies rejected the apparently strategic offer. Some greeted with scepticism all information received from these irregular Jewish sources, about both the extent of deportations and the possibilities for halting them; others either genuinely doubted the credibility of Nazis seeking to deal or dismissed on moral grounds any idea of talking with 'gangsters'. A few recoiled from the spectre of having 'millions of Jews dumped' on them: the British ambassador in Cairo is said to have remarked that he had enough trouble with the Grand Mufti of Jerusalem as it was, to say nothing of the Arab world in general. Then there was the prohibitive problem of how to cope with Stalin should the West suddenly perform a treacherous volte-face. Above all floated the scent of eventual total victory and the rhetoric of 'unconditional surrender', both of which by this time had become irresistible for policy-makers in the West.

Löb cites well-known responses from Eden, Churchill and others in rehearsing the matter. His main purpose, however, is to describe the chutzpah by which Kasztner and associates continued to bargain with competing Nazis, using bluff and counter-bluff, trying to avert or delay disaster for as many as possible. That they were successful for some is beyond doubt. Löb argues that, in addition to his own group, the number may have been as many as 5000 and, beyond that, perhaps Budapest's Jewry at large, which may have been spared partly because of the negotiators' feints and delays. Masses in the provinces were not so lucky, especially after the indigenous fascist Arrow Cross removed Admiral Horthy from power in October '44, letting loose an anti-Semitism whose virulence Eichmann himself claimed not to be able to hold back.

Kasztner's failure to save many, as opposed to his ability to free some, led to suspicions about his motives and methods after the war. He inflamed these by foolishly boasting that he had been responsible for the de-nazification of SS Obersturmbannführer Kurt Becher, with whom he had dealt even more closely than with Eichmann and who would go on to become one of the richest men in West Germany. In 1952 Kasztner was denounced as a collaborator in an Israeli newssheet. Close associates to him in the ruling party urged him to sue for libel. The trial, conducted by a prosecutor and judge both hostile to the government of the day, convulsed the nation. Kasztner proved a poor witness and was humiliated. An appeal to the Supreme Court eventually voided the collaboration charge, but not before Kasztner was gunned down in a Tel Aviv street. Three assassins were rapidly picked up and convicted. One was eventually revealed to have worked for Israeli intelligence. He and the others were released by Ben-Gurion a half-decade on, following consultation with Kasztner's widow and daughter, the latter giving her assent on grounds of concern for the assailants' children.

Again, many questions. It is clear that early Israel's Herut vs Mapai politics loomed large behind the libel and affected the trial. It is not so clear, or not fully, what may have lurked behind the assassination. Passionate rage on the part of Hungarian survivors and others who viewed Kasztner as a traitor covers some ground, but it remains hard to see all the wood through the trees. In a recent lecture[1] Löb stated that at the close of the war Becher returned $2 million to Kasztner which had been extorted from Jews to arrange for their escapes. Only $60,000 of this sum ever reached the hands that it had been shaken out of. Where did the rest go? into Kasztner's pocket? back to Becher? on to Zionist colleagues of the former, or postwar associates of the latter? both? all? If any of these are the case, then further

---

1   Institute of Jewish Studies, University College, London. 22 x '09.

extrapolations might be made, including that powerful forces had a motive for preventing one broken former associate from being tempted to spill the beans and/or spread the blame.

Such controversy surrounds these matters that even at this stage further evidence or admissions may not provide closure for those who have long since taken a view. As Löb noted, by the early 1950s the Israeli government, needing grain, arms and cash, was eager for good relations with West Germany. These would develop to the benefit of both nations, the one as it sought to bolster its security, the other as it sloughed its pariah status, both as they became rich. The huge sums that Germany paid in reparations were after all not without economic benefit at home. To cite just one example: the annual rest-cures taken by survivors to *Bad* towns in the Oberbayern and the Schwarzwald, all paid for by the Bundesrepublik, helped not only to restore tourism and create goodwill but also to build one of the world's most advanced healthcare industries.

As for Rezső Kasztner? His name continues to invite attack. After Löb's recent lecture, many asserted that, if he had told other Jews the truth about Auschwitz which he had learned via Eichmann, they might have been able to flee to Rumania or hide from the round-ups or even rise up to defend themselves. To this Löb countered that, if he were to save anyone, Kasztner had to keep confidential what he and his interlocutors had said; moreover, that by the time of his traffic with Eichmann most Jews already knew the terrible truth, otherwise there would not have been panic on his own 'freedom train' when it stopped in a forest to be diverted to Auspitz – a name rapidly transformed into Auschwitz in many minds, causing some to jump out of the unsealed cattle-cars and flee for their lives. Löb argued too that it would have been suicidal for people who might still have been saved, and who were missing most of their men (forced into labour camps) and had no weapons, to rise against their oppressors à la the Warsaw ghetto. Finally, the truth (to which other survivors present testified) may be that most Jews in Hungary, long notably more tolerant than its neighbours, were seduced into a hope that if they just laid low and waited for the storm to pass over they would survive. For many in Budapest this proved to be the case. For others the *Untergäng* of the 1940s kept spiralling on, many refusing to reconcile not only with their racist tormentors but also with those of their own kind who had had the temerity to bargain with them.

Reszõ Kasztner: The Daring Rescue Of Hungarian Jews: A Survivor's Account, Ladislaus Löb. Pimlico, 2009.

A Northern Light for Europe's Darkest Hour

Quarterly Review, 1 v 2014

Sweden is a country whose participation in the trauma of modern European history is of long-standing. Lutheran from early on, it played a significant role in The Thirty Years' War, a catastrophe in which – as Schiller's *Wallenstein* demonstrates – heroics did not always follow the script. Later in the 17th century Sweden began to wrest spoils from a declining Polish-Lithuanian empire, as did its quondam opponent Peter the Great. Not long into the next century, the Nordic land's *Drang nach Suden* was ended by Charles XII's overreaching and the valour of Ukrainian Cossacks, which Byron glamorized in *Mazeppa*. Sweden's receding influence in east central Europe was hastened by the advent of other 'Greats' – Catherine in Russia, Frederick in Prussia – and by the start of the 20th century it was hardly even *primus* among Scandinavian *pares*, having lost both Finland and Norway during a long 19th century of diplomatic manoeuvre set off by Napoleonic upheavals.

Its ancient dynasty was deposed in the same phase that saw downfall of France's ancien régime, but it retains a monarchy in consequence of having invited one of Bonaparte's maréchals to become heir apparent shortly before the collapse of the French empire. This irony is not atypical. Cleverness, coolness and compromise allowed Bernadotte and his heirs to survive the Metternich-ean reaction. Similar characteristics marked 20th century Swedish governments' tergiversations as Europe descended towards its darkest hour. During the interval, great banking and trading families had grown up to be powers in the austere land, not least the Wallenbergs, whose influence over politics, diplomacy, social and cultural life was second to none. Raoul Wallenberg, the 'hero of Budapest'[1], was a scion of this clan. His legend belongs to the genre of what may befall young men of privilege if they are so lucky or so rash as to offer

---

1 I used this epithet in relation to Kasztner. It has been applied to both men.

themselves up in service as saviours.

Raoul's initial expectations in life were perhaps less great than is generally assumed. His father, for whom he was named, died of a rare cancer at age 25 before he was born. Raoul Jr was raised under supervision of his paternal grandfather, a naval officer, diplomat and entrepreneur who took no direct role in running the family bank but by dint of first-born status expected his son and eventually grandson to take it on. Sons of a younger brother's branch, being tracked for the bank from an early age, had a head start on their cousin: Raoul's grandpa, fearing the lure of social life for a rich boy in Stockholm, preferred him to get his education in the outer world. Study in Germany and France was followed by university in the U. S., at Ann Arbor in Michigan not the Ivy League – grandpa feared that similar social lures lurked on the more élite American east coast. From this regimen Raoul gained fluency in four languages (he learned some Russian as well), a sense of self-sufficiency, ease of relating with varieties of people and a penchant for fun. Hitchhiking became his favourite mode of travel; despite being mugged once on a midwestern road, he kept to it.

He studied architecture and once back in Europe in 1938 expressed admiration for the 'genius' of Albert Speer, 'which reflected a striving for "bigness" [that] has long been suppressed in Europe'[2]. He was proud to a point of hubris of a drop of Jewish blood in his veins – 'A person like me, who is both a Wallenberg and half-Jewish, can never be defeated'[3] – though he was in fact only ¹⁄₁₆th Jewish, on his mother's side. Despite this, he seems to have taken little note of *Kristallnacht* or its portent for a people whom he would later be engaged to help save. In common with many in the international élite of the day, other Wallenbergs appear to have had a whiff of social anti-Semitism about them, which may on occasion have been directed at this 'outsider' in the cousinage. In any case, none rushed to welcome Raoul into management of the bank; so with characteristic

2   In a letter to an American friend, quoted by Jangfeldt, 144.

3   A statement to a friend during military service in 1930, quoted Ibid., 146.

chutzpah he threw himself into trade and teamed up eventually with Kálmán Lauer, a Hungarian Jew who had emigrated to Sweden in 1939 yet wished to continue to deal in livestock and foodstuffs with his native country as well as other regions of what was, or soon to be, a Nazi-dominated continent. Given his languages, his connections and charm, Raoul seemed to Lauer a perfect young operative to cultivate.

The Hungarian connection attracted attention from others who by 1944 needed a paladin to rescue what they could of that nation's 800,000 Jews. The relatively mild fascism of Admiral Horthy, who had ruled Hungary since the crushing of Béla Kun's communist régime of 1919, was in process of being supplanted by German occupation and the fanatically anti-Semitic native Arrow Cross party. A War Refugee Board was set up by President Roosevelt at the behest of Treasury Secretary Henry Morgenthau, funded partly by wealthy American Jews; the OSS man in Stockholm knocked heads together with Lauer, the chief rabbi and 'righteous gentiles' to find a man to front an op. Despite a well-publicized speech by the king against actions against Jews throughout Europe, the Swedish foreign office was not uniformly eager to associate itself with a project which could be construed as less than wholly neutral. Even so, once a Wallenberg had been recruited, it agreed to give him cover as one of its civil servants on an official humanitarian mission.

Thus began a six-month descent into an inferno – the final machinations and collapse of fascism, with all the terror, starvation, rape and pillage entailed, followed by even more shocking rampages on arrival of the Red Army in frigid January of '45. Wallenberg's mission between the early summer of '44 and this end-game was to round up such Jews in Budapest as could be shown to have a link to Sweden, thus to save them from being transported to the labour camps and death to come for their fellows in the countryside. Exploiting a non-combatant status which Sweden shared with the Vatican, Switzerland and Spain, he used bribery, fiction, fraud, back channels to the Arrow Cross, cat-and-mouse games with Eichmann, promises of postwar protection for 'good Germans', indulgence of Himmler's offers of 'blood for goods', pliability of the SS man-on-the-ground Kurt Becher and playing off of one actor against another[4]. He was a Wallenberg and many Germans saw Sweden as the best hope for facilitating a separate peace with the Western allies, or at least leniency from them as they faced annihilation from the East. Horthy had supported Hitler mainly out of fear Bolshevism and loathing for the post-WWI Treaty of Trianon, which had reduced Hungary to a rump, and Wallenberg was not above playing to these emotions in order to hide chattels and stockpile food for his ghettoized protégés. In his months in Hungary, he also architected a plan for the country's rehabilitation after the war – a scenario in which, it is fair to assume, his experience as a trader with Lauer and his link to a leading international capitalist family played their roles – i.e., it would be far-fetched to suppose that he envisaged a Marxist satellite state, let alone return to anything like the revolutionary Leninism that had flamed up however briefly under Béla Kun.

We can never know. The plan went with him when he 'crossed the line', evidently to treat with the Soviets as they entered a city which their mortars were turning to rubble. From his bunker in the vault of a bank as well as other no longer safe Swedish houses, Wallenberg collected and packed into his car's petrol tank currency, jewels, gold – booty from Jews he had been sheltering, which otherwise might have vanished in the chaos. The Russians proved to be captors, not saviours. The car was stopped; treasure and documents vanished; Wallenberg was held without charge by the counterespionage unit SMERSH. He found himself shortly in the notorious Lubyanka prison in Moscow, to be interrogated on suspicion of being a German collaborator, a trafficker in stolen goods, a Western spy with conspiratorial agenda against the USSR and/or all of the above. His protests of diplomatic status proved of no avail and his claims of working only to save a threatened people evoked derision from some in an increasingly anti-Semitic Stalinist

---

4 I wrote about contingent matters re Kasztner in the chapter above.

milieu. Did he infuriate his jailors by the self-confidence and aura of superiority with which, it is said, he had sometimes cowed their equivalents of the Arrow Cross or even the SS? Was he beaten? tortured? injured? disfigured? From the time of his disappearance until his supposed death, by heart attack, aged 34, in March 1947, nothing is clear. This was a time of the miasma of gulags and closing of an 'Iron Curtain'.

Other forces at work, or not so, were also opaque. Such is the conclusion of Bengt Jangfeldt in his formidable account of the affair, a narrative thick with detail of the Budapest inferno but never bogged down in its pursuit of the many threads as to whom Wallenberg truly was[5] and what occurred between his last sighting and reports of his demise. Jangfeldt portrays an exceptional adventurer fully capable of being a double-dealer if needed, even 'triple thinker' to use Edmund Wilson's term[6]. This makes it quite easy to understand how his captors might have viewed him as playing for personal gain or an enemy spy. But Jangfeldt also wonders about the role of official Sweden, eager for trade deals in Stalin's new east central Europe and under a socialist administration of its own. Why didn't it push harder for information about this illustrious son? And why, to raise Jangfeldt's most barbed final question, didn't influential members of the Wallenberg family do more?

One answer may go like this. Great families, like great corporate entities of all kinds – political, commercial, covert – have their essential economy. Individual members grow up to slot into roles or not as the case may be, for better or worse: the

---

5   One aspect in which Jangfeldt's account is too sketchy is Wallenberg's private life. Girlfriends are mentioned but the nature of relationships with them is not made clear. The impression is that Raoul was a 'young man in a hurry' with too much to accomplish to have time for more than dalliance and, after all, his grandfather had consistently warned him off falling into the clutches of women, unless and until he was ready to marry. Perhaps a postwar Raoul Wallenberg might have found a wife and become a paterfamilias in traditional mode, but for all one can tell a playboy nature might have led him in quite other directions.

6   Wilson's term became a title of a book of essays which appeared some years after his classic on the genesis of Communism, *To the Finland Station* (1940).

flourishing or at least survival of the group depends upon it. There is inevitable ruthlessness in this process, if not always quite conscious. Raoul Wallenberg, like Byron, could not have been an organization man in an establishment mould: the absence of a father and eccentric tutelage by a grandfather destined him for a more romantic agenda, even if romance was part of what the tutelage was meant to discourage. In the end Raoul (his name is said to derive from a character in Dumas[7]) *had* to behave like some latter-day Sidney Carton, a Christ-hero amid scenes of ghastly upheaval. His cousins safe in Stockholm running the bank were perhaps not overly fussed that they did not have to share desk-space or boardroom with such a flamboyant rival and lifted only a few fingers to discover what had happened to him. The Swedish F.O. likewise, even while others – in Hungary, the U.S. and Israel – busied themselves in raising a new young man of privilege into the status of a latter-day Don Carlo reaching down to help *les misérables*, a Byron breathing his last to combat tyranny. Glorious apotheosis! Yet what comfort for a body rotting away and perhaps finally poisoned in some noisome cell out of *Darkness at Noon*?

This is often the real end of daredevil service. And while the bravery of Raoul Wallenberg seems beyond question, the legend surrounding him may be misleading, in this respect: whatever he did, whatever he achieved, whatever heroism he displayed – even his martyrdom, if it was that – involved the efforts and interests, good and bad, of countless others operating on the same ground at the time; and much of what he accomplished may have come to pass via them anyway. He was no doubt exceptional – certainly few appear to have given up such comfort as his pedigree promised. But the sacrifice was rich in incentives: he had at his command vast resources and was invested with extraordinary insurgent/official authority. The mission was heady. He took it, presumably in full knowledge of the risks, for that reason. It would be disingenuous to suppose

---

7 The son of Athos in *The Three Musketeers*. Jangfeldt takes the idea from Wallenberg's half-sister, 4.

that there was not an element of vanity in his motives, possibly even competitive (familial) pride. Dreamers on heroism of the future should take note: read this life as a cautionary tale, not just for inspiration to go out and get yourself recruited.

The Hero of Budapest: The Triumph and Tragedy of Raoul Wallenberg, Bengt Jangfeldt, trans. Harry D. Watson and the author. I. B. Tauris, 2014.

Faut-il brûler Céline?[1]

Quarterly Review, Spring 2012

I was once asked by a Bavarian what region of Europe was furious at not being annexed by the Nazis. The Südtirol was the answer: Hitler was loath to annoy Mussolini, with whom he shared a passion never to return to the territorial arrangements of the hated Hapsburgs.

One might similarly ask what world-famous author of the mid-20th century was furious that German occupiers didn't do more to get rid of Jews? Céline is the answer: he liked to make out that the administration of Paris, even Foreign Office in Berlin, was infested by 'youtrons'[2].

It is well to remember such shocking trivia. History is rarely as uniform as the received narrative would like to have it, nor is any totalitarianism total. Céline made a career out of cynicism, bad taste, insult and every form of transgression he could imagine. Yet he was able to thrive during the Occupation, pouring obloquy on the rump régime of Pétain as on the 'youtres, cocos et pédés alcooliques' whom he caricatured as surrounding that British puppet De Gaulle[3]. After the war, following a spell of exile and incarceration in Denmark, he was allowed back to Paris, re-published by Gallimard and posthumously included in the Pléiade edition of canonical greats, between Bergson and Cervantès. Many *whys* are thrown up by this. Someone of Céline's twist of mind might posit a Jewish plot in which the

---

1 The editor ran this as 'Céline Redux' and suggested translations of the French, which we agreed to put in notes. Needless to say, it is a mug's game to try to translate a mentality, especially one as rebarbative as Céline's; thus we offered only rough approximations – in this case, 'Is it necessary to burn Céline?'

2 See Alméras, esp. chapter entitled 'Occupé' and its section 'Les Juifs à toutes les places, les Français dans les Steppes'. Céline's slang might be 'yids' or 'yidders'.

3 The patter vs De Gaulle is as one would expect of a 'collabo' or 'mangouste [mongoose]'; it extends into to an idea that 'Dogol' was a concocted name, with implications re impure French ethnicity. Ibid., 268. The phrase approximates 'yids, pervs and drink-sodden faggots'.

anti-Semite is promoted precisely so that *their* world domination might be advanced – didn't he mutter about Hitler as Nazi Europe collapsed, 'Hitler juif ou demi-juif machinerait le cataclysme'[4]? And wasn't his rehabilitation due in part to efforts by New York Jewish academic Milton Hindus? Nowadays few self-interested writers would cite Céline as a model, but Howard Jacobson knows it will not hurt *his* reputation to declare preference for the incontinent Frenchman over housebroken upper middle-class English types who proclaim philo-Semitism while never inviting a neo-expressionist Jew like himself to Sunday lunch at their *gîtes* in the Home Counties[5].

Céline was not a literary end-point in the style of Modernist precursors such as James Joyce or Gertrude Stein. Henry Miller famously shared in his aesthetic, as would the Beats, especially Jack Kerouac, who was of French descent and would end in his own slough of racist grumblings[6]. Céline's *Voyage au bout de la nuit* was an epoch-making book in the 1930s, *Mort à Crédit* not far behind; and both regained status in 1950s America, the latter in part because of inspired translation of its title to *Death on the Instalment Plan*. Like his Beat successors, Céline had a knack for appearing to write spontaneously, to record exact speech and to drop the mode of the novel into the gutter where – in the context of the thriller – Raymond Chandler said it belonged[7]. Like Miller and Kerouac, Céline specialized in not quite fiction, not quite memoir, but a sort of hallucinated life-experience.

---

4 Ibid., 271. Alméras draws a parallel between Céline's ideas and those of the conspiracy theorist Nesta Webster; the phrase approximates 'Hitler, Jew or part-Jew, would engineer the cataclysm'. After the war Céline hardly modified his analysis: in a letter of 14 Feb 1950, he observed that Jews 'tiennent la France en domesticité absolue, créant les antisémites pour assurer leur position des victimes' ('hold France in their clutches, creating anti-Semites in order to assure their position as victims'). Ibid., 400.

5 At an event for English PEN, Free Word Centre, 15 Jan 2008.

6 Including anti-Semitic, despite his famous friendship with Allen Ginsberg. See Tom Wolfe's description of a pilgrimage to Kerouac by the Merry Pranksters in *The Electric Kool-Aid Acid Test* (1968).

7 Re the achievement of Dashiell Hammett in 'The Simple Art of Murder'.

Unlike them, he was neither a proletarian nor near to it: his real surname, often rendered 'des Touches', suggests haut bourgeois pretentions. He qualified as a doctor and served as such in both wars, as well as in the French civil service in Africa. In the 1920s and after he worked for the Rockefeller Foundation on public hygiene projects: a much-reproduced photo shows him leading a delegation for it to meet with Mussolini[8]. In this phase, he lived in Montmartre with a dancer from Los Angeles, Elizabeth Craig, who aspired to the Ziegfeld Follies. When her family lost a fortune in property schemes in the 1930s, she returned home. Céline followed, hoping for marriage and a film deal. What he got was rejection in favour of one Ben Tankle, 'plus jeune, plus entreprenant, plus optimiste' and possibly Jewish, though Céline chose to depict him as a mini Al Capone[9]. Rejection might explain Céline's embittered tone in his début as author were it not for the facts that *Voyage* had come out two years earlier, dedicated to Craig, and that the swagger he had gained from it as literary lion was part of what killed her attraction to him. Years later Craig would explain that she could not revert to 'cette attitude de supériorité dans la décadence comme si était quelque chose qu'il fallait chérir', especially not after having reattached herself to 'l'imbécillité américaine... cette fraîcheur bête... dans la nature, dans les collines ensoleillées de la Californie du Sud'[10].

Rejection perhaps *did* colour the 'style vengeance' in books Céline would write in years following. A tone of 'l'imprécateur devenu pestiféré'[11] invaded memories of his Rockefeller experience, including exposure to Henry Ford's notorious anti-Semitic tracts of the '20s and frustration under a Jewish boss

---

8   The photo is unfortunately not included in Alméras's biography, which is not 'official' and lacks pictures.

9   Ibid, 174. Phrase approximates 'younger, more enterprising, more optimistic'.

10   Her words come from an interview taken in English but published in French. Returned to English they approximate, 'that attitude of superiority in decadence, as if it were something necessary to cherish' and 'American craziness... the wild freshness... in nature, in the sun-drenched hills of Southern California'.

11   Ibid., 472. Literally 'the imprecator become pestiferous'.

in Geneva. Recycling these via the language of a fascist New Man culminated on the eve of the war in an anti-Semitic polemic *Bagatelles pour une massacre*. Like Hitler in *Mein Kampf*, the leitmotif for Céline was degradation of his own race. The French were to blame for their *enjuivement* and would lose in their struggle with that ethnic group and its fellows, which dominated the world from Wall Street to the Kremlin and especially in the City of London. Such views, shared by so many anti-Semites of the day, including Anglos, were pushed to an extreme worthy of Nazi ideologues and Yankee prohibitionists by Céline's canard that the rot had begun in the 13th century when Saint Louis had collectively baptized three or perhaps six hundred thousand Jews and other 'mongrels' in the south, thus rendering France into a kind of *suralgérie*, and was assured in modern times by the proliferation of booze, manufactured and distributed by Jews. A solution lay in non-aggression with Germany, but Blum's *Front populaire* had put France on an unstoppable path to conflict, and the Nazis in victory had made the error of reincorporating Alsace-Lorraine into their Reich and occupying only a northern part of the country instead of forging a full *Anschluss* and creating a franco-allemande army. After the war, arguments would be made, not least by Céline, that his outbursts circa 1938-40 were meant as Cassandra warnings rather than incitements; and *rigolade* and exaggeration *do* make them slippery to pin down, much as irony does various precepts of Nietzsche's which the Nazis liked to adopt, and like that philosopher Céline clearly had some grudging regard for the race he contended to have degraded his own. Yet despite a phase of philo-Semitism in the years when Hindus was trying to restore his reputation[12] and James Laughlin at New Directions was releasing translations of his work, Céline continued sarking and sniping – not least in his correspondence – putting visceral antipathy beyond doubt.

---

12 Hindus eventually published a memoir *Céline as I Knew Him*, which was less than laudatory. Céline's reciprocal attitude had long since descended into invective. See Ibid., especially 359-77.

What is the value of such incontinent expressionism in our era post-Osama bin Laden/post-Anders Breivik – or, at a popular level, post the self-lacerating eruptions of Mel Gibson, John Galliano and Lars von Trier? Philippe Alméras tries bravely if inconclusively to reach a verdict on Céline in a 'Postface' to the new edition of his vast 1994 biography. Here as elsewhere we are reminded that some will continue to try to justify Céline's excess by his training as a physician – 'le désir de savoir ce qui se passe dans le dedans des hommes… le sécret des choses… [duquel] la masse refuse la vérité'[13]. We are also reminded that many French intellectuals are inclined to take Céline less than seriously, as a grand *farceur* in a tradition of Rabelais[14], and that critics still praise him for leading a vanguard in destroying convention so that the voice of the writer could ventriloquize previously unmentionable musings in a tradition of Baudelaire's 'Mon coeur mis à nu' – though in this case less of heart than of bowel, genitalia and organs of rage. Céline has been seen as a case of that modern extension of romantic license whereby 'L'artiste tout-puissant préfère sa personne et sa fonction à son œuvre… l'œuvre est, non une fin, mais le moyen de construire, ou de détruire, sa personne'[15]. In erecting a 'mythe personnel', he in fact tends to seem, ironically, most at one with the great 'pédés' among French *auteurs* of his era, Gide and Genet, whom he despised; but whereas pre and during the War this allowed him to play at 'l'autobiographie remplit d'imaginaire, de rêves, de fantastique', afterwards it brought him crashing to the ground of real history and its effect on an errant self with the message – as De Gaulle's Minister of Culture André Malraux remarked –

---

13 Ibid., 468. 'Desire to know what goes on inside men… the secret of things, of which the mass is in denial'.

14 Gide was one of these: re *Bagatelles* he believed that Céline 'se rigolait' (Ibid, 212). Céline placed himself in a tradition of Rabelais, Villon and Breughel and spoke of its 'formule nordique'.

15 Jean-Yves Tadié, *Le Roman au XXe Siècle* (Paris : Belfond, 1990), 9. 'The all-powerful artist values persona and function above his work; the work is not an end but a means to construct, or deconstruct, that persona.'

of 'Ayez pitié de moi'[16].

Might we surgically remove genuine values from Céline's oeuvre, as perhaps we can from *The Cantos* of his Fascist-admiring contemporary Ezra Pound, whom Laughlin was promoting in the same era? Possibly not. There is a chasm between the spectacle of degeneracy probed by the doctor-*romancier* and the programme for regeneration the American poet wished to drill into his readers. Master of prose of a kind, as Pound was of prosody, Céline deserves recognition on a basis of style; yet one might argue that the style itself is corrupting – not quite the same as Gore Vidal saying of Kerouac's practice 'that's not writing, it's typing'[17], but akin to it. Without a reasoned organizing principle, what follows? Céline *did* have a genius for recording the interior monologue of a type of his times, even of the potential for the abyss in Everyman. He *was* trenchant in exposing hypocrisy as well as dishing it up, yet hardly reliable at assaying true good and evil, or making a pattern, or attempting to inscribe some system to live by. That aspiration, which a messianic Modernist like Pound cracked his mind over, or W. B. Yeats attempted in *A Vision*, would seem too much like hard work for this progenitor of Miller-ian looseness. Yet, does it matter? Must the role of an author always be ethical after Auschwitz, as so many have contended, or is this mainly a persuasive slogan for what by extension becomes a censorious political correctness?

Pound appeared to be slouching towards redemption when he said to Allen Ginsberg, 'The worst mistake I made was that stupid suburban prejudice of anti-Semitism' and in his late assertion that the demon he'd been fighting was not 'the Jew' but simple human greed[18]. Céline on occasion had the ingenuity

---

16 Ibid., 14. 'Have pity on me.'

17 'Textes en écriture automatique ou lettristes méritent à peine le nom de roman,' Tadié argues (Ibid., 81 ['Automatic and letter-style writing hardly merit the status of novel']). Having chased rejection by one dancer with marriage to another, Céline would liken his style to that of contemporary dance, a piquant (Dionysian?) notion which there is not space here to investigate.

18 Conversation in Venice, 28 Oct 1967. An account of it is given by Humphrey

to observe that what he meant by 'Jew' did not refer to race or ethnicity so much as to a turn of mind or set of attitudes and associations, a kind of opportunism among those who wished to exercize power in certain ways[19]. The connotation will be familiar to those who knew Eastern Europe or Russia of the day before yesterday, or know the Arab street now. But co-opting a part for the whole in this manner is at the least an abuse of language, and what author can be maintained as a classic who juggles the meaning of words to malign effect? There may be approaches to the world, impacted by history and tradition, that are or have been common to some Jews; but in an era when it is demonstrably false to assert that 'Jew' equals Zionist or market-manipulator or media-meister *tout court*, such generalizations seem either deluded or adopted purposely to gain notoriety – and that is not to mention their latent consequence in respect to pogrom, terrorist act or eugenic policy.

Simone de Beauvoir in the '40s wrote an essay in favour of authorial freedom famously entitled 'Faut-il brûler Sade?' The similar question 'Faut-il brûler Céline?' must be answered post-Nazi book-burnings *non*. Yet post-Holocaust one may feel obliged to add to this bien-pensant liberal attitude, **but**...

Céline entre Haines et Passion, Philippe Alméras. Pierre-Guillaume de Roux, 2011.

Carpenter, *A Serious Character: The Life of Ezra Pound* (Faber, 1988), 897-9.

19   In the letter mentioned in note 3, he wrote, "Un sur 1000 est réellement juif, c'est une secte, un gang comme les Templiers, ce qui ambitieux devient juif' ('One in a thousand is truly Jewish – it's a sect, a gang like the Templars. Those who are ambitious become Jews'). Far from being a Poundian recantation, this identifies the category 'Jew' as having little to do with ethnicity or religion and everything to do with self-interest.

Packed verbal baggage

Jewish Chronicle, 3 xii 2010

By virtue of linguistic skill and geographical displacement, the Lithuanian Jew who called himself Romain Gary was able to devise a storybook life. Born under Russian imperium prior to World War I, he grew up in renascent Poland, only to move to Franco-Italian Nice before the Nazi-Soviet pact brought catastrophe to his region. War rendered him French in a way that prejudice might have disallowed had catastrophe not turned west. He joined De Gaulle in Britain, had a 'good war' as an airman and was able to exploit Slavic origins in an 'authentic' novel about resistance in the East. By 1946 he was a French diplomat and married to English *Vogue* editor Lesley Blanch.

Like Joseph Conrad, the Polish speaker moved from French to English as writer, yet without giving up a nationality and language necessary for his job and for winning kudos from the likes of Malraux and Camus. Sartre, whose fictions were thinly disguised representations of life, was envious of Gary's existential material; but Gary rarely used life-matter directly. As if some literary Chagall, he animated his work with the fantastic brio of the East; if it failed to reach highest accolades, this was from lapses in what Sartre excelled at – *les mots*. 'Style does not interest me', Gary claimed. Nonetheless, he won the Prix Goncourt twice, the second time under a hoax identity which caused a furore that may have contributed to his suicide in 1980.

Gary's carelessness was deliberate. He believed in the 'total' – that is, the compendious, open-ended, human as well as humane – as opposed to the 'totalitarian', which in his formula denoted the constricted formality of closet classicist *auteurs* of his day. His 'rebirth' as Émile Ajar was intended to show up this establishment for its cabalism and false values. It retaliated by branding him as a sloppy purveyor of sentimental page-turners suitable for the middle-brow taste of his English first wife or the Hollywood friends of his second, Jean Seberg, whom Gary met in his mid-forties when he was posted to L.A. as French Consul and she was fresh from teen stardom as Joan of Arc.

As celebrity and writer, Gary had 'antennae that picked up the trend and direction of current affairs'. At the same time, he never lost his Russian angst and Polish/Yiddish sense of humour. His great creations – his own mother in the memoir *Promise at Dawn* and Mme Rosa in *Life Before Us*, as well as the picaresque 'Sganarelle' whom he placed at the centre of all his narratives – hark back to these sources rather than to the milieux he operated in. Writing in English reflected his transnational status as much as desire for wider audiences and more money, but the 'Free French' label opened doors for him too, first when he was being promoted by the Brits in the '40s and later via connections made during his postings in New York and L.A..

Gary's forays into film were as disastrous as his marriage to Seberg, but his novels sold well in the States where their 'total' character anticipated sprawlings by Mailer, Bellow and Thomas Pynchon, whom Gary tried to sue for use of his character Genghis Cohn in *The Crying of Lot 49*. David Bellos chronicles all in a sprawl of his own, with brilliant critical insights meeting the organization of the card file. Chapters are devoted to categories – politics, sex, books and so on – and readers hoping for a life told in compulsive sequence may be disappointed. Lesley Blanch said of her husband's writing that it was 'an organic necessity'; Gary characterized it as 'une évacuation quotidienne'. Bellos follows by characterizing it as 'bullshitting', a term the Princeton academic uses a dozen times in as many pages. His objective is to vindicate a remarkable figure whose bête noire was 'the well-made book'. This is admirable, but more readers might be persuaded had he adopted a French classical injunction to be 'clair, précis, rapide au but... puissant, hautain, sublime et net'[1].

Romain Gary. A Tall Story, David Bellos. Harville Secker. 2010.

---

1 Formula iterated by the Franco-Jewish poet/critic Catulle Mendès in the 1880s to distinguish French practice from German, notably Wagnerian, which he saw as 'long-winded, lacking vivacity, laboured in development of character and idea'.

Jean Améry and multiple identities

Quarterly Review, Autumn 2011

Among national stereotypes, the stolid Germanic burgher ranks high; yet in inverse proportion to his supposed dominance, eccentricity, extravagance and madness have regularly broken loose. The mild-mannered philology professor who became Dionysian scriptor of *Also Sprach Zarathustra* is a vivid example of the phenomenon[1], but his early idol – the composer whose Pilgrim's Chorus degenerates into a Venusberg bacchanal – could also serve. Music describes the antipodes often: the hammer strokes of Beethoven smashing the classical symphony, massive clown formations in Mahler chasing quiescent adagios. There are curdling cries from blood-spattered Elektra to counterpoint waltzes in *Der Rosenkavalier*. And what of Brecht and kind? What of the Schnitzlers and Schieles, Schönbergs and even sex-deviance-tracking Freuds of the Viennese Secession and after, all of whom worked in a greater German tradition? Farting witches of Walpurgisnachts from Mann to Goethe back to Dürer; the metaphysics of Kant and weird musical mathematics of Bach – put them against, say, Vico and Vivaldi and you have a contrast akin to the Gothic vs Romanesque cathedral. Which embodies imaginative extremity and which order? As to politics; great Visconti's *The Damned* demonstrates how National Socialism emerged as an expressionist exaggeration of what in Fascism could be taken as modernist brutalism longing for classical form.

Can such generalizations be useful to understanding? Can we spy their shadows in Jewish responses to the Holocaust, between say German-speaking Hans Mayer, who would rebirth himself 'Jean Améry', and Piedmontese chemist Primo Levi? Both experienced Auschwitz, only to commit suicide after

---

1 Mayer/Améry's first important essay, 'Zur psychologie des deutschen Volk' (1945), generalized on such matters in light of his experience in the camps. He blames Nietzsche for descent of German morality into 'a notion of exerting power divorced from any ideas or aims'. He acknowledges irony in the philosopher's most barbaric pronouncements, but does not see it mitigating their baleful influence.

decades of trying to make sense of it. Though fellow founders of what the late Tony Judt called 'that republic of letters formed against their will by survivors of the great upheavals of the 20th century'[2], they viewed one another with courteous wariness. Like an inconsolable mourner for a lost beloved, Améry semiconsciously felt that no one else was entitled to a grief that *belonged* to him. Levi treated the matter too smoothly, he grumbled, being too willing to forgo resentment, even to reconcile with former tormentors[3]. But then Levi had been able to go home to a land where he was well-planted and which had participated in evil only half-heartedly. His compatriots were not guilt-ridden; he could get on with his profession; time and place encouraged an elegant dealing with the past and moving on. This of course he could not do, having made himself into what Améry would brand 'a victim to be put on show, an example of Jewish suffering'. 'If you gaze for too long into the abyss,' Nietzsche had written, 'the abyss will gaze into you.'[4] Rash heroism it was for survivors to drag themselves back through experiences which self-interested Yea-sayers to life might have blocked from the instant of regaining liberty – cf. Nietzsche's further quip that the power to forget is 'always the one thing that makes happiness'[5].

Améry's path was tortuous. Hans Mayer had grown up by the Alps, ever the landscape of his heart, though Nazis tore identification with it away from 'cosmopolitan' Jews. A cabaret year in late Weimar Berlin was followed by literary apprenticeship in the Vienna captured so luridly in *Auto-da-Fé* by his future admirer Elias Canetti. Anschluss impelled Mayer and a young wife to Belgium; he joined the resistance there and in 1943 was picked up, tortured, eventually sent to the

---

2 *Reappraisals: Reflections on the Forgotten Twentieth Century* (Penguin, 1908), 14.

3 Améry's assessment, confined mainly to private letters, is one with which Judt among others would disagree. See Ibid., 'The Elementary Truths of Primo Levi'.

4 *Beyond Good and Evil*, 146. *Complete Works*, xii.

5 *Thoughts out of Season*, II, 'The Use and Abuse of History', I. Ibid, v, tr. Adrian Collins.

camps. His wife disappeared while he was away, never again to be found. Postwar Austria, the ex-imperial rump which to this day is riven between a cultured/decadent capital and uplands where peasants host ski-/biking daredevils (to say nothing of the *sitzfleisch* which the *kuchen kultur* of Central Europe is so adept at producing), was not eager to welcome back 'outsiders' of Mayer's stripe: though briefly part of the Weiner Kreis in the '30s, he had never had time to establish himself there anymore than in his boyhood home, Bad Ischl. After flirting with residence in the Paris of his new idol Jean-Paul Sartre, Mayer returned to the neither-here-nor-there of Belgium, to settle like a resident in a transients' hotel until the end of what seems like a simulacrum of life. Hack journalism under French reinvention of his name followed a phase of non-success at writing novels. He married a supportive friend of his late wife, but poverty, overwork and living on edge continued, aggravating a chronic heart condition. In 1965, through a sympathetic programmer at Bavarian state radio, he landed a commission to write about his experience in the camps. 'Auschwitz – An der Grenze des Geistes' made him famous overnight. He could, within limits, write his own ticket ever after.

The story at this point becomes partly one about Germany, indeed West Germany as it progressed in the decades after the war. Améry had not set out to 'play the Auschwitz clown', as he would seethe in the last year of his life[6]; he had wanted to be a literary artist in the tradition of Mann or, short of that, a philosopher à la Sartre. But what sells drives, and what sold to German commissioning editors of the 1960s was a more radical look-back at errors of their parents' generation and deeper inquiry into man's inhumanity to man. Revisiting the Holocaust provided a native equivalent to the soul-searching France was going through in relation to Algeria and America would shortly enter into re Vietnam[7]. Why, one must ask, had the horrors

---

6 In a letter to Hans Paeschke, his sometime editor at the *Merkur*.

7 German publication in 1961 of a translation of Levi's 1947 *Se questo è un uomo?* played a role in this process and was an incitement for Améry to enter into it.

Améry came to speak about not got fuller airing in the late 1940s or '50s? Conventional wisdom is that the escapees from death wanted simply to live again, while those who had meted it out and been shackled in consequence wanted simply to break free and rebuild. That such resolutions don't last may be natural, up to a point; it may also be artificially motivated. Media need material; editors want stories to command attention, shock, move. Helmut Heissenbüttel was pushing the envelope in the most conservative *Land* in Germany by inviting Améry to make the successive programmes that would become chapters of *Jenseits von Schuld und Sühne* (1966). Ostensibly he was helping the survivor by providing him with a forum. In personal terms, the effect was increasingly less happy.

By the 1970s Améry had turned back to what he had set out to do in 1945: write novels. Did Heissenbüttel want to know? Did the critics? Not much. Here is the moment when the bitter penny dropped: in literary terms, he was victim *tout court* – *that* was his identity, his final branding by Nazis, more indelible than an Auschwitz number on the arm. We are sympathetic, ran official thought-processes; still, you are not just a man, but a Jew we mistreated unspeakably, a representative of those to whom we must make amends, even obeisance, before moving on. Simultaneous to his mini-Proustian *Lefeu oder Der Abbruch* (1974) being panned or ignored, Améry was erected into a star-turn on talk-shows and panel-discussions, to be set against rehabilitated victimizers like Albert Speer. 'There is no one else in this country who can think in public as seriously, as profoundly, and with such awareness of problems as you,' he was told[8], but this was not what the imaginative writer wanted to hear. His spirit, long wounded, began to turn on his material being. Levi's question re Auschwitz '*Se questo è un uomo…*' spread out into 'If this is a life…' Améry wrote *Hand an sich legen* (1976), subtitled *Diskurs über den Freitod*, the word chosen deliberately instead of its synonym *Selbtsmord*. Nothing is natural about living into the ignominy of death, he argued; it is neither 'redemptive' nor a 'peaceful sleep'.

---

8 By media colleague Horst Krüger, in letter, 1971.

'Free death' becomes the logical end to Enlightenment ideals of personal liberty. In a world beyond 'God', man has the right to choose his time for himself, without sanction. So he did, in 1978. So Levi would, in 1987. So in between would the writer who called himself Romain Gary, another Jewish déraciné in the 'republic of letters' branded by war, though without the precise mark of the camps.

Gary won the Prix Goncourt twice, second time under a further assumed name, a 'lie' contributing to the stress which may have hastened his end. He was granted the kudos as novelist which Améry craved, yet denied the esteem as intellectual he had aspired to[9]. Was this wrong? In Améry case, *was* there an overlooked Thomas Mann? Irène Heidelberger-Leonard rates his fiction more highly than contemporaries did, arguing for it a status equal to the essay-novels of Sartre, with which it shared existential themes and in one case a literary-critical subject. Améry's *Charles Bovary, Landarzt* (1977) is a direct retort to his onetime idol's *L'Idiot de la famille* in style as well as in content (166 pages to Sartre's nearly 2500). It attacks what Améry sees as malice in the supposed realist Flaubert who, though bourgeois, freighted his fictions with faux-aristocratic elitism. The cuckolded husband whom the author of *Madame Bovary* found too boring to grant an inner life is recast by Améry as all-seeing and suffering, thus vindicated. The exercize is fundamentally political: Flaubert's haughty scorn had resurfaced in the New Left of the '60s, Améry believed, and became a referred target for his ire. A further target may have been self-directed: deconstruction of the literary tradition in which Mayer had begun and Améry had found his only true 'home'. *Charles Bovary* was his final complete work, but a further novella was projected[10]. In this the narrator, provoked by a dream, would take a journey to locate a lost beloved; en route he would meet characters created by

---

9   Gary's main effort as an intellectual writer, *Pour Sganarelle* (1965), was largely panned by his peers.

10   Sole work set in the country he had lived in for decades, it was to be called *Rendezvous in Oudenaarde*.

authors he at one time or another had revered, but none would be able to help him find his destination, which, when he reached it at last, would turn out to be a rendezvous not only with his beloved but with death.

If Améry as novelist seems underrated to his recent German biographer, Améry as philosopher may seem less attractive to some in our era. Loyal supporter of Israel, though with trepidation after 1974, he treated torture and especially 'Freitod' in ways which take on a new tint when considered in the light of a régime that has used whatever is at its disposal to extract intelligence from enemies and has been plagued by bombers only too willing to opt for 'free death' to wreak vengeance on their 'torturers'. What Améry troubled his way through can, alas, be adopted, not just deplored; that is a consequence of the Enlightened 'free thought' he continued to espouse long after Sartre had dropped it in favour of principled engagement. Sartre may have been wrong in some of the principles he engaged in but perceptive in analysis that contemporary politics could no longer permit all choice to be free. If Améry had lived on into a world in which Jew would (again?) be equated with victim less than with victimizer, how might he have reacted? Did his growing disenchantment with the left in the '70s suggest that, like others of his kind, he might have morphed into a neo-conservative? Perhaps fortunately the question cannot be answered. Unexpected intrusion of passion into his shadow-life – an adulterous liaison with a younger woman – conspired with illness, artistic rejection and moral stress to bring on an ultimate suicide attempt. Breaking off a promotion tour for the poorly-received *Charles Bovary*, he retreated to the Österreicher Hof in Salzburg, a nicely pivotal locale in the schizoid divide of his birth country, and, having achieved a final 'homecoming' thus, carefully overdosed himself.

For the insecure Germanic Balt Alfred Rosenberg, *kapo* of Nazi ideologues, Jews were Jews and, if German or Austrian-based, even for generations, not Germanic[11]. For Germanic

---

11   In *Der Mythos des Zwanzigten Jahrhunderts* as elsewhere.

Jews, many of whom shared their compatriots' distaste for the Östjuden fleeing into their midst, they were often German or Austrian first or – in cases of atheists and converts – only. Old Hollywood hands recall how German-speaking refugees arriving in the '40s took a *de haut en bas* attitude towards their fellow émigrés and descendents of pogrom-escapees from lands further east: 'Jewish or not, they acted as if no Czech or Hungarian had ever composed a line of music,' the widow of a leading concertmaster of the era, Rumanian by descent, told me[12]. One might infer that in this respect too, ironically, 'the Germans won the war', as grumpy Brits like to grouse: not only via the *Wirtschaftwunder* of relatively ethnically-cleansed natives after 1945, but by the excelling of Germanic Jews in other places, notably the United States. Such generalizations form up, then dissolve at 'the mind's limits', to adapt Améry's phrase. The idea stated baldly may seem partial at best: German and Jew may be less an opposition than a symbiosis, as Mayer/Améry's career partly shows; and Germanic *and* Jewish may not be a wholly fantastic description of the *Leitkultur* in a post-British Empire, post-Sartrean/existentialist Western world. Certainly like Améry's our arts, letters and politics continue to turn on the wheel which the catastrophe of the mid 20th century lashed them onto. Expressionist eccentricities regularly break loose – they are encouraged! – but the pieties of what we have 'learned' channel and corral them, so that updated versions of stolid bourgeois values may *sitzfleisch* their way on less disturbed than before. Genuine threats to them, assuming they truly exist, seem nowadays to come from elsewhere.

The Philosopher of Auschwitz: Jean Améry and Living with the Holocaust, Irène Heidelberger-Leonard. I. B. Tauris, 2010.

---

12 Annette Kaufman, who completed her late husband's memoir: *A Fiddler's Tale: How Hollywood and Vivaldi Discovered Me* (University of Wisconsin Press, 2003). Louis Kaufman played violin on some 500 classic films and is credited by many as having created 'the Hollywood sound'.

Pre-eminent (and anti-Semitic) modernists

Jewish Quarterly, Winter 1995/96

During the period we associate with the rise of modernism, a narrowly defined and largely new ethnic group rose to pre-eminence in literature in our language. This was of old Yankee stock, chiefly New English in origin, with puritanism in the depths of its spiritual ancestry and transcendentalism in the Weltanschauung of its recent predecessors. It was relatively well-off, well connected to the political and cultural leadership of the young nation, well-educated (often with connections to Harvard) and well-travelled from early days on a version of the classical grand tour. Patrician, though not quite aristocratic in a European sense, it was increasingly remote from much of the population in a country which had quadrupled in size from its original thirteen colonies: not only from the southerners whom its fathers' generation had defeated in the Civil War, but also from the new westerners and immigrants arriving in its native northeast, owing to a voracious appetite for cheap labour of the rising class of Robber Barons.

Out of this background came two of the three greatest poets of the early 20th century: Ezra Pound and T. S. Eliot. From it had also come two of their most influential precursors in prose: Henry Adams and Henry James[1]. All of these writers turned to Europe as adults and stayed there for much of their lives, in body if not spirit. All took on European attitudes and traditions while at the same time retaining a sense of a native ethos which they thought more idealistic and relevant to mankind's future. This combination of attachments, or detachments, put them in a unique position in the cosmopoles they came to inhabit. They saw themselves as more civilized and worldly than their American fellows, yet more energetic and original than their

---

1 James was the only one of these not directly of English ancestry or connected with the early colonial period, his people having been Scotch-Irish and arrived in New York around 1775.

Old World confrères. Regarded by some back home as turncoats against a nascent national culture, they struck many in Europe as breakers of old forms in ways which were singular, if not revolutionary.

Yet something disfiguring happened in this process; and particularly in the cases of Eliot and Pound (though it is presaged in Adams and James), this showed itself in a grimacing, sometimes scatological anti-Semitism. Long noted by some critics, this has become a central feature in studies of both poets in recent decades, despite efforts by even some Jewish admirers to sweep it under the carpet. Among those interested in what Harold Bloom calls 'the western canon', it is especially troubling, given that Pound and Eliot represent a pre-eminent point of access for American poets into that august category. Ironically in view of their fanatical zeal for tradition, both are now exhibits in 'politically correct' arguments against the culture of the White European Male. For scions of their caste, old WASPs like myself, the discovery of attitudes so alien – indeed evil in relation to values we are brought up on today – can be deeply demoralizing. How could such proponents of high culture have been complicit in views which led to the Holocaust? And what does this say about our literary heritage at large?

To address these questions, we must first establish the nature of the offence: when it occurred in the opus, how it developed, whether in the course of two lengthy careers it transformed and, if so, into what. This is the subject Anthony Julius, now a lawyer, takes up in regard to Eliot in a Ph.D. thesis turned into a book, *T. S. Eliot, Anti-Semitism, and Literary Form*. The last part of this title is misleading because, on the matter of form, about which a great deal might be said – New vs. Old Testament models, Gospel-like concision vs. loose historical collage, Eliot vs. Pound in short – Julius says almost nothing; and from a literary critical point of view, this is the book's most disappointing lapse. If he had considered the matter of form closely, Julius might even have concluded that Pound – the apparently more anti-Semitic of the pair – created in *The Cantos* a work which has much to appeal to a Jewish aesthetic tradition, which perhaps is a crucial, if largely subconscious, reason why so many Jewish poets of the Allen Ginsberg generation admired Pound's work to a point of making him into a father figure (cf. Harold Bloom's 'anxiety of influence') whom they had to overcome.

But Julius's subject is not literary form really, at least not in this book. Anti-Semitism is, and about that he is unequivocal and exhaustive. Eliot was a Jew-hater. In the opus, principal evidence comes in *Ara Vos Prec*, later called *Poems, 1920*, the volume including 'Gerontion', 'Burbank with a Baedecker: Bleistein with a Cigar' and one or two other short works with unflattering allusions to Jews. Prior to it, Eliot had published *Prufrock and Other Observations*, in which no anti-Semitism is apparent. After it, he went on to *The Waste Land*, which had further anti-Semitic passages of the *Ara Vos Prec* type, cut from the final draft ironically at the suggestion of Pound, only to appear decades later after Eliot's death and arguably against his wishes. That Julius cites them in evidence may strike some as inadmissible, but in his role as prosecutor he argues his case without qualification or signals of self-doubt. After *The Waste Land*, Eliot as poet published *The Hollow Men*, *Ash Wednesday* and *Four Quartets* among large works. About these, Julius says little or nothing. In them the prejudice seems to have disappeared, or at least to have been moved on to other, largely Christian, concerns.

Regarding Eliot's prose, Julius cites the famous swipe in *After Strange Gods* (1934) about the undesirability of having too many free-thinking Jews in what Eliot regards as a coherent culture; Julius also cites essays marked by possibly anti-Semitic asides or neglect of support for Jews during their agon, these presented as part and parcel of a noxious conservatism. As his concern is anti-Semitism, Julius pays little heed to the fact that Eliot's principal targets in *After Strange Gods* are 'heretics' among his literary contemporaries: Yeats with his occultism, D. H. Lawrence with his religion of Life, even Pound with his Hell 'into which only a few usurers are condemned'. Nor does Julius note how Eliot deplores non-Jewish free-thinkers, including in the same book George Eliot and Thomas Hardy, who started the 'rot' in English literature in his view, or in another essay the most famous of all near-contemporary *Freigeister*, Nietzsche. Within this larger context, Eliot's anti-Semitism might be seen as only one element of a generally hysterical reaction to a civilization which appeared to him, as to his guru Charles Maurras of Action française, to have strayed too far from Christianity and royalism into multiculturalism and democracy.

I do not argue with Julius's case for Eliot's anti-Semitism. Inasmuch as the most ambiguous of writers was ever capable of convictions as firm as he proposed, Eliot was an anti-Semite at a crucial juncture in his career – ironically, his most interesting phase as a poet, between 1917 and 1922. *The Waste Land* may reflect this even more than Julius maintains, despite the cuts: in my own thesis-made-book, *Wagner to the Waste Land*, I argued that a Zeitgeist to which anti-Semitism was central hangs over the poem, buttressed by allusions to precursors like Wagner, the French *symbolistes* and Arthur Symons, and by attitudes shared with the quasi-religious and economic theorists Eliot had encountered since arriving in Europe in 1914. An analogy may be that, as Ginsberg and his generation found a father-figure in Pound and to a lesser degree Eliot, so Eliot and to a lesser degree Pound found one in a composite *décadent* poet-philosopher of the 1890s in whom Holy Grail-ism, theosophy, hermeticism, Paterian paganism and anti-Semitism were mixed. *The Waste Land* represents a critical farewell to these fragments shored against what Eliot saw as Europe's ruins. None of them, bar the formal debt to symbolism, appears in his later poetry.

If we add to this the fact that Eliot worked in a bank during the period in which he wrote *Ara Vos Prec* and *The Waste Land*; that he was suffering from material, marital and health difficulties; that he was involved in financial transactions caused by dislocations of the war, the Versailles treaty, the Russian Revolution, the German reparations and hyper-inflation; that he was exposed in the bank and elsewhere to petit bourgeois mutterings about international financial conspiracy, replete with racist jibes such as had marked it since at least the heyday of Marx (Julius puts on his cover a picture by Degas of two Jews whispering conspiratorially at the Bourse), we see how his poetry of the time could come to incorporate anti-Semitic imagery. On one level, Eliot was merely reflecting what was 'in the air'. On another, he was joining in an ethnic thuggery which intellectuals of the day aped from Houston Stewart Chamberlain in Germany, Maurras in France, even Adams back in the States (his *Education* was first published in England in 1918); also an unsystematic snobbery typical of the English upper-middle classes, among which he was trying to get on.

Why should this anti-Semitism have proved irresistible to Eliot? In James's *The American Scene* (1907), we see how an elder of his type had anticipated Eliot's distaste for the entry into a supposedly refined, homogenous culture of industrial capitalists and labouring masses from Eastern European with their odd languages, habits and agitations for social change. Where Pound was brought up, in a Philadelphia suburb, WASPs were already beginning to be ploughed under, as it were, by new and 'foreign' money. In Eliot's case, the germ of prejudice was probably present when he set out for Europe, but it is clear that Europe's malaise combined with the struggles of the déraciné to turn mere infection into disease. It is equally clear that after the disease had raged for some years, it began to wane. Whether it was ever entirely cured is another matter. Julius puts no more faith in Eliot's statement that once he became a Christian he could no longer be an anti-Semite, as anti-Semitism was a sin, than in Pound's of later years that he had 'botched the job' and that 'that stupid suburban prejudice [had] spoiled the whole thing'. Such disclaimers strike Julius as insufficient, even opportunistic. Why did the two poets not apologize with forthright unambiguity? Can a few off-the-cuff phrases to Allen Ginsberg, or the change of a 'j' in 'jew' in an old poem to a 'J', really constitute remorse, let alone atonement?

Maybe not. Still, these documented slouchings towards apology *do* qualify the excesses of both poets' works. Nor can a careful reader miss the elements of naïveté and foolishness that were always present, obviously in Pound's ranting which led to his incarceration and confinement in a mental hospital, but also in Eliot's too-clever little game with stereotypes which might have appealed to Dr Goebbels. On the charge of opportunism: in Pound's case, if it existed, it was ham-fisted: no thorough opportunist could have been so self-defeating. In Eliot's, on the other hand: 'old Possum' was always more practical in the politics of social and literary worlds; if at one time anti-Semitism seemed a help in shinnying up the greasy pole, so at another an appearance of regret may have seemed called for. A more just view, I suppose, would be that, by the end of his career, Eliot saw it as not only his Christian duty, but also in the best interests of a civilized society to accept orderly, God-fearing Jews on an equal footing.

Many Jews of this stripe have been among his supporters since, just as many of a more free-wheeling, anarchic kind have been Pound's. This may strike one as too generous, but it is not wholly inapt. As with many artists who have passed through the fevers of anti-Semitism, both poets placed the situation of the Jew in western culture at the centre of attention; and there is some evidence that, given further time, each might have gone on to become anti-anti-Semitic. Eliot satirized jack-booted Jew-haters in his fragment *The Rock*, as Julius points out; nor should Pound's remark that the real evil he was fighting was not Jews or usury but plain avarice be dismissed wholly, as Julius wishes. Such qualifications deserve to be emphasized for students of the future when studying these writers. That both should continue to hold an important place in the canon seems desirable still. For apart from their significance to literature in the 20th century, they represent, if interpreted thus, classic examples of that other victim of anti-Semitic prejudice: the self-tortured anti-Semite himself.

T. S. Eliot, Anti-Semitism and Literary Form, Anthony Julius. Cambridge University Press, 1995.

Hemingway & D'Annunzio

Quarterly Review, Summer 2011

> 'You haven't a picture of then, have you?'
> 'No. There weren't any pictures except with Mr
> d'Annunzio in them. And most of the people turned out
> badly.'
>
> *Across the River and into the Trees*

In 1918, the 18-year-old Ernest Hemingway went to Italy to participate in his first war. He wanted to be a writer. The theatre of war was in the northeast of the country, on the plains of the Veneto and Friuli regions, bordering Istria and mountains formerly Austrian. Hemingway was wounded, an experience he would write about in different ways in his first two great novels, both set in Europe, first Paris and Spain, second Italy and Switzerland. The latter would incorporate his Italian war experience. The last major novel published in his lifetime[1] would return to the region and theme following his 'last' war. Set almost entirely in Venice, it is seen through the eyes of a demoted American brigadier also affected by war, wounded and reminiscing about having been wounded in the same theatre in the first war. Hemingway's contemporary and alter ego Colonel Cantwell has a bluff, amateurish interest in writers, especially in a tradition of them associated with the spirit of a place to which he has returned semiconsciously to die.

This is indicated in an early chapter devoted mainly to a boat trip along the Grand Canal to convey Cantwell to his favourite address in 'my town', the Hotel Gritti. D'Annunzio is mentioned by the venerable boatman, whose brother fought in the same theatre when young: 'He was a patriot and inflamed by hearing D'Annunzio talk', so he marched off to war, in his case to death. The morbid note buries itself in Cantwell's musings, which are busy flicking over personalities evoked by the view:

---

1 In dimension and content *The Old Man and the Sea* is a novella.

an octogenarian countess whose milieu might have come out of D'Annunzio's fin-de-siècle Venetian novel *Il Fuoco*; the mother of his eventual host, an ambiguous aristocratic huntsman, Barone Alvarito; Byron, on whom Cantwell's thoughts linger, savouring the poet as a 'tough boy' loved by Venetians, in contrast to his successor Browning. The reflection gives Cantwell a chance to ponder his own version of the famous Hemingway code, which will dominate this book as much as any: 'A tough boy... a man who will make his play and then backs it up. Or just a man who backs his play.'

The boat moving on, Cantwell eyes a 'little villa... ugly as a building you would see on the boat train... coming into the banlieue before Paris... overrun with badly administered trees'. He thinks 'there *he* lived', italics portentous. Only two words in English, *really* and *didn't*, have appeared thus up 'til now; few will after. D'Annunzio has been referred to only in passing, so we hardly can jump to the conclusion that he is *he*. Closer in context is Byron, though his palazzo – beds slept in mulled over – has receded from view. Browning? He, wife and dog have been dispatched in a few phrases. So who is *he*? a character to figure later in the novel, Alvarito perhaps? another poet in Anglo expatriate succession? Hemingway's Parisian mentor Pound for example, long associated with Venice but now locked in a mental hospital in Washington DC for supporting Italy during the war? Despite the author's recent efforts on behalf of his compatriot, *he* does not refer to this Fascist-linked man-of-letters, rather to one who aped 'tough boy' Byron so closely as to name the heroine of his Venetian novel – based on the actress Eleanora Duse, about whom Cantwell muses – with nearly the same tag as the baker's wife with whom Byron had a notorious affair, over which Cantwell muses also. Then D'Annunzio re-enters his mind, to be considered for over two pages – i.e., something beyond one percent of this short book. Why? mere stream-of-consciousness? scene painting? Or does the allusion indicate themes to arrive: the fatal attraction of Fascism perhaps, the aesthetics of Venice / Venus and love? – Cantwell ruminates:

They [the Italians/Venetians] loved him for his talent, and because he was bad, and he was brave. A Jewish[2] boy with nothing, he stormed the country with his talent and his rhetoric. He was a more miserable character than any that I know and as mean. But the man I think of to compare him with[3] never put the chips on the line and went to war... and Gabriele d'Annunzio (I always wondered what his real name was... because nobody is named d'Annunzio in a practical country and perhaps he was not Jewish and what difference did it make if he was or not) had moved through the different arms of the service as he had moved into and out of the arms of different women.

Arms as weapons, arms as lovers' limbs – the same binary reference which had animated Hemingway's first Italian novel, in whose title they are memorialized... Cantwell's evocation summons a further and other or obverse alter ego: a ghostly standard by which he and his creator can measure themselves and be judged. With its bravery, chutzpah and fraudulence, it also suggests recrudescence, possibly subconscious, of the Robert Cohn/Jay Gatsby type so annoying yet galvanizing to a young contemporary of Scott Fitzgerald's trying with nothing but his raw talent to storm the literary citadels of the 1920s.

Cantwell's musings move on to focus on D'Annunzio's wound – wounds always being iconic in Hemingway – in this case to an eye, ever after covered with a patch; his Byronic pallor, 'white as the belly of a sole'; his haranguing of troops

---

2 I have been unable to find corroboration for this, which appears to be Hemingway's own supposition.

3 The referent may be Hemingway himself, reflecting an irritation military men felt with his antics as war correspondent, or self-contempt that he had not seen important action. It may be the writer, based on Sinclair Lewis, who annoys Cantwell in the bar/dining-room of the Gritti. At a further stretch it could denote Pound, who never 'went to war'. A most exotic choice would be Dante, whom Cantwell imitates in his accounting of heroes and villains of the war, but describes ambiguously as 'another *vieux con*'.

– '*Morire non a*[4] *basta*' – his adulation even from those who, like Cantwell, 'did not believe in heroes' (do we trust this?) – '*Evviva d'Annunzio*'. As the dingy villa fades in the boat's wake, a typically Cantwellian/late Hemingway twist of emotion rises: pity for 'the poor beat-up old boy' and 'his great, sad and never properly loved actress' – a magnificence ending in dust. The colonel laments that he does not know where they are buried; also that his companion, a U. S. Army driver, will never even have heard of them, nor that the man was a

> writer, poet, national hero, phraser of the dialectic of Fascism, macabre egotist, aviator, commander, or rider, in the first of the fast torpedo attack boats, Lieutenant-Colonel of Infantry without knowing how to command a company, nor a platoon properly, the great, lovely writer of *Notturno* whom we respect, and jerk.

This coda, lush in its semi-Joycean[5] listing, might also have come out of D'Annunzio's brashly overwritten Venetian novel, while the depiction of writer overreaching as soldier recalls Hemingway's own grandstanding with the American liberators of Paris and the Ardennes. There is, in short, an identity.

What did a younger Hemingway know of his Italian precursor beyond what Cantwell sketches in here? Had he read *Notturno*, D'Annunzio's postwar novel, partly about wounding? Hemingway's personal copy of *Ulysses* – whose 'great, lovely writer' he claimed to respect more than any other – had only

---

4   This seems incorrect Italian – i.e., 'a' should be 'è'.

5   The appeal of D'Annunzio, *Il Fuoco* notably, to young Joyce is suggested in 'The Day of Rabblement' (1899), Joyce's callow assessment of contemporaries before he left Ireland. The ambition of *Il Fuoco*'s hero is shared by the young writer Joyce struggled for years in Trieste to depict and rings through Stephen's declaration at the end of *A Portrait of the Artist as a Young Man* (1916), 'I go for the millionth time to… forge in the smithy of my soul the uncreated conscience of my race.'

half of its pages slit[6]. If Hemingway did read *Notturno*, he could not have done so in one of the 'fair English translations' Cantwell recommends to his driver: among D'Annunzio books it was one of the few *not* translated then. Did Hemingway try it in Italian, or in the French into which like all D'Annunzio's oeuvre it was published simultaneously? If Hemingway read it or part of it in either language, when and where? It could not have been during his earliest days in the region because, though dated 1916, *Notturno* was not released to the world until 1921[7].

Young Hemingway would have heard of D'Annunzio and his wounding when at the front. Given the Italian's repute, his books would also have been lying around, and the future creator of Frederic Henry could have picked one up or borrowed it or had it pressed on him. Later, when in hospital recovering from his own wound with nothing but time on his hands, Hemingway may well have taken a serious look at some work by the flamboyant Italian. Hemingway's reading has been traced as far as evidence allows; catalogues exist of his library; but 'for 1920-1925, crucial years when he was learning to write, there is no complete data'[8]. We know even less of what he may have attempted during his Italian rite of passage. Could he have dipped into D'Annunzio's early novel *L'Innocente*, about a youthful love affair, unexpected pregnancy and the hero's fury against a child whose arrival imperils its mother's life? This inversion of the Oedipus complex resurfaces in *A Farewell to*

---

6 'Only the pages of the first half and of Molly Bloom's soliloquy are cut.' (Kenneth Lynn, *Hemingway*. Simon & Schuster, 1987), 161. This of course does not prove that Hemingway did not read the entire novel in some form, either piecemeal before publication or in another edition years later.

7 He may have been introduced to *Notturno* by Pound, who reviewed the French edition for his 'Paris Letter' in *The Dial*, Nov 1922, praising its superior 'vitality', especially vs work of Proust. Hemingway could have borrowed Pound's copy – they saw one another nearly daily – and read it in French, as D'Annunzio's anglophone admirers had long done, George Moore for example (see *Letters to Lady Cunard*, Rupert Hart-Davis, 1957), with whose work Hemingway was familiar (see the banter about writers in *Green Hills of Africa*).

8 Michael Reynolds, *Hemingway's Reading, 1910-1940* (Princeton, 1981).

Arms. Convalescing in Milan, Hemingway would write to his beloved, model for heroine of that book, that he intended fill his hours of missing her by going to a production of D'Annunzio's *La Nave*, a historical drama set in Venice[9]; and after the war, when back in Chicago and courting his first wife, Hemingway urged her and others to read *The Flame* (*Il Fuoco* in translation), of which he 'found it easy to project himself into the role of the hero'. In his apprentice mode he would write a poem and two short stories parodying D'Annunzian attitudes; a character in the latter, Rinaldi, reappears in *Farewell to Arms* as well as in *Men Without Women*, the book of tales published just prior to it, including 'Che Ti Dice La Patria', whose title was a D'Annunzio slogan. All this suggests what one biographer calls a 'lifelong fascination with the Italian poet, playwright and soldier of fortune' and supports a hypothesis that the famous Hemingway persona was built up partly out of motifs borrowed from him.

A telling link is to the aesthetical stance Italian critics dub *dannunzianismo*[10]. In this, the chief fictive persona and author's identity are blended, and intense prose-poetic brooding – a kind of talking-to-oneself, self-apology or special pleading – contributes to formation of a Byronic cult. The mode was fixed in Hemingway by time of his 1929 novel, over which D'Annunzio looms unnamed. Pre-Fascist nationalism such as would lead the Italian and his followers to stage their coup at Fiume is foreshadowed in Hemingway's depiction of the retreat from Caporetto, in which fanatical officers ('Italy should never retreat') pull stragglers out of the crowd and execute them on the spot as cowards / traitors. This is the cause, triggered by a foreign accent, for Hemingway's hero to desert: his first 'farewell to arms'. His

---

9   See James Mellow, *Hemingway: A Life without Consequences* (Houghton Mifflin, 1992); Lynn's *Hemingway*; and Reynolds' *Hemingway: the Final Years* (Norton, 1999). Reynolds says Hemingway gave copies of *The Flame* to 'every young woman of interest'. Others posit that the middle-class young American was intrigued by the relationship between D'Annunzio's hero and the somewhat older, fictionalized Duse on the grounds that he was shortly to marry a slightly older woman.

10   See Giansiro Ferrata's Introduzione to *Il Fuoco* (Mondadori, 1967).

second farewell is to the embrace of his beloved as she dies bearing his child, an agon filtered through an interior monologue marked by intense self-examination and rationalization similar to what D'Annunzio's hero thrashes around in in *L'Innocente*. Textures of masculinity are also similar, as are youthful themes of how to 'be a man' and navigate the emotional high seas of love. The *cloître à deux* D'Annunzio projects is more extreme and productive of transvaluation of values than the one Frederic Henry will enter into with Catherine Barkley, but the latter is hermetic and obsessive too, as much as a provincial middle-class American male of Hemingway's day and type might allow. If the wannabe writer had indeed picked up *L'Innocente* at the front or in hospital – and of D'Annunzio works, it is most likely to have been lying around – *Farewell* would have been a logical place for its atmospheres, simmering in the subconscious for a decade, to resurface. There may even be hints strewn around in it of the Italian as a tutelary ghost, for instance in a priest's hope that Frederic will visit his native Abruzzi when on leave, Abruzzi being the 'half-barbaric' province of Italy that D'Annunzio had emerged from, fond memories of which colour evocation of the rural dignity he depicts in *L'Innocente* and elsewhere. Frederic does not make it to the Abruzzi but in a passage lamenting the fact, he paints a picture reminiscent of the rural, forested Upper Michigan so dear to the heart of his homesick young creator, to be memorialized in the stories written in a Parisian garret a half-decade on:

> I had wanted to go to Abruzzi. I had gone to no place where the roads were frozen and hard as iron, where it was clear cold and dry and the snow was dry and powdery and hare-tracks in the snow and the peasants took off their hats and called you Lord and there was good hunting. I had gone to no such place but to the smoke of cafés and nights when the room whirled and you needed to look at the wall to make it stop... [The priest] understood that I had really wanted to go to the Abruzzi but had not gone and we were still friends, with many tastes alike,

but with the difference between us.

Note the contrast between rural virtue and urban vice. It is typical not only of young Hemingway but also of D'Annunzio, not least in *L'Innocente*, where he embodies it in portrayal of a mild, stoical, taciturn *carbonaro*[11] whom the hero asks to stand as godfather for the infant son he himself lacks the maturity to love or to protect properly. The D'Annunzian male ideal had not by this stage reached the decadent verge that it would in *Il Fuoco*, let alone the proto-Fascist extreme that would follow the author's hands-on experience of war.

Hemingway was ever enamoured of Europe and its great languages, but it has never been established fully[12] how much Italian he knew as a teenaged ambulance-driver. Enough to get on in a soldiers' mess surely. Enough to read a sophisticated novel? It would be odd if the aspirant author had *not* tried some work in the original by the most notorious writer of the time and place, even if he had laid it aside unfinished once the post had brought a letter from home, along with his favourite sports page. Cantwell jokes in Italian with his interlocutors and spouts

---

11   The importance of the *carbonaro* figure to Byron and to a tradition of hero extending down to the 'spaghetti westerns' in which Clint Eastwood fixed his persona may be insufficiently recognized.

12   Mark Cirino (*Hemingway Review*, Fall 2005) made a case that, despite bombastic letters home to the contrary, Hemingway didn't get far with the language in 1918 or after. Cirino bases this mainly on 'faulty' representation of Italian in *Farewell*. But reading, speaking and writing a language involve various levels of skill, and it is unclear how far each went for Hemingway. Moreover, they may have altered over the years, not least after much experience of French and Spanish, both possibly helpful in reading the sibling language but damaging in speech of it. Mary Hemingway (*How It Was*, 1951) notes that en route to Italy in 1948 Hemingway spoke with a steward in a mix of Italian and Spanish – just what Cantwell uses with staff at the Gritti. Among 7368 items listed in *Hemingway's Library* (Garland, 1981) hundreds are in French and Spanish, about 100 in Italian and over 50 Italian in translation. This implies a writer who read foreign authors in the original, at least later in life. But needless to say, inventory of a library taken after a man's death provides only limited evidence of what he may have read and when.

Venetian dialect when rumbling an ex-Fascist; he then lapses into Spanish – easier for Hemingway with a decade of Iberian war and Caribbean navigation behind him – and admits that as 'a punk kid' on the front he had 'insufficient command of the language'. If this is a Hemingway admission, it reveals little about what the young man may have tried, whether ending in failure or not. Struggle in a first foreign language, however poorly mastered, may be as compelling as reading Stendhal or Tolstoy in translation. Moreover, in Italy in 1918, with the Parisian avantgarde of Joyce and Proust (the latter expanding themes and styles developed in *L'Innocente* and *Il Fuoco*[13]) not yet available, D'Annunzio, after native forbears like Jack London, may for young mannish, existential and stylistic inspiration have seemed the one game in town.

Hemingway's return to Italy in *Across the River and into the Trees* raises related questions. How did the aging author prepare himself to write a version, as he evidently hoped, of the great Venetian novel? Portentous allusion to D'Annunzio suggests a dip into the Italian writer again, and why not in the original when boning up on a language for months *in situ*? What to put in a book bag? Location suggests *Il Fuoco*, and *Across the River* shares motifs with it: paeans to the spirit of Venice; confinement to a short, imaginatively intense space of time, months in one case, days in the other; devotion to conversation and rumination on life, fate, ethics and aesthetics; concentration beyond the protagonist on one focal character, a beloved female to some degree anagogical. But whereas *L'Innocente* and *Farewell* share universal young mannish personae and concerns, *Il Fuoco* projects a middle period, extravagant artistic type wholly D'Annunzian

---

13 D'Annunzio impressed Proust directly via his novels and indirectly via social lionization between 1910 and 1915 when he escaped his Italian debts by living in a Paris suburb (cf. the odd aptness of Cantwell likening his Venetian residence to a house in a *banlieue* as seen from the boat-train). Proust would have been aware especially of the fascination D'Annunzio exercised over Le Comte de Montesquiou, model for his Baron Charlus, during an era when Proust himself was struggling to begin (self) publishing his great work.

and not shared by Hemingway, while *Across the River* essays a brusque, self-condemning yet justifying, later period type which the world could only take as Hemingway's own. Of course late Hemingway was more of an aesthete than the public persona pretended[14], and middle-phase D'Annunzio already harboured the pre-Fascist who would revel in the hard-boiled; still, contrast is pronounced, and it carries on into style. While both early novels share in types of interior monologue, anaphora, painterly forms and prose-poetic devices, the vast wave-like paragraphs and Wagnerian periods of *Il Fuoco* could not be further from the *Time*-magazine era strictures of *Across the River*. Cantwell counterpoints his lush evocation of D'Annunzio with the anglo-saxon epithet *jerk*. 'What is a jerk?' his beloved will ask him some time later. 'It is a little rough to state,' the aging lion growls; 'but I think it means a man who has never worked at his trade (*oficio*) truly, and is presumptuous in some annoying way.'

If this refers back to use of the term re D'Annunzio, it would seem more apt for the author of *Il Fuoco* than for that of the later novel set in Venice, sole work Cantwell sees fit to mention. *Il Fuoco* is swollen with what Hemingway once called 'erectile writing'[15]; *Notturno* – part journal, part visionary tract – is by contrast hybrid, spare and from the heart, marking a revolution in style recalling the later Nietzsche or Dante[16] or

---

14   Reynolds says backgrounds in *Across the River* show 'a sensitivity to place worthy of Pater', view shared by George Monteiro (*Hemingway Review*, Fall 1985) who sees a link between Hemingway's and Pater's aesthetics. (Set against *Il Fuoco*, this needs major qualification.) Late Hemingway's general interest in aesthetics is indicated by a correspondence with Bernard Berenson which he 'took over' from Mary, who had visited the art critic at I Tatti during an interlude of the 1948 trip to Italy when she left Ernest in the Veneto to get on with research for *Across the River*.

15   In *Death in the Afternoon* (Scribner, 1932), 53-4.

16   The Nietzsche who became stylistically *contra* Wagner: aphoristic, pre-modernist. Re Dante: Cantwell is aware of resonances of the '*vieux con*' in his account of the war. Dante suggests Pound and *The Cantos*, which may be presence behind the novel, unacknowledged unless via allusion to a writer like D'Annunzio who never went to war (note 3 above). Hemingway would have been most exposed to Dante via Pound in Paris in the early '20s – epoch of *The Waste Land* as

looking forward to Hemingway's own noted breakthroughs in the 1920s, which it anticipated by years. Shades of *Notturno* behind *Across the River* indeed stretch beyond Cantwell's praise. Hemingway's protective, beloved young heroine shares in name, age, function, designation (Daughter) and even hair with La Sirenetta of D'Annunzio's book[17], portrait of the author's child by a mistress preceding La Duse. Both works are composed in short paragraphs, often no more than single sentences, and use simple language drawn from quotidian concerns. Quotidian content permeates each, viewed through eyes of a military man of middle age consumed by 'wrath and agony' over the death of his comrades and debilitated by seizures as he wanders across the wintry city, partly in solitude, often 'addressing no one, except, perhaps, posterity'. What comfort he finds – in ministrations of 'daughter', in an 'order' of old fellow warriors who suffer and endure, in aperçus about time and fate – are strikingly similar, as are his aesthetic preoccupations: in food, quality of air and light[18], intensity of memory and its power to redeem, simple acts of living, seeing, feeling and sensing[19]. Both works track a process of overcoming the traumas of war; both depict the cost contingent on codes of active masculinity; both are hyper-sensitively *felt*. In *Notturno* Hemingway could not have seen D'Annunzio as 'not working at his trade truly' or 'presumptuous in some annoying way'. The writer who would help to propel Fascism was not a *jerk* in this case; and to intimate

---

well as publication of *Notturno* (note 7).

17   Adeline Tinter connects them (*Hemingway Review*, Fall 1985). She also links emeralds given to Cantwell by Renata to similar stones given by La Duse to D'Annunzio, a detail Hemingway could have picked up from Tommaso Antongini's *D'Annunzio* (Little, Brown, 1938), of which he had a copy.

18   The Colonel's admiration of the 'wonder light on the ceiling' in his room at the Gritti as it refracts up from shimmering waters of the canal evokes imagery of a type that abounds in *Notturno*.

19   At the start of *Notturno* this is especially pronounced: the focal character is bandaged and bed-ridden from having been wounded, and every step he takes seems as if for the first time.

as much – elements of virtue within enemies dead or defeated[20] – emerges as prime motive for the 'beat-up old' American writer to have composed what would be his last war novel, whose theme is *healing*. It seems a pity that many critics, both at the time and since, have dismissed him as a 'jerk' as defined in his fractured and yet brave attempt to do so.

---

20 Examples include respect for Rommel and other German generals in contrast to contempt for Leclerc, Montgomery and the administrators of SHAEF; also simple sympathy for Italians moved by 'love of an old country, much fought over and always triumphant in defeat'. Of the embittered, Cantwell muses: 'It must be quite a difficult trade being an ex-Fascist... I can't hate Fascists.' Near the end of the book he comes to empathize with a gamekeeper who 'seemed to hate me from the start' when his host explains: 'It was [your] old battle-jacket. Allied uniform affects him that way. You see he was a bit over-liberated... When the Moroccans came through here they raped both his wife and his daughter.'

The Übermensch States of America

Quarterly Review, Summer 2012

In his early, portentous *Schopenhauer as Educator*, soon-to-be ex-philology professor Friedrich Nietzsche observed, 'Most of the learned works written by university philosophers are badly done, without any real scientific power, and generally are dreadfully tedious.'[1] Tedious Nietzsche was not. Escape from academia helped save him from that, though not the fate of a Promethean unbound. Freed from father-gods' supervision, he fell like Lucifer; and the spectacle of a luminous spirit's descent fascinated more than one generation. 'I read Nietzsche until my eyes went bad,' W. B. Yeats wrote at a crucial stage in his progress towards becoming the great bard of a new century[2]. His eventual rival for that title in Anglophony would avoid what their common mentor Ezra Pound called 'neo-Nietzschean clatter'[3]. But T. S. Eliot had studied at Harvard under the quintessential 'university philosopher' Irving Babbitt, who alone among Nietzsche-struck sages at America's pinnacle of higher education – William James and Josiah Royce, for example – warned of the dangers to classical order posed by a German 'Romantic' to whom 'Greek' meant Dionysius as much as Apollo and Socrates was 'a symptom of decadence'[4].

In her ambitious, well-researched account of Nietzsche's reception in America, Jennifer Ratner-Rosenhagen, associate professor at the University of Wisconsin, risks adding a new tome to the category her subject deprecated. Tedious she is not: there is ever a felicitous phrase here or remarkable insight there. Yet often she is unable to escape vices not unfamiliar in work

---

1 In *Thoughts out of Season*, II, I.

2 Yeats read Nietzsche avidly in 1902-3. He knew of the philosopher from Havelock Ellis' 1896 essays.

3 In *Hugh Selwyn Mauberley* (1920). Pound's relationship to Nietzsche is not often explored. Eliot wrote in 1916 that Nietzsche's philosophy 'evaporates' when stripped of its author's 'demogogic' gifts. See *Wagner to the Waste Land*, 206.

4 *The Birth of Tragedy. Complete Works* ii, tr. W. A. Haussmann, esp. Appendix 2.

from America's academies in our time: over-comprehensiveness and over-adherence to a dogma of 'good' expository writing. An alert reader need not be detained at the end of each chapter with a pedestrian summary of what he has just read. The intellectual *Frei Geist* does not wish to have his trek through mountain peaks of Idea impeded by arbitrary boundaries. Forced into detours via suburban foothills, he is liable to become impatient. Hot to emerge for a cool plunge in the sea, he may even take flight.

The Nietzsche of Èze[5] may well have tossed Ms R-R's book into the maquis. But he first would have spied in the large eyes peering over the author's credentials on its back flap a longing to be freed from constraints of university press publication and grant-body approvals to fix subsidy. The book has bulk and production values connoting 'serious', though the size of its typeface might have sped Yeats to his oculist, especially if he had read it in a place lacking North America's transcendental light. Its effect, which shades into a blessing, is to hurtle a reader back to Nietzsche's own oeuvre, there to breathe fresher airs, spy wider vistas, track pacier pathways and enjoy more glamorous glimpses of destination. For despite the confusion of direction of which the philosopher has often been charged, his work is overarched with a sure, radical drive towards a *Beyond*: transcendence. And Ms R R, whatever her short-comings or long-windings as a guide, repeatedly points us to it.

It makes her work partly radiant too. How refreshing it is to feel *positivity* again in Nietzsche's 'anti-foundationalism'; to see his individual 'perfectionism' as a boon to men and women, not mainly an incitement to narcissism; to view his scepticism as wisdom, not mere sneering; to find in the open skies at the end of his road hope, not just emptiness; to locate in his legacy a 'new world' (cf. Ms R-R's title) as well as elements of an old – We Mediterranean ones, We Europeans, We Free Spirits[6]. There

---

5 The cliff-top village near Nice where he wrote part of *Zarathustra* and from which he would hike on an old smugglers' trail down to and up from the sea.

6 Such invocations run throughout Nietzsche's 'Mediterranean' books, reaching a crescendo in the last part of *La Gaya Scienza*, finished near Genoa.

is evident cramping in Ratner-Rosenhagen's focus – the great thing surely is Nietzsche's universality, not just his relation to or effect on developments in one culture. But to have him freed, as he must periodically be, from over-identification with his sometimes despised German roots, as well as his more recent possession by French post-modernists, is essential. And to have him brought 'home' to inspiration in the essays of Emerson secures an intrinsic link to the finest of American spiritual-philosophical traditions – of the Transcendentalists proper.

This attention is not new: Stanley Cavell is a recent figure to have paid it. Nor is citation of links between Nietzsche and pragmatists like John Dewey and W. James: Richard Rorty made this. But Ms R-R highlights what more flamboyant genealogists of American philosophy have tended to pass over: the centrality of German-Jewish émigré Walter Kaufmann to Nietzschean discourse since World War II[7]. She lauds Kaufmann for rescuing Nietzsche from an abyss he fell into due to his lionization by fascists. She rehearses Kaufmann's combat against Elisabeth Forster-Nietzsche's emphasis on her brother's paeans to *Wille-zur-Macht*, the Blond Beast and Master vs Slave Morality as well as his rants against democracy and Christian ethics. She describes Kaufmann's effort to relocate Nietzsche into a forerunner of existentialism and to re-interpret his Übermensch as projection less of an amoral Superman than of an all-too-mortal striving to overcome limitations. *Ecce* the Nietzsche of individual self-realization who might, like successors such as Hermann Hesse, have had his books banned by Nazis. Quite right too, because there is little in this Nietzsche's progress to suggest that he could ever have allowed himself be turned into a mouthpiece for one race or political party.

Via Kaufmann, Nietzsche became iconic to liberation movements of the 1960s. Huey Newton of the Black Panthers is among the devotees R-R cites, noting how his book *Revolutionary Suicide* co-opts the idea of self-realization to a collective as inaptly

---

7 R-R focuses on Kaufmann's 1950 book about Nietzsche but does not judge his quality as translator or the merits of his editions vs the Levy *Complete Works*.

as the Nazis had. This tendency has more than once surfaced in American radicals who 'thought with Nietzsche'[8]: anarchists Benjamin Tucker and Emma Goldman in the 1890s, socialists Upton Sinclair and Jack London in the 1910s, right-wingers Ayn Rand (whom R-R does not mention) and Leo Strauss in the '40s, feminist and gay coteries in the '70s. All looked to a powerful forerunner who in the end ran away from them. For it's in the nature of Nietzsche – what Stefan Zweig called 'ihren stündlichen Veränderungen meteorologische Natur'[9] – *not* to remain tied to a group or a faith. Nietzsche's truth is variable, 'perspectivist'. However – and this separates him from the Derrida crowd which sought to claim him for 'play' towards the end of the 20th century – the fact that it is variable, possibly unascertainable but in any case beyond grasp, does *not* mean that it cannot exist and that thus there can be no ultimate meaning. Pursuit is the point, goal 'real' or not. Nietzsche credits the force of illusion: thus the Platonic completion of his most partially quoted apothegm, 'God is dead *but for millennia to come people will spy his shadow in their caves*'[10].

His 'hero' Zarathustra illuminates this. So do his near-mad and Jesus-like personae in *Der Antichrist* and *Ecce Homo,* written shortly before his fatal collapse. Ever present is a questing self, a fighting self, an unquiet self-overcomer launching into Dionysian dance before lapsing back into Apollonian contemplation, removing and protecting what Jack London calls his 'silk'[11] from damage by *Kultur-philisters,* banalization by bourgeois convention or routine society. It is this cultural insurgent that appealed to tetchy commentators on the state of American civilization from H. L. Mencken in the first decade of the 20th century to Allen Bloom in the penultimate. Looking

---

8 R-R's formula for the process of insight and dialectic Nietzsche may provoke.

9 'His hourly-changing meteorological nature'. *Baumeister der Welt* (Frankfurt: S. Fischer, 1951), 309.

10 *Gaya Scienza*, III, 108 (italics mine).

11 In *The Game* and elsewhere. It refers to physical perfection but implies also purity of spirit.

about them and finding a herd-like, anti-intellectual, materialist avidity – a plasticized social order based partly on carelessness, if not outright lies – they took comfort from a precursor who had seen the same in his time and place and shouted to like-minded 'brothers'[12] then and in future: WHAT IS TO BE DONE?

Ms R-R devotes her epilogue to Bloom and his agon, the best-selling *Closing of the American Mind*. She underlines his identity as 'midwestern gay Jewish atheist', as if the categories lent special force to his views. Perhaps they do for R-R's audience. If so, they may relate to omissions in her tale of the transit of Nietzsche, two of which evoke another celebrity Bloom of her formative years – Harold, colossus among American literary scholars and author of *The Anxiety of Influence*, promoting the idea that great poets (read also artists and thinkers) must kill their 'fathers' – i.e., giant foreshadowing precursors – in order to 'father' their own best work. In Nietzsche's case the titanic father figure was Wagner, to whom he devoted four major books and argued *pro* or *contra*, named or not, in others. R-R mentions him only in passing and seeks to erect Emerson as the father of note, though not so overweening that the son had savagely to deconstruct him[13]. Her decision may have to do with a wish to skirt dangerous associations – Wagner as anti-Semite, beloved by Hitler – or an urge to downplay European motifs in favour of American, which threads through her book, induced perhaps by an unexplored apprehension that American culture

---

12   'O my brothers' is Zarathustra's repeated form of address to his 'companions'. The phrase WHAT IS TO BE DONE?, made famous by Lenin, is anticipated by Nietzsche in many guises, especially in later work – cf. the famous opening of *Beyond Good and Evil*: 'Supposing that Truth is a woman – what then?', also the title & several-times-repeated first sentence of the Third Essay in *Genealogy of Morals*: 'What is the Meaning of Aesthetic Ideals?', which must have been known to Tolstoy – as indeed much of Nietzsche would have been to the Russian intelligentsia of Lenin's generation, who will have seen Nietzsche as exactly what he claimed to be: a great 'forerunner' of an epoch's call for radical cultural change.

13   Relative importance of the two to Nietzsche may be gleaned by the fact that Wagner takes up six and a half pages of *Index to Complete Works* whereas Emerson has three lines. Walt Whitman, unmentioned, may be yet more important.

is still seen as unformed, half-formed or partly ill-formed by an older world. Her failure to deal with Nietzsche in the light of Wagner seems a chance missed. Not only was there an 'American Wagner' to shadow 'American Nietzsche', but the shadow never ceased looming over the great questions which haunted the philosopher, from the time he first eyed the score of *Tristan* as a youth to a decade after the 'stellar friendship' had ceased and he wrote nostalgic lines about 'ships passing in the night'[14].

Beyond envy, hurt and offense, as well as incompatible talent for coping with a 'philistine' public, what is illumined in Nietzsche via Wagner includes a conundrum which has vexed every even half-responsible enthusiast R-R cites. In a world beyond moral foundations where men and women are left to 'create' themselves, what principle exists by which individuals can relate – i.e., whither 'society'? R-R quotes Rorty on Nietzsche's posture: 'His ironic self-perfection has "nothing particular to do with questions of social policy"; he enables us to "drop the demand for a theory which unifies the public and private."'[15] With Wagner this was progressively not the case, and what upset Nietzsche perhaps most in his onetime idol was his 'last word': *Parsifal*. Wagner's earlier *Ring of the Nibelung* had seemed to unmask via drama what Nietzsche would articulate: futility and mendacity in civilization's belief systems. What survives in *Götterdämmerung* is beyond structure or government, whether of earthly or heavenly making: only Nature, fire and water, as well as one fully amoral individual – i.e., no more than was there at the start of the cycle, with one exception. Hope for redemption via Love floats in the final motifs: a melody once heard when a mortal woman praised a demi-goddess for shielding her so that she could give birth to a hero – the Übermensch. But the finale of the cycle shows how this would-be transcending individual is fated to end: as a betrayer betrayed, on a funeral pyre.

With triumph of the Übermensch revealed as an illusion – a phantom of *hope*, the 'worst of evils' in Nietzsche's self-

---

14 *Gaya Scienza*, IV, 279. The passage is entitled 'Stellar Friendship'.

15 *Contingency, Irony and Solidarity*, quoted and discussed by R-R, 292-3.

hardening code[16] – the Bloomian 'son' of Wagner fled Bayreuth and began his fertile agon of wandering. The lure of an Übermensch did not leave him, however – *Zarathustra* came a decade after première of *The Ring* – and its persistence suggests how in an existential sense it may be the transcendental idea par excellence. Nietzsche blamed Wagner's debunking of it on need for a theatrical ending and characterized his programme for a way forward in *Parsifal* as relapse into 'the Christian lie'[17]. But the moral of Wagner's 'last word' goes beyond religion. The free spirit, if he is to have a chance to succeed, must learn some degree of self-abnegation, purity and devotion to principles beyond self – to great spirits who have travelled his path before (a Grail Order) and cosmic sympathy. *This* 'beyond man'[18] qualifies his predecessor (Siegfried) as little more than a brute, distinguished from the amoral survivor (Alberich) most by a 'blond beast' beauty vs. dwarf ugliness. Though Nietzsche professed to loathe *Parsifal*, it seems implausible that, had he not lost his wits and lived to its creator's age, he would have clung to a discredited Siegfried projection and continued to damn its corrective[19].

A second notable omission in a book entitled *American Nietzsche* may come from urges similar to those which sideline Wagner. This is Pound, the literary figure and American most resembling Nietzsche in temperament, career and

---

16 *Human, all-too-Human, I*, 71. *Complete Works* vi, tr Helen Zimmern.

17 See *The Case of Wagner* and *Nietzsche contra Wagner, Complete Works* viii. Wagner himself described the *Ring* as his Old Testament and *Parsifal* as a necessary revision of it (Conrad, *Verdi and/or Wagner*, 229).

18 Alternative to 'Superman' or 'Overman' as translation of 'Übermensch', 213.

19 Nietzsche's agon may have been on Wagner's mind when composing his tutelary scenario. Normally *Parsifal* is seen as tailored for young Ludwig II, who suffered from the 'sex wound' of homosexuality; but Nietzsche, who was the same age as Ludwig, had a 'wound' too, Wagner believed – compulsive masturbation. Wagner shared this theory with Nietzsche's doctor in 1877 – i.e., when setting down to work on his last drama (see Ronald Hayman, *Nietzsche*, Weidenfeld: 1980, 203). Nietzsche's discovery of this 'fatherly' intrusion into his private life is taken by some as a partial explanation for the fury of his reaction against Wagner.

programme. If Pound is avoided because of anti-Semitic and Fascist enthusiasms, or because his expatriation to Europe makes him seem 'un-American', so much the worse; because what in Nietzsche encourages provincialism, let alone native bias? The author of the post-Wagner 'Mediterranean books' of *Human, all-too-Human, Dawn of Day* and *The Gay Science* was transnational by conviction, troubadour by sentiment, classicist by tradition – all affiliations which the poet of *The Cantos* took up with zest. Allied with Emersonian and Whitmanesque instincts, these impelled Pound out onto a greater American road, one which led to Nietzsche's beloved European *south* as well as to cultures further afield but still within a transcendentalist scope – Fenollosa's Cathay, Frobenius' Africa; landscapes to which, as Nietzsche foresaw, 'other birds will fly farther'[20], ever seeking, ever wishing to locate and assess new modes of being to get *beyond* what they began as: conventional little Western men.

Pound's quest led out of 'safe' academe and entailed an assault against what he saw as a native philistinism: domesticated, feminized, ineffectual 'taste'. Supported by and promoting radical journals – *The Little Review* of Chicagoan Margaret Anderson, whom R-R cites, *The New Age* of A. R. Orage, who (like Mencken) edited a slim volume of Nietzsche's *mots* – Pound blasted the foundations of tradition with 'fearless independence' yet also a 'deep reverence for the mysterious laws of our being'[21]. Like Nietzsche he became an intellectual nomad and teacher-as-provocateur: hortatory, adopting personae and perspectives, unmasking them as needed, ever in pursuit and attempting – at the risk of madness – to break through to some new, if illusory Truth. In contrast to the Harold Bloom trope, he collected father figures rather than killing them and in a maturity Nietzsche never achieved tried to apply the best in them to a public policy to serve aesthetics and promote, not curtail, development of

---

20 Final passage of *Dawn of Day*, 'We Aeronauts of the Intellect', *Complete Works* ix, tr J. M. Kennedy.

21 Phrases used by Maude Petre in articles about Nietzsche for *The Catholic World* in 1905-6 (R-R, 83).

great individuals. Pound's misjudgements in this project would give way beyond breakdown to a perception shining through the later *Cantos* of a need for sensible law – hence celebration of the writings of Sir Edward Coke.

It is a solution Nietzsche might have foreseen: beyond debunked foundational moralities, there must be some code by which individuals can treat with one another as other than Darwinian beasts. Yet the *nil admirare* of a 'son' ever at war with the 'father' partly blinded him to what shadows his work and is celebrated in Pound's: great spirits of many ages and places; a 'grail order' of Übermenschen defined as those prepared to weigh conduct and values against some such transcendent projection. Ms R-R's pantheon of Nietzsche admirers has distant kinship to this. That it is not quite as inclusive as could be may be inevitable for one of her identity: to paraphrase her on A. Bloom, a midwestern female Jewish associate professor. These categories define limitation: fear of being taken as provincial; feeling of disadvantage in history made by white European males; aversion to whatever has trafficked with prejudice; bondage to 'philology', if not *Kultur*-philistinism. Seven pages of acknowledgements at the end of her text testify to not only its care in scholarship but also its lack of free flight, while the adjective in her title hints at an occasionally inferiority-inflected nationalism recalling the one Nietzsche grew up in. We must hope that this does not augur a larger cultural drift leading to ghastly error. In any case, it is hard to imagine a sceptical critic not seeing in the lady's wave of the flag traces of some editor's well-calculated marketing scheme.

American Nietzsche: A History of an Icon and His Ideas, Jennifer Ratner-Rosenhagen. University of Chicago Press, 2012.

The 'Flying Salzburger'

Quarterly Review, 5 iii 2015,
amalgamating *Jewish Chronicle*, 20 xii 2013 and 14 xi 2014

Among German-language authors of the early 20th century Stefan Zweig is now being re-positioned near the top. Some contemporaries saw him as in 'the first rank of the second rate', to use Somerset Maugham's self-deprecation; Hugo von Hofmannsthal, whom Zweig succeeded as Richard Strauss' librettist, put him several rungs beneath that.[1] In moments of depression which darkened his later years, Zweig may have seen truth as well as envy in such relegation. He was lucky however to have huge numbers of admirers, a public which bought his books in the hundreds of thousands, fellow humanists who shared his ideal of a finer pan-European order and above all an adoring young second wife, who followed him in restless search for a final resting-place and finally joined him in suicide there.

From a literary point of view Zweig belonged to the last great era before writing was overtaken by other media as a principal means of telling tales and promulgating ideas. From a political point of view he belonged to a last gilded age before world war disfigured Europe. Child of privileged Jews in fin-de-siècle Vienna, he was one of its most famous sons by 1920 when with a fellow-writing first wife he decamped for a hill over Salzburg. There he busied himself on novellas and plays such as he had churned out since his early twenties. He worked indefatigably, travelled peripatetically and cheated on his wife shallowly. In a life devoted to the written word, he was a manic collector as well as producer. He gave public readings and lectures about culture far beyond his imploding Germano-phone world. As his fame spread, this tendency deepened to explore of acts of danger, daring and will.

He wrote mini-biographies of great men – Balzac, Dostoyevsky, Nietzsche – building them into the popular

---

1 Hofmannsthal called Zweig sixth-rate. See 'Yesterday's Man', note 25.

Baumeister der Welt series, based not so much on research as on analysis. He sought to discover what he called the *lebenskurve* and in effect to create literary-historical equivalents to the psychological case-studies being written by his friend and fellow Viennese Sigmund Freud, a reluctant inclusion among his subjects. Analysis of great men morphed into pinpointing crucial moments, the *Sternstunden* as Zweig called them, on which history pivots. High-risk explorations, visionary inventions, inspiration via mass emotion, creation against physical odds, vain leaps after fortune, persistence in face of defeat... Zweig zeroed in on the obstacles he saw men as having to face if mankind as a whole were to move forward: Balboa in sighting the Pacific, Scott in the Antarctic, Lenin in Petrograd.

One can hardly read of these heroic cruxes, all in the present tense, and not feel their author's febrile excitement. Zweig was a man in a hurry in an age which had an appointment with destiny. His vignettes, full of hope of beating the odds, were also haunted by spectres of downfall. Rouget de Lisle composing 'The Marseillaise', Grouchy's lack of initiative at Waterloo – Zweig had a vast interest in upheavals of the previous century, and naturally he sensed that in a few years' time some of his readers might be burning his books. Anxiety stalked, but he did not let it impede the drive of his prose or choice of topics, which belonged to the frightening Zeitgeist. Like Freud, the child of Austro-Hungary reviled Woodrow Wilson for 'the failure of Versailles'. He grew as ardent in promoting pacifism and European unity as malign contemporaries were in inciting war and race hatred. Hitler was a contemporary compatriot. Goebbels and Rosenberg read Zweig books. Suicide with younger wives would happen in the Berlin bunker too. Victim and victimizer came from contiguous milieux.

In fiction Zweig specialized in the long story and wrote only one novel. Like his *Sternstunden*, his collected tales have recently been made available in English by Pushkin Press. Clothbound and printed on good paper, with decorative colophons to demarcate the text, these books are objects which the bibliophile in Zweig might have approved of. The tales match their covers in quiet smartness, with a variety of styles and subjects including something to seduce a life-savvy aunt as well as wide-eyed boys. Like Maugham, Zweig had a knack for narration and feel for human nature; yet unlike that often spiteful ironist, he had a suffering soul. Hard hearts accuse him of sentimentality, but few now will be able to read 'In the Snow' – a Jack London-like tableau of the people of a ghetto freezing to death while fleeing pogrom – without appreciating the prescience of this carpet-slippered son of Vienna to the catastrophe others of his kind were shortly to undergo.

By the mid-30s Zweig was in full flight from the arrival of the mad expressionism of National Socialism, with which his overwrought style and enthusiasms had traits in common. In a book recently published about his last years, George Prochnik does not flinch from recognizing this irony. *The Impossible Exile* shows Zweig as a figure in whom the disease of the age was ever apparent, and never more so than at his end. Where in a world beset by furies could an individual of devout European culture turn? London took him, for a time; he retreated to Bath, tried to idealize it but finally found an English sang-froid insipid. New York took him also, for a time; he retreated to a quaint hamlet on a bluff overlooking Sing-Sing but found it a prison. America enjoyed bounty while Europe convulsed in war and its citizens starved. Zweig, rich from both inheritance and book sales, was beleaguered by indigent fellow-refugees wishing introductions, begging cash. On top of it all, where in the U. S. could one find a proper café, that institution so central to Viennese cultured life?

If the detail sounds banal, it is crucial to the tale Prochnik tells. For it is not just Zweig in exile whose plight he analyzes but the condition of flight from Hitler's Europe altogether, especially for Jews who within a few generations had gained and now were losing the *splendeurs et misères* of high civilization. Where to go, who to be, what language to write in? One may have been 'saved' – that is, to have found shelter in *Amerika* – but what then? The world they knew had vanished. They wandered hither and thither, haunted, bickering with one another, hating while at the same time being obliged to love where they had come to. Zweig's solution? to penetrate further into new worlds, another land of the future – Brazil. Nature in the hills overlooking Rio was gorgeous, the coffee to die for. And that was it. Fully cut off. Utter deracination. At the age of sixty, the man was played out. And worse tragedy, whose promptings can never quite be understood, is that his young wife should like some Brünnhilde of grandiose opera or myth have chosen to cast herself into a personal *Götterdämmerung* with him.

This finale has caused much speculation. Laurent Seksik published a novel about it in French in 2010; it is now available in English from Pushkin and as a graphic text from Salammbô. The latter makes Zweig's story accessible for those unlikely to read his massive oeuvre or more challenging works proliferating about him[2]. Whatever the dominant motive for his melodramatic end, the novel musters probable elements: exhaustion, his wife's asthma, the melancholia of exile, horrors engulfing those of his kind left behind, a killing nostalgia, temperamental allergy to the new and a bourgeois mittel-European fragility in face of carneval masses... A pagan 'new age' birthed no 'terrible beauty' for Zweig. It was no 'country for old men' in either metaphysical or physical senses. Suicide is a pathetic response, however, and surely no country for a loving young wife. On the basis of the evidence, it is hard not to construe that this great writer was at his exit neither a worthy exemplar nor a responsible husband. But let us be kind. Zweig's end, like Jack London's, was above all the Faustian price to be paid for having poured out popular books of relative brilliance year after year.

Shooting Stars: the Historical Miniatures, Stefan Zweig, trans Anthea Bell; Pushkin, 2013. *Collected Stories of Stefan Zweig*, trans Anthea Bell; Pushkin, 2013. *The Impossible Exile: Stefan Zweig at the End of the World*, George Prochnik; Granta, 2014. *The Last Days of Stefan Zweig*, Laurent Seksik, illustrations Guillaume Sorel, trans Joel Anderson, Salammbô, 2014.

---

2   Such as Rudiger Görner's critical study. See 'Yesterday's Man', note 17.

La Bohême[1]

Quarterly Review, 1 xi 2013

There is a mystique about Prague which makes it for some the most alluring of European cities. This may have in part to do with geography. It stands at roughly the centre of the continent, occupying more or less the same position as Kansas City in the United States, a centrality which persuaded President Wilson to choose the otherwise relative backwater as locale for a monument to Allied victory in World War I. That catastrophe, along with Wilson's war aims of the Fourteen Points, brought into being the hybrid nation 'Czechoslovakia' and made Prague a capital city for the first time since arguably the greatest previous European catastrophe, the Thirty Years' War.

Prague's hinterland had always been called Bohemia and was a major part of Hapsburg and Holy Roman empires. Bohemia's history is illustrious and tragic. One of its native heroes, Karl IV, was elected emperor in the 14th century, but his imperial capital was demoted and reduced to a backwater after the Battle of White Mountain in 1618. Germanic dominance for centuries kept Czech preponderance at bay, though Bohemia never stopped being a crossroads, with shifting populations of Poles, other Slavs, Jews, Gypsies and refugees sharing its urban if not rural spaces with the two larger ethnic groups. This polyglot mix with its variety of religions, generously seasoned by heresy – another local emperor, Rudolf II, made Prague 'the magic capital' of Europe in the late Renaissance, attracting alchemists and other seekers for a philosopher's stone – no doubt contributed to our modern transmogrification of 'Bohemia' into a Cockaigne of the mind.

In eclipse for three hundred years, Prague's reversion to capital status in the 1920s and '30s was followed by re-demotion

---

1 After some disputation my editor agreed to use the circonflex rather than the grave, following a French convention (notable in Gérard du Nerval) that the one refers to the land (whether actual or of the mind) and the other to a native of it.

under the Nazis. Liberation was succeeded by communization in the late '40s. The glorious 'Spring' of 1968 gave way to occupation by Soviet tanks. Finally Prague re-emerged as unmolested capital in the Velvet Revolution of '89, but only two years later lost nearly half its territory in a 'velvet divorce' with Slovakia. All of this may place it at the centre of the grand sweep of events which marked what the late Eric Hobsbawm called 'the short 20th century', but whether it justifies a book entitling Prague 'capital of the twentieth century' is another matter. Several rival European cities come to mind for this title – Berlin, Rome, Moscow, even in a different colouration Warsaw or Vienna. The book itself makes a case for Paris as truer 'surrealist' capital, with New York and possibly even L.A. – particularly after World War II began – not far behind.

What then is the point Derek Sayer is making in *Prague, Capital of the Twentieth Century*? Or is his title just a provocation, akin to the surrealist antics that are its true subject? I may just have answered my question. In any case, where we are going with Sayer isn't Prague exactly, rather an iconoclastic cultural fantasy-land whose emergence counter-intuitively came in an epoch when totalitarianism was bestriding the continent like a colossus. Or maybe on inspection 'counter-intuitive' is not the apt term. Sayer's subtitle is *A Surrealist History*, but Surrealism was never quite the anarchic, free-spirited movement it seems. Adherence or not to Stalinist dogma fractured it in the 1930s; and like fascist aesthetics, contrasting Futurism in Italy of the '20s with the anti-*Entartete Kunst* 'cleansing-war' in Germany of the following decade, its practitioners diverged in product as in prejudices. Salvador Dali, the 'surrealist' probably thought of first and foremost by posterity, languished for a spell under excommunication by the movement for his apparently crypto-fascist attitudes. Meanwhile, the two great ideologues of Surrealism proper – André Breton and Louis Aragon – spent much of their maturity not speaking to one another.

For those who need a Virgil to guide them through the labyrinths which this book's author, as well as its subject, evidently favour, Breton is the man, alternatively his onetime mate Paul Éluard, with whom Breton travelled to Prague for a Surrealist *internationale* in 1935. The event is a pivot on which the book balances its dual subject – 'the reception they found in the city merged to create a single rose-tinted memory' – but the pair would soon embody their movement's fissiparous tendency too. Breton was in '35 undisputed commander-in-chief, Éluard his loyal aide-de-camp. The double-entendre seems à propos: though Surrealism saw itself at the forefront of sexual liberation, Breton was like many Communists homophobic, and Éluard's more ambivalent nature contributed to their split. Aragon, who fell afoul of Breton's political line in this pivotal year, was equally 'confused' when it came to sexual dogmata. On one occasion when the group was conducting 'Recherches sur la sexualité', Breton said, 'if this promotion of homosexuality carries on, I will leave this meeting forthwith'. To which Aragon retorted:

> It has never been a question of promotion of homosexuality. This discussion is becoming reactive. My own response, which I would like to elaborate upon, isn't to homosexuality so much as to the fact that it has become an issue for us. I want to talk about all sexual inclinations.

It is surrealistic in itself sometimes to observe the tergiversations of these quondam friends and allies in the *sillons* of a cultural revolution. The Communist Party had no time for what it regarded as 'pornography' by the '30s, and the author of *Irene's Cunt* was called to account. Breton meanwhile was happy to alter the name of the movement's journal from *La révolution Surréaliste* to *Le Surréalisme au service de la révolution*. On another hand, Aragon would continue editing a magazine for Le Parti Communiste Français during the epoch of show trials in Moscow, while Breton had scarpered to Mexico to pen manifestoes for Leon Trotsky. If this seems to bespeak a less than Stalinist posture, consider that when Éluard dared to publish a poem in Aragon's journal, Breton not only made a final break with him but enjoined his colleagues to 'commit themselves to sabotaging Éluard's poetry by any means at their disposal'. Those who imagine this movement to have been more or less a blithe child of Dada and/or grandpa to postmodernist 'play' are wearing very dark glasses. 'Disgusted,' Sayer tells us, 'Max Ernst and Man Ray followed Paul [Éluard] out of the group.' Breton managed to get away to New York after the war began. His arrival there, according to Marcel Duchamp, 'was the moment when the American avant-garde was born.'

Has 'Bohemia' then always been something other than the land of Cockaigne of our fond imaginings? On evidence of this incarnation of it, one might say yes. But that is not the book's message, and such attention as it devotes to the other half of its subject – the capital of Bohemia proper – tells a different or at least more sympathetic tale. The Prague surrealists, so less well known, had their own political and aesthetic schisms, as one might guess, which Sayer catalogues. Yet Prague in his view, echoing others', has a claim to embodying surrealism itself. Of all cities, anyhow in the European world, it is the best example of it – that is the argument, taken in descent from Walter Benjamin, who (also in 1935, as it happens) labelled Paris 'capital of the Nineteenth Century'. Benjamin's touchstone was Baudelaire, whose great book begins with the phrase 'fourmillante cité', metamorphosed by T. S. Eliot in his great poem to 'Unreal City', from which provenance it should not be much effort for us to accept 'surreal city' in continuation. 'This book,' maintains Sayer, 'tries to do for our recent past – which is to say for Walter Benjamin's present – what *The Arcades Project* did for his: to rummage amid the rags and refuse of yesterday's modernity in the hope of uncovering the dreamworlds that continue to haunt what we fondly believe to be today's waking state.'

The rags and refuse Sayer ransacks in Prague include works of Kafka and *The Good Soldier Svejk*; of Milan Kundera and of Václav Havel. They include the Starry Castle, the Hradčany and Suicide Lane. They include bartered brides from Smetana, 'Granny' from folk tradition and circus girls playing with penises in cartoons by Toyen. They include remnants of old street grids from the time of Karl IV, gnarled alleys of the Ghetto, a modernist monumental Trade Fair Palace, Frank Gehry's and Vlado Milunić's contemporary Dancing House. Nowhere is Sayer more adept than in describing architecture and its role as a symptom of and comment on cultural progress. That Prague is a mishmash of ages he extols. That a building designed for merchandising should become a seat of communist officialdom is just the kind of oxymoron he likes to see as typifying. 'Prague doesn't let go... This little mother has claws,' Kafka famously said, and its metamorphoses are evidence of intrinsic strength more than of tragedy. Sedimentary layers are the city's essential identity. Compare them to the marvellous rigidities of Haussmann's Paris and the point becomes clear: Prague *is* 'bohemia'; Prague *is* 'surreal' – more so evidently than predominantly modernist New York, Huguenot/Wilhelmine Berlin, 18th/19th century imperial Vienna, even a Rome whose three ages are quite clearly demarcated. Go to Prague, the book urges. See for yourself.

For those who have been there, Sayer's intellectual, historical and geographical excursion may call up memories, phantoms, desire, *nostalgie*. For those who have not, it may seem somewhat hallucinatory. There is no easy path through it, and its great walls of rhetoric scintillate and distract the reader from his way. That, one presumes, is part of the intention: to envelope you in an ethos from which there is no sure egress; to hold you there long enough so that a kind of Oblomov syndrome sets in. Nerviness to get on – to the point, to an exit – begins to lose its grip and, as if you were sitting over some greenish libation in a smoky café, with fog out the window and the dank of river water on the air, you start to slip into a mild acceptance. A fiddle plays somewhere, or accordion. And who is that pallid creature loitering over in the corner, and what language is it – or is it many – massaging my ears? You begin to think yes, this is where I belong, or anyhow where I find myself, and am inclined to stay. It may be a bit weird or disjointed, but in a quite seductive way, and besides I'm inexplicably beat or, no – oddly content – so why should I stir? I have come to a place which seems to accept me, for now. Maybe it's just shrugging its shoulders, or doesn't care. Whatever, it is enough. Let the rest float. Tomorrow may be tragic, but... what is that aura descending? sheer whimsy? dolce far niente? No, I recognize it. Isn't it our old and sweet shape-shifting friend – *la vie de bohème*?

Prague, Capital of the Twentieth Century, A Surrealist History, Derek Sayer. Princeton University Press, 2013.

Goodnight, Vienna

Quarterly Review, 12 v 2013

Edmund de Waal had a succès d'estime a few years back with his family memoir *The Hare with the Amber Eyes*. His Ephrussi forbears, a grand European Jewish clan, produced among other exquisites a model for the protagonist of the overture volume of Proust's epoch-making *À la recherche du temps perdu*. Fine manners and taste allied with great wealth characterized a type and an ethos summoned up with gentle, if perhaps not quite unintentionally polemical, nostalgia. The Palais Ephrussi had stood prominent among similar piles along the top-drawer Ringstrasse in pre-war Vienna – a street known as 'Zionstrasse' among less privileged types. This was in retrospect a harbinger of trouble, as de Waal notes in his preface to *The Exiles Return*. Yet in the heyday of the Ephrussi and kind such insults were nobly ignored. As late as the Anschluss in 1938, de Waal's great-grandparents hung on, only to be rescued by an efficient daughter who had begun her own exile to the west fifteen years earlier as Rockefeller Foundation fellow in economics at Columbia University.

Elisabeth von Ephrussi became 'de Waal' upon marrying a Dutchman. Although trained as an economist, she had from an early age wanted to be a literary writer. She penned poems in her husband's language, two novels in her native German and three in adopted English. Following her time in America, she lived in Paris, where she wrote for *Le Figaro*, and later in London, where she reviewed French novels for *The TLS*. A true cosmopolitan, she could recite swaths of *Faust* and of Rilke, her favourite poet, with whom she had corresponded. She owned an original copy of Joyce's *Ulysses*, published by Shakespeare and Company, and may even have read much of it – her grandson tells us its pages are cut up to 563. Above all her master was Proust; and in *The Exiles Return*, a novel left unpublished at her death, we see a version of his milieu, if not style, filtered heavily through the anaesthetic of 'the American century' and transferred from belle époque Paris to a postwar Vienna, whose sombre atmosphere will forever be branded on the Anglo psyche by the Carol Reed/ Alexander Korda/Orson Welles film of Graham Greene's *The Third Man*.

As an evocation of what once had been and would become of that city in the last days of Four Power occupation, de Waal's novel penetrates further than the Greene spy scenario. Because she had lived to adulthood amid its glories, now flattened, de Waal could feel the place as an insider as well as outsider, victim as well as new dominator. Her exiles returning provide a three-way split of her psyche: a scientist/academic who fled with his wife to America, where she flourished but he felt alien; a Greco-Viennese magnate who also fled to the U.S. and flourished but now seeks to thrive again in a milieu where his people strode like colossi before the calamity; a daughter of another noble émigré to the States who has grown up in a plasticized suburb where she never feels quite at home, thus is sent to 'find herself' among relations of the surviving Austrian aristocracy. Action takes place for these three respectively on *Third Man*-ish mean streets and in an un-renovated university laboratory; in art and antique shops and a rebuilt, if somewhat hidden, palace; at a down-at-heel country estate and in a noble townhouse now turned into flats. The impact of American upon Old World values is pervasive, yet shallow. Resistance of the latter to the former is deftly depicted. The mix of the two in an emerging new order is painted with subtle brushstrokes.

Gore Vidal once entitled a book *Pink Triangle & Yellow Star* to underline the mutual interest between gays and Jews in the aftermath of a common persecution by Blackshirts. He relocated to Europe to ply a congenial lifestyle among the decadent aristos of, in his case, Italy. This very New York-ish new/old alliance – gay, Jew and ancien régime – is the matrix into which de Waal places her personae, interweaving their destinies as they ply semi-expatriate lives in a new (for them) old world. The scientist departs from his wife in Manhattan where she is making a fortune as corsetière to the nouveau riche, whom she despises with a verve resembling Leona Helmsley's later on; yet he finds only begrudging welcome from native academics at his old institute. As a result of imposed policy, he is restored to his former position but granted no recognition for his achievements in exile. He finds contentment only via the affection of an aristocrat who, dispossessed, has buried herself in research; too grand to think in terms of rivalry, she can recognize his genius without fear of being overshadowed by it. Her brother is a beautiful scamp who, penniless, becomes bisexual bait for the rich. He is taken up by de Waal's second persona, the Greek collector, who wishes to create a salon for what remains of, or can be made into, a beau monde in the half-deadened city. De Waal's third and most intimate persona, the American girl sent to discover herself in ancestral Austria, falls under the spell of the scamp and becomes pregnant by him. He refuses to marry her, being after wealth only; but she is offered salvation via engagement to the Greek, whose motive for taking her on is to increase his own attraction through her beauty and pedigree, thus to exercize further sway over the lothario-scamp, who turns out to be not only bait for his salon but also the object of his own rarefied erotic interest.

In this imbroglio, ethnic, class and sexual prejudices all play significant roles. There is something pot-boilerish to the ending, and one senses a whiff of Hollywood – say, James M. Cain (*Mildred Pierce* comes to mind) – affecting an otherwise ambient scent of, say, one of Louise de Vilmorin's contemporary Proust-lite efforts. That said (and one wonders if it may be an explanation for why the book was not published in Elisabeth de Waal's lifetime), the ending does have portent. Not all is as it should be in this New-World-within-Old paradise. The gay/Jewish/aristo alliance turns out to be a 'golden bowl' with fine fissures; and it is fortunate for the principals that American authorities are still in charge of their district, if only just. Along with carefully vetted police and under supervision of a mysteriously omniscient priest, they are able to cover up a tragedy which might lead to scandal – even to reactionary sanctions were the natives back in control, as they imminently will be.

Elements in *The Exiles Return* are strikingly of the 1950s and might alarm monitors of political correctness now. Homosexual intrigue as a cause of a naïve young woman's demise is one example. Depiction of the plutocratic Greek as all-manipulating is another: he would doubtless seem an anti-Semitic caricature were he to have been cast as a Jew, as he readily and possibly more credibly could have been. But Mrs de Waal was clearly driven by desire for *recherche* of her own Proustian province as much as of this new Old World at large, and the picture she paints of postwar Vienna's apparatchiks and ideologues, only partly de-nazified natives and nostalgists, is sketchy in comparison to the detailing of her own kind. Thus we must not rush to hail the book chiefly or only as the historical portrait it appears to be at first glance. As that, it is atmospheric, intriguing, suggestive and rich; but as novel of personality and development it has a more insistent pull and intrinsic truth. This may a chief explanation for why Edmund de Waal, with his family agenda, persuaded Persephone Books to release it now for the first time. It is a credit to both that they have done so, and in an inexpensive, yet highly attractive edition.

The Exiles Return, Elisabeth de Waal, with a new Preface by Edmund de Waal. Persephone Books, 2013.

Twentieth Century Sociology – made (mostly) in America

Quarterly Review, 16 iv 2013

Why write a book of almost prohibitive dullness? to keep away those who won't like the message? discourage readers who can't face strenuous analysis without an inducement of lollipops? In the case of Christian Fleck's tome on the social sciences, this may exclude some libertarian *Luftmenschen* who believe that our western democracies are institutions of un-freedom, not so different from the régimes which flourished in central and eastern Europe in the mid-20th century by managing to control the responses of their citizens. That those régimes fell apart may be an omen for ours, runs the logic. A prophetic analogue is what Fritz Lang projected in his classic *film noir* in the heyday of Weimar Berlin: an Ayn Rand-ish structure in which everyman is a cog in a capitalist machine kept running smoothly on schemes and advice from a mad Old World new scientist. In the end the great city is unmasked as wholly dystopic, and with uneasy pleasure we watch it come down.

It is a pity that Fleck's live version of the *Metropolis* scenario is not told more accessibly, as it is fascinating, and important. After the World War I, the Rockefeller Foundation distributed bounty in Europe to develop institutes, projects and seats in universities for study of social matters that would gradually separate into disciplines of psychology, economics, political science, social anthropology and sociology proper. Largesse was dispensed in a spirit of philanthropy typical of the progeny of 'robber barons'. The Carnegie Foundation joined the RF in this pioneering work; neither was in bed yet with the U.S. government, though both operated in harmony with Wilsonian ideals for a league of nations (which a conservative U.S. Senate rejected) and Hooverian initiatives to feed, re-house and renovate lives of millions on a war-ravaged continent. Since much of the displacement and devastation had been in the centre of that continent and – as the Dawes Plan simultaneously recognized

– the core of that centre was in Germany, and to a lesser extent Austria, it is where the greatest effort was focussed.

Money was spent, perhaps not quite consciously at first, to Americanize Germanic methods. Use of survey, interview and data collection were introduced to buttress theory; collegial projects were underwritten to supersede cults of individual 'genius'; democratized departments were set up to supplant fiefdoms of magisterial professors. Reduction of Austria to a rump following collapse of the Hapsburg empire made recruiting interested academics there easier than in Germany itself: the Weimar republic had inherited academic structures largely intact from its Wilhelmine imperial predecessor; nonetheless German sociology, with its traditions deriving from Max Weber among others, was soon penetrated by American interests too. Friends were made and scholars financed to travel to American universities, to develop new programmes in their own or in both. Ostensibly non-political, these initiatives carried on in the first years of Nazi power; then a darkening situation, especially after the Anschluss, shut down and/or transplanted them to the U.S., where scores of German and particularly Austrian academic friends fled, Jews prominent among them.

Among programmes which grew up coincidental to or consequent on this process was the Princeton Radio Research Project – a misnomer, as it was run out of Newark and later Columbia Universities. Paul Lazarfeld was its director and the sociological writer who styled himself Theodore Adorno its most celebrated contributor. These two egotistical, sporadically paranoid émigrés forged an alliance – sometimes misalliance – to bring 'American empiricism' and 'European theory' together in order to assess the role of the new medium of radio in the lives of its listeners. 'Who listens, When, How, and What to?' were the questions. American sponsors employed these brilliant foreigners and others at half the price of native equivalents; the brilliant foreigners penned proposals padded out to allure maximum dollars from their hosts, a habit already practiced by some in Europe during the pre-Nazi phase. One commentator would describe Lazarfeld as a 'con-artist'. Certainly Adorno capriciously pursued his own star, cultivating an old European profile as 'genius' to the extent that a credulous New World would allow. Setting such Machiavellian characteristics aside, what was accomplished?

Quite a bit, it would seem, in the analysis of effects and what was likely to cause them. Now familiar techniques were developed: panels of listeners, button-pushers and what we call 'focus-groups' to gauge what types of music were likely to lull, stimulate, infuriate or be turned off, and what types of voices would best appeal – the latter spelling an end for 'the intellectually superior type', 'the know-all', 'the stuffed shirt' and 'the grumbler'. Beyond music and its commentators, such diagnostics aided in development of the new science of political prognostication – Gallup, Roper and Daniel Bell all worked on the fringes of the programme now and then; and general effects of media began to be predicted with as much acuity as by their contemporary magicker back in Germany, Josef Goebbels. Results could be provoked, Adorno later observed, 'according to the ideal of a skilled manipulation of the masses' with self-evidently 'exploitative' or 'benevolent' consequence.

An era of mass advertising and mass 'fads' was simultaneously growing up, with proliferation of new professions feeding it. The U. S. War Information Office became involved; the Rockefeller Foundation was eclipsed as premier funder by the American Jewish Congress. Max Horkheimer became maestro of huge investigations into the nature of the authoritarian personality and the typologies of anti-Semitism. Preferring California to New York, he manufactured health excuses to shift the centre of gravity west; Adorno, meanwhile, attached himself to Horkheimer's burgeoning équipe, as too from time to time did other 'stars', such as psychologist Erich Fromm and Marxist/Freudian philosopher Herbert Marcuse. New purpose suffused once supposedly objective research, a fine sense of The Enemy and of mentalities to be re-formed, if not extirpated, or at least marginalized. Horkheimer saw himself as directing a social research organization analogous to the scientific one at Los Alamos developing the atomic bomb, and the shift in world morality it advanced – towards zero toleration of racism and prejudice – would arguably become an even more potent force in postwar history.

If the cause was just, many of its promoters were all-too-human. Fleck's account of Horkheimer and Co. often recalls the famous quip about academic disputes made by another émigré promoted via Rockefeller largesse: 'The reason they are so vicious is because so little is at stake.' But Kissinger's wit is not in Fleck's bag of tricks. He plunges us into tables comparing salaries, publication rates, recognition status – measures that today might boil down to the number of clicks a name gets on the web. Possibilities for distortion were present then as now. On collective publications, which most projects spawned, the author listed first often became the one it was known by; thus Adorno's profile was artificially raised. Networking helped, not least among émigrés, especially those associated with the RF or AJC; elements of European prejudice persisted, Germans whether Jewish or not displaying a traditional *de haut en bas* attitude towards Czechs, Romanians or refugees from other 'less advanced' cultures. Vienna was top among origins for some, despite or perhaps because of its dramatic decline; within those combating 'the authoritarian character structure' or 'psychodynamics of anti-Semitic disease', it was not hard to spot traits that might have jumped off a page of Elias Canetti's 1936 novel about that city's unsacred monsters, *Die Blendung (Auto-da-Fé)*.

After World War II many players went back to Europe, either with sponsorship or by choice or both. The RF by now was working in concert with U.S. government agencies, as were Carnegie, Ford and other foundations; occasionally, as Frances Stonor Saunders exposed in *Who Paid the Piper?* (2001), they operated as fronts for schemes directed by the CIA. From initial postwar days of the Control Commission in Berlin, planning and implementation of a new world order progressed. Techniques of the diagnosticians were applied: profiling, acquisition of

166

assets (i.e., competent, loyal friends), re-education. Social sciences, seen as having 'suffered more than any other individual disciplines' under Nazi rule, were 'rebuilt', though in Austria they were allowed to slide back into a pre-war condition, Americans apparently believing the self-serving line of the natives that the country had been the 'first victim' of Nazi expansion. Proud as some were to have come from Vienna originally, few were eager to return to a rump *heimat* – they were too cushily ensconced now on American university campuses.

As Germany prospered, its homecomers increased. By the early 1950s Friedrich Pollock, Adorno and Horkheimer himself were back. Frankfurt was chief beneficiary of this reflux; its Institut für Sozialforschung re-arose. Berlin was another: by the 1960s, it boasted the Max-Planck Institut für Bildungsforschung. Women ranked low in these new citadels of social engineering, nor had all the old vices vanished – hyper-reverence for authority, theory and 'genius'. But data collection was now implanted into the system, modes of analysis imported and refined, tools by which to bolster a new 'social market' economy and order, user-friendly, open to continuous modification, embedded with and within the desires and anxieties of a 'reoriented' *Volk*. What 'robber barons' had incepted a new Europe inherited. Given that as early as 1913 American per capita GNP was 50% higher than that of developed Europe (by 1950 it was double), it is no surprise that the flow should have been in this direction. However, as Fleck points out, by the end of the 20th century the discrepancy was back to a 1913 level and 'other indications going in the same direction'. So what now? What to come?

Thirty-five years ago as the above process proceeded, libertarians and radicals in the U. S. fretted about the supposed hegemony of the Trilateral Commission, a group set up by David Rockefeller to bring together leaders from the then most powerful entities: America, rebuilt Europe and Japan. Resentment was voiced about how this directorate seemed to shape events, advancing its protégés Carter and Bush as government leaders at home and their equivalents abroad. Who rules the world, it was asked, and to what end? In those days it was the defeat of Communism, which succeeded. But after? Some questions remain evergreen. Who advises our masters? What scientist-geniuses are employed by *Metropolis*-style bosses to maintain sway over the suggestible mass? How different *is* their mentality of control from that which devised bread and circuses for denizens of the totalitarian states we opposed? How much less eager are they to root out an 'enemy within'? Doesn't the will to control always carry bacilli of paranoia in it? Did the sociologists of Fleck's study not flourish in an era that also produced Joe McCarthy?

It was an era sufficiently 'plastic' – i.e., opposed to man's organic nature and freedom – that male babies were regularly mutilated, i.e. circumcised, on hygienic grounds later found to be bogus. Along with kid sisters, they were fed on powdered formula in preference to breast milk so that their mothers might nurture in padded push-up bras busts to rise to the level of desirable womanhood advertised by iconic Ja(y)nes, Russell and Mansfield. Unsurprisingly, the 1960s brought revolt in the form of bra-burning, let-it-all-hang-out hippies, descendents of Nietzschean *Wandervögel* and Kibbo Kift kindred of the European 1920s. But the drive to assess and direct individual activity in the name of social cohesion, order and marketing carried on into our era, facilitated by the tracking of credit card transactions, email, social media pages and so on. It is, after all, an instinct as old as the king or his spies going in disguise among the people to hear their complaints and deal with them.

Libertarians know that their cherished freedoms can be protected only by perpetual vigilance. Current hegemons and social diagnosticians preside over a world order in which there is, as there doubtless always has been, an echelon of individuals whose driving urge is to probe the system, evade, slip the net, hide away, change locale and/or identity, adopt a low profile – do whatever is necessary to pass under the radar of what is easily regarded as a near universal control industry. Totalitarian China is this new age's premier success story. Yet even it must co-exist with a rival phenomenon equally characteristic of our times – neo-robber barons, oligarchs, tax-haveneers, commodity speculators and their unwitting (or witting?) foot-soldiers: terrorists who shelter in an ever-evolving list of 'failed states'. What answers do the messianic data-gatherers and mind-benders have in this situation for us simple *bürgers*, if any of us in absolute honesty still exists?

A Transatlantic History of the Social Sciences: Robber Barons, the Third Reich and the Invention of Empirical Social Research, Christian Fleck (2007), trans. Helen Bleister. Bloomsbury Academic, 2011.

The Americanization of the Holocaust

Jewish Quarterly, Autumn 1995

When the controversy about whether Martin Amis should be nominated for the Booker Award was raging in the fashionable ghettoes of literary London some years ago, a grand lady novelist said to me: 'I'm sick of authors trying to make a success out of somebody else's misery.'[1] The Amis oeuvre in question was *Time's Arrow*, a clever narrative in reverse chronology about an American doctor who turns out to have been a Nazi physician in a concentration camp during the war. Should Amis have not stuck to his usual fare of young-mannish sex-and-cynicism romps, set on the mean(ish) streets of Notting Hill? Wasn't he merely trying to 'cash in' on fascination for the trendiest of the century's moral horrors and identify himself with the politically correct attitude towards it?

What should be the response of non-Jews to the Holocaust? They are asked to remember. Many regard the tragedy as theirs too in some sense. Unquestionably, this catastrophic act of genocide has determined important features of everyone's postwar existence. It seems absurd, if not worse, to speak in terms of divisions of race in its aftermath. All the same, there remains for non-Jews an unwritten sanction that perhaps they shouldn't talk about it too much, or at least not write about it authoritatively. However it may have affected their lives and whatever solidarity they may feel with the sufferers, it was *not* their tragedy in any direct way. Their ignominy in part, perhaps – but that is a different, less comfortable burden to bear.

And if non-Jews do 'cash in' on the Holocaust, or in some other way make it their own, what is the effect? de-Judaization of the memory? dispersal of its significance? Judaization of non-Jews in general, with consequent dilution of what it is to be a Jew? new polarizations like those that produced anti-Semitism in the past? These were some of the issues crossing some of the

---

1 Alice Thomas Ellis, who wrote a column for *The Spectator*.

minds of those who attended inauguration of the United States Holocaust Memorial Museum on 22 April 1993. The irony of the moment is captured by an image of Holocaust survivors having to wait to approach the site until after the limousines carrying President Clinton and Vice-President Gore, their wives and other dignitaries, had arrived and disgorged these neo-Roman potentates to perform their ceremonial functions.

As this occurred, a cynic remarked that the real purpose or erecting a Holocaust memorial adjacent to the symbolic centre of the most powerful nation on earth was 'to remind congressmen on how to vote on issues regarding the State of Israel'. Others contemplating its placement next to edifices enshrining the founding principles of the Republic (the Washington Monument and Lincoln and Jefferson Memorials) asked why such a negative and essentially foreign (i.e., European) event should be remembered here at all. And didn't the modernist construction violate the architectural integrity of the place? It hardly conformed to the classical plan Pierre L'Enfant had laid out for the city. And wasn't a memorial associated with one ethnic group or religion at odds with the nation's secular, inclusive ideals?

Underneath all this, a banal yet ominous rumble produced inchoate complaints: why should a preponderantly Jewish project have been underwritten by 'a federally sponsored council operating on appropriated funds and built on federally donated lands, [which] would, after opening, rely extensively on federal appropriations for annual operating costs'? It could never have happened in Thatcher's Britain, some Republicans muttered. But then, for all her admiration of President Reagan, the Iron Lady (still a pin-up of the American right) hardly shared the Great Communicator's notion that, when in doubt, a great nation must *spend*. The world economy, and the dollar, still reel from his lush dependence on deficits. That was one of many things a right-wing restoration would have to correct.

Political considerations marked the Memorial project from the first. In his exhaustive, if sometimes repetitive account of a fifteen-year struggle to get it off the ground, Edward Linenthal shows how, step by step, it danced cheek-to-cheek with partisan ambitions. It was made 'official' during the Carter administration because presidential advisors saw it as a way to counteract suspicions among Jewish Democrats over Carter's evangelical Christianity and sympathy for the Palestinians. It was nudged from the realm of 'dreamers' (like Elie Weisel) to 'developers' in the Reagan years because Republican strategists wanted to curry favour with wealthy Jews making their progress to the right as part of a 'neo-conservative' trend.

Both Carter and Reagan advertised themselves as populists. Neither, however, quibbled much about the expense of a project that never was seen, even by its promoters, as popular or all-American. Was this to their credit, or was it another feature of financial and political opportunism? Few congressmen objected; plans went ahead. The suggestion that it all be done with private finance, as Mrs Thatcher was advocating with everything from the Channel tunnel to the National Health Service, was never a player. Why? In an era in which aggregates of private wealth make even great nations look financially puny, this might have been prudent accounting. Surely the mega-bucks boys in New York and Chicago tucking away billions off torching currencies could have forked out and let the American budgeteers save a few extra hundred million to create a health system to keep poor Blacks from dying on the streets?

So ran the argument in the ghettoes, among the Muslims and Jesse Jackson supporters – ominous mutterings come from left as from right. But it is not as if they were overlooked. Indeed, the deliberations of the committee which initiated the project, recorded in detail by Linenthal, anticipated such criticisms before they were raised; and they were debated with rabbinical zeal. It would be hard to think of any national project, even the atom bomb, undertaken with more premeditation. And given as much – and given the risks – it is worth stopping to consider what this was really about in larger terms. For the issue of money was not the main one, nor indeed was the issue of Israel. The point of the Holocaust project was overarchingly moral. That is why, arguably, it deserved to be undertaken in the symbolic heart of the most moralistic (if not moral) nation on earth.

We live, many think, in a fallen age: an age in which moral values have vanished. The United States itself is often depicted as responsible for this: with its inordinate freedoms, its violence, sex, drugs and so on, it is leading the world towards a decadence not seen since the collapse of the Roman Empire – so the argument runs, often heard in Europe. Yet, as the Roman Empire saved and transformed itself by taking to heart the morality of a cult of a crucified Jew, so that American one may find a rudder through the next thousand years by 'sailing to Byzantium' in an analogous way. The Holocaust, socio-politically speaking, may provide a 'second coming' for the U. S.. It may prove the moral complex by which it can continue to instruct the world in how to live: an ultimate standard by which it may measure all future actions, external as well as internal.

At the end of his book, Linenthal tells a story about events that happened two thousand miles away in Billings, Montana at Christmas in the same year as the Holocaust Memorial was dedicated. Though Washington may be the capital of the U. S., the heart of the country, as everyone knows, is elsewhere – not least in the mountain states. In recent years this area has seen migration from both coasts of middle-class folks, including Jews, disaffected by pollution, taxes, crowds, violence and the inconvenience of urban sprawls like Los Angeles and New York. The mountain states, however, have also long been a bastion of backwoods WASP racist groups, particularly Montana and neighbouring Idaho (birthplace coincidentally of America's most famous literary anti-Semite, Ezra Pound).

Confrontation was waiting to happen. When it did, it was organized. Skinhead groups disrupted Afro-American church services. They distributed hate literature. They painted swastikas on the door of the synagogue. (Only forty-eight Jewish families live in Billings, in a population nearing 100,000.) They broke windows of Jewish homes, threw in leaflets denying the Holocaust and fomented a situation that the conductor of the Billings symphony orchestra likened to *Kristallnacht*. Jewish houses were identified by Hanukkah menorahs sitting in their windows. Focusing on this, Christian ministers called on parishioners to put menorahs in their windows too, as a way to retaliate. The strategy succeeded. Menorahs were soon everywhere in town, in homes, shops and even cars.

At first the skinheads responded by spray-painting messages against 'Jew-lovers' and by anonymous phone threats. Eventually, however, these Ku Klux Klan-ish tactics were marginalized by the solidarity of a large number of normal, decent citizens. The people of Billings were, in Linenthal's words, 'willing to "become Jewish" as an act of engagement'. In the last sentence of his book, he adds: 'They spoke with a very loud voice, the kind of courageous and compassionate voice that will need to be raised again and again if Holocaust memory is to serve us well.' We are invited to extrapolate that 'becoming Jewish' in this way is what the Holocaust Memorial betokens for the United States in its deeper structure: solidarity with all sufferers from race hatred, now and forever.

The moral decline of the New World Order is thus reversed. To be American becomes subtly, in part, to become a legatee of the Holocaust: that is, to feel vicariously in flesh and bone what it was like to be incinerated for nothing – for someone else's frustration or free-floating hate – and not for anything you yourself did. From the point of view of personal ethics, this may be a signal benefit of the great catastrophe of the century. From an 'official' point of view, however, it has its uses too. For if to be American becomes in some symbolic way to be a Jew and a victim, then anti-Americanism becomes a logical successor to the anti-Semitism of a discredited past. And if that anti-Semitism continues to be held out as a paradigm of unreason and evil, then anti-Americanism by implication becomes so as well.

The result is that, by further implication, Americanism re-establishes itself beyond reasonable question as *good*. Thus the subliminal logic of the 'official' adoption of the Holocaust in national iconography. And so in the end one might demonstrate that American taxpayers have not been swindled, as closet anti-Semites of right and left may wish them to think. Indeed, it is they above all who, through the opportunism – or at least mixed motives – of their leaders, will 'cash in'. Meanwhile, some Jews – a few of the 'dreamers' – may be appalled, especially those who see neglect by the United States as part of the reason that the Holocaust happened in the first place. At the same time, others – doubtless many of the 'developers' – may see it as one of the benefits they set out to achieve with this epoch-making project.

Preserving Memory: The Struggle to Create America's Holocaust Museum, Edward T. Linenthal. Viking, 1994.

World War Three

Quarterly Review, 1 xii 2013

We do not live in an era of moral certainty. In Anglo-Saxon countries questionable wars – Vietnam, Iraq – have left more than one generation drained of faith in the adage *Dolce et decorum est pro patria mori*. Some excitement persists for the idea of spying – James Bond films continued to spin money during decades when spun dossiers became our expectation of politicians. At the same time, American films have taught us that the agent who believes in the probity of his deployers may be being set up as a patsy. Be your own man and adhere to higher truth is the message. Country – nation – is too often in hock to this mafia or that. Indeed, nation itself may no longer be much more than a concept of mafia writ large.

Perhaps it was ever thus. However, there was a time when nation could be conceived of as a higher good, at least in contrast to what else was on offer – ancien régimes, dominance solely by power, supranational groupings given to corruption or debauch. Such was the case for many in our grandparents' and great-grandparents' generations. Two world wars were fought in a context where national virtue was not subject to grave doubt, and many rushed to serve without apprehension that winds of change might blow one into becoming a free agent. Nowadays many feel nostalgia for the certainty of those eras. Loyal service is longed for even as scepticism morphs into cynical disbelief. And there are establishments ever keen to revitalize values by which they once flourished. Vested interests don't just die; pressed to the wall they may, however surreptitiously, fight back.

Once secret archives are not, one assumes, open to authors liable to cock a snook at their revelations. Authors given access may be expected to have proven tried and true. This is not to imply that they must be ciphers or 'owned', only that they can be relied on to be 'sound'. Nothing wrong in that; it is at least a way in and, once in, the best may turn out to be their own men or women. An example is Peter J. Conradi, whose biography of SOE agent Frank Thompson, *A Very English Hero*, tells how a poetic young man from a distinguished Anglo-American intellectual family died in the Balkans, age 23, while attempting to assist an uprising against a fascist puppet régime. Conradi's sympathy for his subject – a civilized soul who was theoretically 'engaged' to Iris Murdoch[1] – leads him to follow Thompson's path in ruminative detail and to postulate that a life given up to such a cause, however noble and ethically sure, may be on balance a life thrown away, neither *dolce* nor *decorum*.

The sadness Conradi evidently feels for his young victim is in a tradition well-known from World War I – Rupert Brooke, Wilfred Owen and others who died in that catastrophe, to wit. Conradi, who has also written about Buddhism, displays what Allen Ginsberg described in another context as a 'bodhisattvic heart'[2]. This is contrasted by the brio with which Carole Seymour-Jones treats her SOE operative, Pearl Witherington, in *She Landed by Moonlight*. This book is also a close account enlivened by an author's identification with subject; but whereas sensitive males have been sacrificed at the altar of conflict for so long that it may be, as in Conradi's case, difficult to view them going off on their missions without a tear in the eye, brave women have been 'allowed' into these 'male' roles so seldom that it may prove equally difficult for a female author not to feel a curiosity bordering on enthusiasm and, in a case when tragedy is not the upshot, a touch of the triumphal. Seymour-Jones' tale is far from the 'girls' own' adventure that its title may imply, but it is not being invigilated by the sweet melancholy and higher irony that, for some, Conradi's title evokes.

Both authors are tested biographers. In Seymour-Jones' case, Pearl succeeds two forthright women in competition with men: Vivienne Eliot and Simone de Beauvoir. The first was suppressed by her husband, the second never granted more

---

1 Conradi's book was conceived partly as a sequel to *Iris Murdoch: A Life* (2001).

2 He was speaking of Jack Kerouac.

than co-equal status by her partner in 'dangerous liaisons'[3]. Pearl in her war-work exceeds both in individual glory, and her eventual husband, with whom she operated, played second fiddle to her. (He would later say to her, 'If I hadn't met you, I would have been a hobo.') Coming from shabby genteel origins in the Anglo community of prewar Paris, Pearl rose to become 'warrior queen' of the Indre, a Joan of Arc to her *maquis* and an unqualified hero in guerrilla war with the Nazis – in her case, we need not change the term to feminine gender. 'As good as a man' is how one may respond to her acts as Seymour-Jones recounts the dangers, deceptions, secrets and sabotage at a pace in contrast to the admirable contemplativeness with which Conradi views Thompson. It is hard to believe that these two young people, Pearl and Frank, were working for the same bosses in the same war at the same time, if half a continent apart. One is a Slavic tale, full of eastern downdrift, the other a Gallic one marked by *esprit* and *rigueur*.

In fact, the success of Pearl owed much to her gender. Women were (perhaps *are*) less visible in covert ops, less expected to supervise parachute drops, dispense weapons, control funds, destroy phone lines, electricity cables, train tracks and bridges. They may be less ready to live off the land, rough it in the Massif Central without washing, proceed by blackmail, coercion and theft. On the other hand, they may be more able to manoeuvre out of instinct, scenting traps and evading capture by charm or even clairvoyance[4]. More than men they may know how to make themselves loved, thus to command loyalty, even when needed evoking Mills & Boon emotionality: Seymour-Jones implies this of Pearl and on occasion offers a neat double-entendre – Pearl is given cover by the uniform of the First Aid Nursing Yeomanry, abbreviated FANY. Yet all these 'female' skills might have profited Pearl little had she not had a near native feeling for things French, and Seymour-Jones is adept at leading us through

---

3   The title of Seymour-Jones' double biography of Sartre and de Beauvoir was *Dangerous Liaisons*.

4   Seymour-Jones ascribes this metaphysical power to Pearl.

the terminology of the epoch – *attentisme* (waiting to see which way the wind blows), *clandestinité* (cardinal talent for résistants), *gros bonnet* (Gestapo who can be corrupted), *baignoire* (water-boarding, to avoid at all costs), *résistants de la dernière heure* (late comers to the right side), *naphtaline* (fighters whose uniform has 'the smell of mothballs').

Above and beyond Pearl's mission loom machinations among the gods on the faraway Olympus of London. Chief of these was the *engueulade* between Churchill and De Gaulle, an antagonism which at one point led the bulldog PM to explode to his erstwhile protégé: 'Every time we have to choose between Europe and the open seas, it is the open seas we shall choose. Every time I have to decide between you and Roosevelt, I shall always choose Roosevelt.' Churchill kept secrets from De Gaulle, ran ops in competition with the Free French and told SOE contingents not to cooperate with them. This became easy once the death of Jean Moulin virtually eliminated Gaullist resistance in France, and many in SOE often seemed to prefer to deal with the rival Communist résistants. But much went on in a grey area where allies and even national operators could be cut off from aid or expended. SOE was Churchill's pet; the SIS loathed it and tried to shut it down. However, the 'old spook' (Seymour-Jones' tag recalls young Winston's service in the Boer War) was as shrewd at power intrigue and playing organizations off one another as at setting up clandestine 'controlling sections' for Deception, for Destruction and for Double-Cross. Much is summed up by his apothegm: 'In wartime truth is so precious that she should always be attended by a bodyguard of lies.'

Seymour-Jones is excellent on this, as she is on a predictable post-liberation reaction. In September '44 De Gaulle told the SOE man in Bordeaux, 'Vous êtes anglais, votre place n'est-ce pas ici.' Later that day his Minister of War told the same agent 'quitter la France dans les deux heures'. Pearl and her French husband-to-be were not treated with much more decorum – a shock, given their close relations with *résistants* on the ground. Officialdom to come became less and less congenial. A Wehrmacht division, surrounded by but unwilling to surrender to the maquis, was allowed instead to do so to an American general, who behaved with his German counterpart as if 'two great gentlemen making an agreement in circumstances marred only by the presence of some troublesome Frenchmen'. To Pearl's dismay, the division was escorted to safety north of the Loire and greeted as POWs with oranges and chocolate. The great adventure was drawing to a close, and Pearl like many of her kind would soon return to a civilian life where no moral certainty existed, no good job was on hand and – because she was a woman – honors were offered that seemed derisory in comparison to those given to men for equivalent service. Pearl refused an MBE and set about scrabbling a living for her feckless husband and new child by working as a secretary at the World Bank.

Seymour-Jones tracks Pearl's tale to its end, noting the rectification of her honorary status before her death by the present Queen. The book, however, is really about Pearl less than about the great, grim adventure which was covert service in occupied France. It is history and Pearl an illustrative 'figure in a landscape'[5], one of thousands once ignored or viewed as 'second rate' on whom an edifice of victory was built. Pearl is never inward – she was no Frank Thompson – and would, one feels, not have been so effective had she been. Blunt, capable, charming, clever, she would, one may guess, not have fired the imagination of a Peter Conradi, who in the course of his portrait grows as half-in-love with his 'very English hero' as that poetic spirit seems to have done with a prospect of 'easeful death'. Seymour-Jones is exhilarated by her tale, which is always on the outside, about '*that* war', and familiar as such: we know how it will end. This reduces its forward drive not a jot, because the accomplished author understands instinctively what Hitchcock taught about the successful thriller: audience is driven just as readily by anticipation as by suspense.

Neither is at play in Elisa Segrave's account of her mother's

---

5   Conradi's phrase for what he was trying to paint in his Murdoch book.

wartime service in *The Girl from Station X*. Like Conradi, yet more so, Segrave writes from inner compulsion as much as desire to flesh out a history oft-told. Her book is a voyage of discovery into another soul, strange yet familiar, to whom she is emotionally tied.

Anne Hamilton-Grace came from a family which had made a fortune in shipping and the guano trade. Her father died in action, aged 34, in World War I, when Anne was an infant. An amateur writer, he sent her a letter from Flanders on her first birthday with this advice: 'Others will judge you by your own estimate, so it will be well to have plenty of self-respect – but above all avoid being proud with nothing to be proud about. Let your motto be "Play the game and make life for others happier by your presence."' The high-minded upper middle-class code is countered later by Anne's mother's more ruthless quip: 'Never do anything if you can get someone else to do it for you!' Segrave sets out to understand how Anne found and lost her way throughout life between this moral Scylla and Charybdis.

Segrave is helped by having inherited after Anne's death in 2003 a cache of diaries kept during most of her 89 years. The book might indeed claim dual authorship since Anne's diaries make up nearly as much of it as her daughter's commentary on them. They lead into a realm that Pearl Witherington's tale escapes and Frank Thompson's only discloses through surviving poems and letters: the turns and twists of a struggling psyche. These are doubled as Anne's qualms, wonders and hopes are matched and measured in analysis by her daughter and often lead to the daughter's analysis of herself. What we have is not a war story so much as the story of lives in which '*that* war' figures. Nor is wartime an end as in Thompson's and effectively Pearl's cases, it is rather a portal through which the postwar world is entered, or perhaps more precisely a vortex through which the prewar world is spun and reformed into what would be much the same, yet so different.

Anne was a debutante who grew up in grand houses – in Belgrave Square, in East Sussex – and holidayed in glamorous places such as Palm Beach and Rome. War did not provide her a chance for advancement or flight from middle class inhibition or impecuniousness; it was a matter of *oblige* and national duty. It did not offer diversion in foreign parts and tongues, but ended both. She went to work in one of the huts in the warren Churchill arranged at Bletchley Park for the essential matter of code-breaking. At one point the PM visits and she records: 'It really was rather a thrill to see him, in our office, sitting at Humphreys' desk and looking at our Middle East reports!... [He] said, "It is amazing that a place that looks so simple can really be so sinister."' This, one supposes, refers not just to Bletchley's arts of code-breaking but its facility for code-making – false codes to deceive enemies. It was detail work, sedentary, taking long hours, dreary and in a setting anything but congenial. 'The whole proceedings [sic] is the essence of discomfort and sordidity,' Anne complains. 'It is a queer life! The atmosphere of intellectuality, of abnormality... is so depressing. I loathe every moment of it.' And later, by contrast: 'When one meets someone from the outside, one breathes a new atmosphere of common sense, gaiety and the things that matter in life... One feels ashamed of being part of the Park.'

This is no tale told to glamorize service; on the contrary, it provides a vivid corrective – spying, as often said, is ¾ quotidian grind. Anne complains of everyone growing 'unhinged'. At one point she feels as if she is in 'a concentration camp one can never get out of'. Yet after a spell of liberty in London, she returns to Bletchley to feel 'a strange kind of peace again... as though I no longer exist any more and am just a shadow with no thoughts or feelings, safe from this terrible mental torment that overwhelms me like a cloud.' Do we glimpse here an equivalent of Churchill's 'black dog'? If so, one may wonder if there is some link between the deep, anti-social actions of spookery and depressive states. Like Churchill, Anne drinks, often too much. She finds relief in writing. Starved for sensual pleasure, she becomes fascinated by a handful of strangers who surface, a Pole, a Jew – 'These foreign men have minds like women and yet they are not effeminate.'

She grows hyperconscious of odd 'second rate' females around her with their WAAF 'nicknames of ambiguous gender: Andy, Paz, Bunty, Knotty, Kiwi, Ronnie, Doc, Dovey and Hammy'.

In the cloistered warren, with males off at war, lesbianism peers round the corner. Anne at first claims, 'It revolts and sickens me'; later she confesses, 'I was attracted by the sensuality and exoticness of it.' She finds her Sapphic colleagues to have 'hypersensitive nerves and quick brains and intelligence' and wants to know 'how their minds work and what are the responses if you "are one too"?' She does not become 'one', though her daughter senses a pull in that direction. 'Are we – sophisticated people, always looking for the perverted side of life and trying to explain things by sexual theories, missing something greater that cannot fit into a theory because it is so rare and elusive?' Thus Anne ponders. However, she does not pursue this transcendental apprehension any further than the carnal ones which seem to have triggered it. Rather she seeks to return to a privileged existence, where bohemianism is conventionalized. After the war ends, she does so by marrying a naval officer perfectly straight in his desire for 'making spermia'. Four children, of which the book's author is the eldest and sole female, are the result.

Anne's war work constitutes the headline topic of *The Girl at Station X*, and her last duties – on the continent after VE Day – provide her diaries' most arresting entries. Brussels strikes her as shockingly prosperous – much more so than victorious London and in contrast to Paris, which seems to have lost its soul under Nazi occupation. Northern and western Germany seem so placid and calm that she wonders how total war could ever have visited there. All this changes when she reaches the Russian sector and encounters bombed-out cities, refugees with no food or shelter and of course the true concentration camps. But Anne does not stay in this macabre region for long. Quickly she is back to London, which she now 'hates'; thence she is off to New York, which she loves, and eventually to Madrid, where her husband has been posted as attaché. A few fine years there are among the last she records. In many ways they are the best of her life. They seem also to be so in the memory of her daughter, then only a tiny child.

After Madrid, Anne's husband has no 'proper' job and is 'assimilated into her café society'. Segrave sees this as leading to his decline, but Anne would defend her part in it by using the language of old privilege – 'How could I expect him to work after he'd had such a hard war?' After his death and other family reversals, she too would decline, into alcoholism, dementia and isolation, except for one or two special women friends. This dénouement troubles Segrave, and her book is sometimes anguished, yet no worse for it. She sums up the experience of exploring her mother's diaries thus: 'I was reminded of those "magic" paint books that I had been given as a child – you put a paintbrush in water and gently stroked it over a blank page, then a picture, hitherto invisible would slowly take shape.' The picture that has emerged is of a life partly wasted, yet partly redeemed by having had a chance for work taken and efficiently carried out. The diaries reveal secrets faithfully kept, not only official but personal ones. The last image is of a tiny girl walking towards her mother through the deepening waters of a 'wild' Spanish sea; of her Anne says, '*I was so proud*' – words that a grown daughter admits to have been searching for all along.

'I love only what is written with blood,' Nietzsche said; 'write in blood, because blood turns to spirit.'[6] Minds shaped by journalism may prefer war tales in more official hues, but a book like this *coeur mis à nu* adds telling strokes to the larger picture.

A Very English Hero: the Making of Frank Thompson, Peter J. Conradi; Bloomsbury, 2012. *She Landed by Moonlight: the Story of Secret Agent Pearl Witherington: the 'real Charlotte Grey*, Carole Seymour-Jones; Hodder & Stoughton, 2013. *The Girl from Station X: My Mother's Unknown Life*, Elisa Segrave; Union Books, 2013.

---

6 *Thus Spake Zarathustra*, Prologue, VII.

The Hooligan

Jewish Chronicle, 15 April 2016

Rudolf Nassauer came to London from Frankfurt in 1939, age 14. His father was a wine-merchant, a trade he inherited. He became a novelist and married a novelist, Bernice Rubens. Both published debut works in 1960. Nassauer's took ten years to write and was rejected more than once. It is now regarded as most remarkable among his seven books.

Few of us any longer know what the world felt like in the 1950s, let alone 1940-45. The Zeitgeist into which *The Hooligan* emerged had barely experienced the Winds of Change and was not yet affected by 'All You Need Is Love' or its riposte, 'Sympathy for the Devil'. World War II was a palpable memory, the Cold War present reality, nuclear holocaust a great fear. It was the era of Soviet gulags. Fascists still ruled Portugal and Spain.

In Nassauer's milieu refugees like Elias Canetti impressed literati like Iris Murdoch with treatises on crowd psychology, and 'New Age consciousness' was afoot. By the end of a new decade hooligans proper would bring terror to (and from) Northern Ireland, but it is not them Nassauer had in mind in his title, rather victimizers from a town called Himmlersberg who run a death-camp named Goeringen. His theme is the Dostoyevskian Weltanschauung which impels them, half-sleepwalking 'beyond good and evil', into amoral goop.

The book is ugly, and titanic. The victimizers are like Alberich and Mime in Wagner's *Ring*, yet without their justification. Nothing has been stolen from them; they are not even of society's losers – only its second-raters, its malleable mass. Yet in odd ways they are also individual thinkers, each conjuring his own form of antinomian ethics. Transvaluation of values is at core in the deadly game that attracts them. Their playing of it induces their victims – the most conscious of them – into entering a version of it too.

Wrath against a God who has failed is ubiquitous, so too

against conventions which lie. Yet, if 'God is dead', then (to complete Nietzsche's phrase) 'for millennia to come people will spy his shadow in their caves'. Survivors long for saviours. A starving, grief-addled woman sees a former camp-officer as Christ. Or is he the Antichrist? Whichever, he dispatches her to her death. An old Jew whom he once forced to grovel with pigs testifies at his trial that he has shown intrinsic goodness in releasing her from misery.

The world is beyond Reason. What hope? 'Man will rebuild the ravaged cities, but there will be no more churches, no altars... only the children... I love children.' Thus the way back to morality of a kind – or is it to the paedophilia of a Jimmy Savile era?

No exit from existential confusion is sure, except the ultimate.

The Hooligan, Rudolf Nassauer, reissued with an introduction by Michael Moorcock. Zephyr Books, 2016.

Mission to Kabul, a Footnote on Weltpolitik

Quarterly Review, 27 vii 2014

It does not surprise me that the U.S. National Security Agency should have wanted to tap the telephone of Angela Merkel. A Prussian 'eastie' who becomes leader of the conservative, historically western Christian Democratic Party must be, at least on the surface of it, a riddle wrapped in an enigma. Frau Merkel goes religiously to the Wagner festival at Bayreuth and cheers volubly in Brazil for her World Cup-winning football team while sitting two seats away from Vladimir Putin – a German speaker who spent nine years running the KGB in East Germany's most West-damaged city, Dresden. Following the Iraq War-opposing chancellor, Gerhard Schröder, deposed to become Germany's main dealmaker with Gazprom, Mrs Merkel has been billed as a West-friendly leader, the German Margaret Thatcher etc. She smiled at George W. Bush, befriended David Cameron (though doing little to help him against his Euro-sceptic flank) and appears at the same time to be the originator of Barack Obama's policy dictum, 'Don't do stupid stuff!' She is alleged to have conspired to bring down one crooked European colleague, Silvio Berlusconi, yet overtly campaigned to keep another in power, Nicolas Sarkozy; latterly she is said to have had good relations with the former[1], while formerly it was claimed she had bad relations with the latter. Who is she really? The NSA might be forgiven for wondering, even if a likely answer is that she is a sphinx without a secret.

A German friend asked by an English colleague 'What does Mrs Merkel want?' responded without hesitation, 'To win the war'. This may or may not give the game away. What is reasonable to posit is that Angela Merkel, possibly more than any postwar German leader, is the true face of her country's historic role. In foreign affairs she speaks softly, smiles and proceeds

---

1 By Berlusconi himself, in an interview with Jeremy Paxman on BBC's *Newsnight* earlier this year.

with caution, keeping a bit under the radar with an eye ever on the national interest. But what is that interest, precisely? To the extent to which it is opaque, the NSA would not be doing its job not to try to find out, just as the BND (Germany's equivalent, Bundesnachtrichtendienst) would be failing in its remit not to try to ascertain America's deepest intentions, thus phone-taps on Secretaries of State John Kerry and Hillary Clinton, to which it recently admitted. Full score to both sides on that issue, and quits. It feels like shadow play and is possibly in aid of getting German inclusion into the Echelon system of intelligence sharing, up 'til now restricted to the 'five eyes' of old Anglo-Saxony: the US, UK, Canada, Australia and New Zealand. Who might object to modern German inclusion? Perhaps mainly those who feel that their historic primacy is being eroded: on the American side Britain, which helped set up the CIA in the first place, on the German, France, which has been the postwar face of European military policy for obvious reasons. Old spooks may be cautious about inviting in old enemies. But Germany has by now long been second to the U.S. as the major western economic and political power, so it is only logical that she should be its principal partner in strategic management, even if adjustment to this status must carry on sufficiently slowly so that the others can get used to their new places at the table.

The traditional view is that Germany is a land power which, apart from Lebensraum in contiguous regions, has little colonial ambition. This may have been true before the later 19th century, though the Holy Roman Empire – Germany's First Reich – pushed borders continually west, south and east. Under the Hohenstaufen, it seemed to invade Italy every summer, only to retreat in the autumn, impelled by insurrection or fever or both. The emperors went with other potentates of Christendom on the Crusades – in that context *Barbarossa* is as much of a name to conjure with as *Coeur de Leon* – which arguably marked the start of European imperialism. But the Crusades may be filed in a category of contiguous land grab – Vienna to Constantinople to Jerusalem is an unbroken trek – and in future centuries Baghdad to Persia to Afghanistan merely continued that outreach into 'Aryan' heartlands. This form of German foreign policy is what *The Kaiser's Mission to Kabul* explores, taking the subject from establishment of the Second Reich to the present. There was of course movement in other directions once Bismarck had consolidated that Reich: Germany, while not participant in the carve-up of the New World and Africa with England, France and Spain – even Portugal and Holland – in the 16th-19th centuries, threw itself with energy into the 'great game' under Victoria's favourite grandson, Wilhelm II; and Germany's expats in the Americas and China as well as explorers in west and east Africa had major impact on development of those far-flung regions.

The Moslem world became a major target. In Morocco Germany was involved in a dispute which threatened world war a decade before the first one broke out. In Ottoman lands she cultivated friends from Constantinople to Baghdad, leading the decayed empire to align itself with the Central Powers. Once world war had started, the Kaiser – rumoured for propaganda reasons to have embraced Islam – approved a mission to Afghanistan, impelled by a hope to threaten British India sufficiently that it could not send troops to the western front. The mission was led by a Bavarian soldier, Oskar von Niedermayer, and a Prussian diplomat, Otto von Hentig, the former to train fighters, the latter to persuade the Afghan king to forswear his cession of foreign policy to the Raj and to stop taking the subsidies that secured it. German activity in this guise appeared on the side of indigenous self-determination; the Indian revolutionary Mahendra Pratap was also in the Hentig/ Niedermayer party, which was partly directed from the Oriental desk of the Auswartiges Amt in Berlin by the lifelong enthusiast for anti-colonial jihad, Max von Oppenheim. In Baghdad, German operatives stimulated insurgent elements, as did 'the German Lawrence' Wilhelm Wassmuss in the deserts of Iran. Meanwhile, at Kabul, Niedermayer trained an army of 40,000 while Hentig made far-sighted attempts to influence 'hearts and minds'. After German reversals in 1916, the mission had to be abandoned, and the pair returned home by divergent yet equally perilous routes. Hentig's through China and the U.S. involved arrests and escapes which encouraged the British F.O. to view him as a kind of Scarlet Pimpernel, and Jules Stewart tells his tale as if it were an adventure out of Conrad or Kipling. Stewart's main purpose, however, is to show how the Hentig/ Niedermayer mission laid the ground for major developments in Afghanistan in the postwar epoch and beyond.

Weimar Germans were dispatched to build roads, dams, schools and infrastructure. They provided credits, even contracts at a loss, to get their feet under the table: the Kabul to Berlin air service via Baghdad lost money but was worth doing as a public relations coup. Given the inflation of the 1920s and unemployment of the '30s, German engineers and designers were willing to expatriate themselves at a cheaper rate than their Brit counterparts, with the result was that by 1937 Germany was shipping steel to Afghanistan worth 2.8 million rupees while Britain was only managing 38,600 worth. Hitler, being racist, was loath to back any project that advanced Indian independence – like many Nazis he hoped for common cause with a British Empire made Germano-friendly – so in the second war, Hentig, now at a desk in the Auswartiges Amt himself, was unable to advance any mission of the kind he had fronted for the Kaiser. A footnote to the story is that he *was* apparently able to help persuade the Führer that Germany should take an interest in encouraging a Jewish state in Palestine; though demonstrably not an anti-Semite, Hentig played on the prejudices of his leader shrewdly enough to promote a cause that would otherwise have seemed anathema[2]. The anti-Semitic French writer Céline liked to rant that, whatever Hitler preached, the Foreign Office in Berlin was still run by 'yids'[3]; and while this may be a flagrant

---

2   A memorandum Hentig wrote 'served as a basis for the *Report to Hitler by the Foreign Office*'; this led to a private meeting in which he argued the case to a bemused Führer. Stewart cites among sources Nora Levin, *The Holocaust: the Destruction of European Jewry 1933-1945* (New York: Crowell, 1968), 132.

3   See 'Faut-il brûler Céline?' earlier in this book.

instance of Célinean *rigolade*, Stewart notes that Max von Oppenheim was still partly directing German Middle Eastern policy from behind the scenes: 'There is in fact every reason to believe that [he] was... actively involved in relations and negotiations between officials of the Third Reich and leaders of the pro-Axis Arab independence and unity movements.'[4]

Postwar Germany, once it had regained its footing, continued to ply a path towards Afghanistan, as well as over the 14,000 miles of land separating it from Kabul. The German capital was selected as site for a first major international conference about the future of that faraway country after the bombing of the twin towers by Al Qaeda in 2001 resulted in western action against its Taliban government. Germany provided the third largest NATO force operating in the region and in the tradition of Niedermayer busied itself training army and police, while in that of Hentig encouraging a policy of 'hearts and minds'. One step closer to home Germany has been among the six nations directly involved in negotiating nuclear matters with Iran; and in Iraq, despite Schröder's famous refusal to join in the younger Bush's 'abenteuer', it has now taken a lead in European action against ISIS to defend Kurdistan. Germany's relations with Turkey remain strong, and its links to Israel – though often opaque – are essential. Thus we can see the thrust and continuity of German foreign policy without even beginning to discuss how it operates in regard to Russia, the Caucasus, China, Africa and Latin America. For a nation which still believes it prudent to take a low profile, it is increasingly 'batting at its own weight', if not – to steal the distinction from David Cameron – *above* it. From a strategic point of view intelligent policy-makers in old Anglo-Saxony must recognize the benefit of this development in a fused 'new world order'. One of them, General Sir David Richards, has contributed an appreciative foreword to Jules Stewart's fast-moving account of an Ur-modern German covert op. The book is a page-turner, and I. B. Tauris may be commended for once

---

4   Stewart quotes Lionel Grossman, *The Passion of Max von Oppenheim* (Open Book Publishers, 2013), 232.

again having produced in handsome form fine insights into the historical forces at work in a complex, conflicted region of our contemporary world.

The Kaiser's Mission to Kabul, Jules Stewart. I. B. Tauris, 2014.

Saints and scholars – the Pope's hopes

Quarterly Review, Autumn 2010

There is a leavening of useful fraudulence in myth. George Moore, regarded as the finest stylist in English of his day, pondered the Christ tale for decades. On reaching a biblical age, he adapted a version of it[1] into his play 'The Passing of the Essenes'. Affected by fascination for post-Wagnerian libretti[2], he depicted a Jesus years after being spirited away from the tomb in Joseph of Arimathaea's garden enjoying a simple life tending sheep in remote mountains inhabited by the eponymous sect. One day a traveller arrives at the cave where the brethren eat and sleep. He has lost his way trying to find a shortcut to the coast and a ship waiting to take him to Greece and to Rome to spread news of miraculous happenings in Jerusalem years before. A preacher of new religion – by claim, son of God – was crucified, and, vanishing from his tomb, appeared on the road before his disciples prior to ascending into Heaven. The Essenes tell their guest that one among them has a pre-history resembling this. The visitor scoffs, but then Jesus walks in to sit down to supper. He confirms that yes, in his hot youth he did have foolish adventures, but now he is content with uneventful husbandry in the hills. The guest reacts crossly, accusing Jesus of lying; he insists that miraculous events *did* happen in Jerusalem years before and that nothing will prevent him from spreading the word. All go to sleep. In the morning Jesus guides the man down to a path through the rocks to deliver him to his ship. 'I may have been wrong in what I said last night,' he concedes; 'I may misremember, but in any case who knows the truth?' The traveller, named Paul, is somewhat mollified. Trailing his guide's

---

1 A more grandiose version appeared in his novel *The Brook Kerith* (1916).

2 A regular at Bayreuth from the 1890s, Moore wrote one of his longest novels, *Evelyn Innes*, on Wagnerian themes and attempted in at least one other, *The Lake*, a Wagnerian style. His long correspondence with the former editor of *La revue wagnérienne*, Edouard Dujardin (later exemplar for Joyce), divides itself between investigation of the origins of Christianity and ideas for post-Wagnerian opera.

beatific look, he carries on to his life-work.

Facts morph into legend, legend into myth, myth into religion, serving ego and / or political ends. Two millennia after whatever occurred in Galilee, we are no closer to the truth about origins of the West's dominant religion than about the tales of hundreds of its devotees later elevated to sainthood. History is spun; news-spreaders have agenda; axes are ground. Good men may adhere to an ethical structure while discounting the fables it is built on, yet they do so at peril of ostracism by those who would sustain orthodoxy, scattering liberals to the hills and activists onto a proselytizer's road. Wherein lies truth: the fanatic or the quiescent heart? By the middle of John Cornwell's biography of John Henry Newman, one begins to ponder such questions. The book looks beyond its subject, Newman being in part a pretext, possibly worthy yet never wholly attractive and, as an ideal, deserving some erasure and rebuffing. Cornwell accomplishes this with almost invisible grace. If there is a flaw in his effort, it comes from his tendency as half-journalist to keep one eye ever on a jury of contemporary social response. The other half of him, a Cambridge don, supplies density of texture: a sense of leaving no significant stone unturned or previous geologist un-cited. This involves academic fuss less than an appearance of genuine respect for ideas honed by commentary and over decades. Collegial geniality is exuded even more than faith in his own genius, which as a onetime novelist and a biographer of Coleridge Cornwell might be expected to show, also as keen observer of his own star – the praised memoir of his early life-struggle, *Seminary Boy* (2006). In this new book he achieves a generous persona, quite natural apparently, hard won over years. A matured individual beckons, welcomes and leads us onto the rocky path the journey entails.

It does so in part because of recent church politics, a terrain the author of *Hitler's Pope* (1999) knows well. Like the subject of that controversial tome, Newman was put forward for beatification during 'the long reign of John Paul II', an era so marked by 'inflation in saint-making' that more were created than in all prior history. The strain evident in Newman's case is as great in its way as in that of the wartime pope. While pleased to achieve recognition as cardinal, Newman himself stated that he was no saint. Literary compulsion alone would preclude such a status, he believed: as a writer, he appealed to contemporaries as contrasted as George Eliot and Oscar Wilde and was, as Cornwell's account underlines, an eager participant in issues of his day, entering into its controversies with subtle acerbity, at one point even leading to a conviction for libel. In eras prior to John Paul's 'inflation', moves to sanctify such an individual might have seemed quixotic. But Catholicism is political, history tells us; and the Polish pope's successor, spying manifold problems in a 'heretical' Church of England, has adopted more than one stratagem to gather its brethren back to the fold – notably offering 'fast track' access for those offended by Anglican liberalism re women bishops and openly gay priests. Benedict XVI's recent visit to Britain, preceded by loud fanfare about abuse in his church, was doubtless conceived in part to exploit openings in these troubled realms, akin perhaps to decades of diplomatic push to bring the recalcitrant fringes of Europe back into Christendom under the guise of the EU. With not atypical German naïve optimism, allied with a touch of equally typical *bürgerlich* anglophilia, the Bavarian pope harboured high, even triumphalist hopes; and Newman as saint, apotheosizing the original 'catholic revival' in England after the Oxford Movement, must have struck him as a coup de grâce to set at the centre of his trip – a perfect means for mounting an arguably native riposte to the mouldy muddle of Rowan Williams-ism.

In failing to go a Lollard, fully Protestant, low church direction during the reigns of Elizabeth I and the Stuarts, the Church of England placed itself ever in a position of being open to inner conflict and charges of incoherence – so argument goes. This plagued it in Newman's day, driving him finally from high Anglicanism to Rome, and stutters on in our own. By contrast, the Roman church, barring spasms of liberalism at the start of

Pius IX's reign[3] or in the interlude of John XXIII and Vatican II, has retained counter-reformational zeal, pope-mobiles and pop-star grins notwithstanding. Cornwell embodies a liberal Brit Catholic turn-of-mind. Perhaps out of stress from necessity of having always to straddle divided loyalties, he longs to believe that the two churches have much in common and, being in key ways complimentary, can aid one another on a tortuous but unavoidable path to uplands of perpetual modernization – i.e., adjustment to the world as it exists. This attitude supposes that his church is, or should be, grounded on 'conversation' between all its parts, laity and clergy, bottom-up and top-down. Attractive as the position may be, it appears in conflict with dominant Vatican policy now as throughout history. Newman's progress to Rome – a Rome taking speedy steps away from the liberalism of 1848 towards the ultramontaneism of Vatican I – is a fairly emphatic rebuke to such optimism, a fact Cornwell is careful not to overemphasize in his largely sympathetic account.

What he comes most to praise in Newman are his contributions to the development of liberal education, set out particularly in *Idea of a University*. Cornwell animadverts on the Aquinan ideals Stephen Dedalus apparently adapts from Newman in the last section of *A Portrait of the Artist as a Young Man*[4]; also, more provocatively, on Newman's high concept of friendship. The latter invites comment in our postmodern, politically correct, salacity-seeking time and place – i.e., wasn't this ascetic aesthete, surrounded by male acolytes, in essence gay? Such speculation may be crucial to one-trick ponies like Peter Thatchell, but for the rest of us who must live, die and wonder what It's all about regardless, it seems a bit of a red herring. Newman's prose does partake of a Victorian sensuality resembling that of *Marius the Epicurean* or even *The Picture of Dorian Gray*. Yet as one of his key passages re the attraction of

---

3 I am told that Cornwell is now undertaking a biography of this arch-conservative pope.

4 Like his creator, Stephen studies at an institution Newman's efforts helped to found: University College, Dublin.

the Roman church demonstrates – Cornwell quotes it from Newman's 'conversion novel' *Loss and Gain* – this was never neatly or wholly homoerotic:

> She is our mother – oh, that word 'mother!' – a mighty mother! She opens her arms – oh, the fragrance of that bosom! She is full of gifts – I feel, I have long felt it. Why don't I rush into her arms? Because I feel that she is ruled by a spirit which is not she. But did that distrust of her go from me, was that certainty which I have of her corruption, disproved, I should join her communion tomorrow.

One may detect trepidation of the femme fatale in this and extrapolate a Parsifalian aversion[5]; yet if so, the turn-away must be towards duty, not 'sin'. Cornwell notes Newman's precept that in interpersonal relations one may *feel* but should not *act*. Close friendship, whether with a brother such as Ambrose St John, in whose grave Newman asked to be buried[6], or with a sister such as Maria Giberne, who interceded for Newman against spite in the English Catholic community at Rome, were of special importance, to be honoured and serviced and *not* – as 'ascetical theology' counselled – avoided as inimical to proper devotion to God.

The journalist in Cornwell presents his subject in a way not to discourage Thatchell-esque interest. In a year in which Pelion has been piled upon Ossa re clerical abuse, it would have been a poor publishing wheeze to have done otherwise. Despite that, it is in these areas of high-minded friendship and intellectual pursuit that the collegial fellow finds his most unambiguous grounds for admiring a figure whom he joins the Pope and curia in seeing as the great exemplar among post-Reformation English Catholics and, not incidentally, a fine stylist. Dedication

---

5 Parsifal's destiny as reviver of the Grail Order is, according to Wagner, predicated on ability to resist the sensual indulgence with Kundry which brought his predecessor low, thus the order into decadence.

6 Thus the book's title and photo of the dual-inscribed headstone on its cover.

to a rich, wide life of the mind, of study and expression, and to generous, continuous discourse and intercourse with the world and times in which he lives – not least with those to whom he is most closely associated – make Cornwell's Newman appear a preceptor in good sense, whether religious or not, and of best civilization. This is somewhat different from what others may be after in beatifying the renegade Anglican; but efforts to erect the man into a saint, involving dubious and for mere rationalists off-putting tales that his spirit when prayed to can perform miracles, appear *chez* Cornwell less important than Newman's stature as a devout individual – a type all too unfashionable in our fallen age. Piety, whether secular or more, continues to matter – that is this book's message, reflecting its author's, if not subject's, inclusive temperament. Nor is genuine transcendental quest likely to be assisted by beatific inflation, let alone opportunistic clerical politics.

Whether a frail, soft-spoken pontiff's visit to Britain has helped to engender an atmosphere in which this can thrive is for the spin-meisters of our media *junta* to judge. One or two of them has shown himself not fully rotten with the 'aggressive secularism' Benedict came to inveigh against; and Cornwell, liberal outrider among Catholics, may not be a half-bad exemplar of them. But was the heir to St Peter well-advised to visit Britain at all? Should the mountain ever come to Mohammed? Were the faithful comforted? It was impressive to see 70,000 turn out on an improbably Mediterranean afternoon in Glasgow; but the pope-mobile was a cartoonist's gift, especially when snaking through London crowds often no more than one protestor deep; and competition in funny hats with Queen and Archbishop is no imagery to advance a true Christian cause. Paedophile victims remained unappeased; Italian atheists and statists smelt blood and wondered, like the strident Geoffrey Robertson QC[7], whether the Vatican deserves to exist as a sovereign power, providing immunity for a onetime member of Hitler Youth and his confrères against prosecution for Nixonian cover-up. A few

---

7 'A curious tale of two embassies' in *The New Statesman*, 20 ix 2010, pg. 24.

days after the Pope's return to Rome, the Bank of Italy began investigation of his bankers under anti-terrorist and money-laundering laws, citing among transactions one with an entity owned by Gruppo Valtellinese, name evoking the redoubt in the Südtirolean Alps where Mussolini boasted that Fascism would make its last stand against predecessors of the 'aggressive secularists' whom the Pope sees as dominating our culture from its Western fringes[8]. Mightn't the old man have been better off staying safe in core Europe, quietly tending his flock? What good can come of going on the road like a hyperactive St Paul, spreading a Word which, to an erratic Zeitgeist, may – except in the private spaces of millions of troubled hearts – appear quite fraudulent?

Newman's Unquiet Grave: the Reluctant Saint, John Cornwell. Continuum, 2010.

---

8 See R. J. B. Bosworth, *Mussolini* (Arnold, 2002), pg. 415. In the event the *Duce* was executed when trying to escape to Switzerland; but his remains were stolen by Salò fascists and briefly concealed in the Valtellina.

Orpheus Rising

Quarterly review, Winter 2011-12

Ann Wroe was educated as an historian and has worked for decades as a journalist and an editor at *The Economist*. Her first two books reflected this duality, one being an account of life in a medieval French village, the other a history of the Iran-Contra affair. But Wroe's spirit as writer has always had something *other* lurking in it, and progressively this has come out. Akin to what moved Virginia Woolf to produce her fantasia *Orlando* – love, poetic mania, desire to apprehend an incorporeal force – Wroe is impelled by a shade of the mystic, in fact the Platonic. Through all the big books of her prime, she has been in quest of probabilities: the what may have beens, could have beens or should have beens that shimmer behind what is taken as given.

Firm in belief that history is infested with speculation, she has treated objective truth as an ideal set about by realities made suspect through subjective report. If *Orlando* was life in costume, so Wroe's non-fictions often seem costume-drama made live. Thus her account of Pontius Pilate (1999), subtitled 'biography of an invented man'; her 'mystery' of Perkin Warbeck (2003), entitled generically *The Perfect Prince*; and her investigation of an imagination, *Being Shelley* (2007), subtitled 'The Poet's Search for Himself'. These increasingly inventive books have pushed the boundaries of a genre which she sees as overtaken not so much by what Wilde branded 'the body-snatchers of literature' as its nit-pickers: the easily readable, what-he-had-for-breakfast/ who-she-slept-with-that-night brigade. Standard biography offering as it were the price of everything and value of nothing, Wroe has been determined to dig deep and extract purer ore.

The approach has its perils. The Pilate book flirted with evoking a phantom as surely as the tale of the same Biblical character magicked up by a fictional author in Bulgakov's *The Master and Margarita*. Relying on 'Perhaps...', 'One version says...', 'A later writer thought...', 'As the poet imagined...', buttressed with pedestrian information such as how long it might take to travel from Tiberius to Rome, Wroe fabricated a credible portrait while always allowing the reader know that she knows that no one can say truly even what her subject looked like. Something similar was true of her bold habitation of Shelley, a kind of Gnostic star-child in her view, hardly meant for this earth and all-too-ready to re-ascend out of it. The 'luminous halo' Woolf sought in fiction is conferred here via psycho-diagnosis. A kind of meta-truth is provided even as the sceptic grows more convinced that one can never be sure of the inner life of even the most self-exploring and self-recording *other*.

These books retained a scholar's paraphernalia of bibliography and notes, the historian only lightly afflicted by the journalist's need to gloss over. *The Perfect Prince* got the balance perfect, providing a model for what informed supposition can tease out of history. The narrative was built so that we didn't have to read Warbeck as a fake, even if probability suggested it. We are allowed to grow cosy with the *realpolitik* of James IV of Scotland, Margaret of Burgundy, the Emperor Maximilian and at times monarchs of Portugal, France and Spain as they spin 'Richard IV' into being the legitimate heir to the Yorkists and Henry Tudor as a usurper intent on ascribing his own crimes to the young man's wicked uncle. Yet once Henry has subdued his opponents at home, aided by Warbeck and Yorkist errors, and displayed his mettle in treating abroad, betrothing his eldest son to a daughter of Spain (the Emperor's cousin) and eldest daughter to the cowed Scottish king, we come like Machiavelli's contemporaries to see that the young man must be consigned to the rope and his white rose to a chivalric, European past defoliating into a more firmly focussed English national present.

Something dreamy, even too fey for this world in her 'perfect prince' may be what led Wroe next to Shelley, and here is where her scholarship began seriously to morph into the poetic, 'creative' or mystic. After finishing the book, she collapsed and had to be taken to hospital; the cost of transgressing established boundaries is high, as Shelley himself knew. Nonetheless, the path Wroe had set out on she would not turn back from. She had spied or been entranced by something en route that beckoned beyond mere words: the inarticulable, related to the unknown and unknowable; breaths of expression both inner and outer – indeed, the synapses between them: *that* is what she had been seeking, much like Shelley in his profoundly musical prosody. And hadn't one reader of her Shelley suggested that, if Maurois could call his book on the poet *Ariel*, she might call hers *Orpheus*?

Ecco: the consummate subject. It circled back to *Pilate*. As in that book here was an 'invented man'– indeed demigod. By now Wroe knew the dangers – 'This book is dedicated to everyone who protested, "But Orpheus isn't *real*" – yet like the Nietzsche who had stared into the abyss of his own apoplexy and become reckless, Wroe was now faithful to the genie that allures. Her Virgil would be Rilke, another poet in a Shelleyan mode, if more mystical; one who had given himself to the god, as it were, and received his music first-hand. Rilke's Orpheus sonnets are source and model beginning and end for what really is Wroe's full-bodied leap into prose poetry. Here and there she inserts well-charted or even home-grown scenery – a landscape in Thrace, buskers in the Underground – but at heart what she writes, or wishes to be free to incant, is an impassioned dithyramb.

This may be apt for her subject, but does it help us? Sceptics to whom the book is dedicated still need to know 'Who *was* Orpheus?' Wroe offers an answer, though neither full nor complete. As with the Shelley book, her organization is not wholly chronologic: where that one had used the four elements, this takes the seven strings of the lyre, each tuned to a representative theme. The hero passes through 'Winter', 'Trees', 'The sea', 'Love', 'Death', 'Fame' and 'Scattering', with accounts of his origins in a forbidding, scarcely classical clime; his naturism; his voyage with the Argonauts, more manly than he; his affair with the never-quite-real Eurydice; his trip to the underworld; his grief and development of a cult; his tearing apart by maddened women. Throughout we are given descriptions of his songs, inspired, able to change seasons, tame waves. Some of these come from ancient report, others as imagined by writers through the ages, many conjured by Wroe herself.

Her Orpheus is surprising. He comes to seem a dark spirit, even seedy, neither bright or glorious. Dionysus is in him as well as his father Apollo. His trip to the underworld to regain his dead bride cloaks him in near disillusion. What once was handsomely striving towards the light, a kind of pre-neo-platonist in Wroe's evocation, becomes guru to a shady all-masculine cult, practicing arcane initiations, committed to suspect secrecy. Weird, misogynistic, almost intentionally off-putting, this figure perhaps half deserves to be torn to pieces in the end. To his destroyers he seems a sociopath. By the lights of their society, on whose outskirts he lurks, he may even be one. Nietzsche comes to mind again: the mad, ecstatic dancer on the edge of *Ecce Homo*. And just as in that perfervid emanation, there is a shadow of Christ too, as shaman, or divinely foolhardy avatar.

Wroe's Orpheus' relation to music – the *sound* of life (she says *song*, but her tale suggests more) – is persuasive: music as melody, rhythm, harmony, bliss, terror, cacophony, discord. His status as hierophant of a cult remains less sure. What *are* his rites? the same as those of Eleusis? similar? something like those of Attis, Osiris or Adonis? Wroe seeks to reveal them, but one is left in the shade. There seems a core narrative of a journey to Persephone, with its significance for vegetation and cyclical renewal; but Wroe's Orpheus is not quite of the nature myth that would imply, a spirit who must die that earth may be reborn. He is for her – and here the historian persists, partly subverting the prose-poet – a man who probably existed: a corpus mythologized rather than a myth incorporated. In the end this disappoints, for no real man can co-exist with the transcendental embodiment Wroe appears to be after. Perhaps it is only on the outside of our given world that she may find Him.

Orpheus: The Song of Life, Ann Wroe. Jonathan Cape, 2011.

www.ingramcontent.com/pod-product-compliance
Lightning Source LLC
Chambersburg PA
CBHW072000040426
42447CB00009B/1412